How Zombies C
Popular Cul

Contributions to Zombie Studies

White Zombie: Anatomy of a Horror Film. Gary D. Rhodes. 2001

The Zombie Movie Encyclopedia. Peter Dendle. 2001

*American Zombie Gothic: The Rise and Fall (and Rise)
of the Walking Dead in Popular Culture*. Kyle William Bishop. 2010

*Back from the Dead: Remakes of the Romero
Zombie Films as Markers of Their Times*. Kevin J. Wetmore, Jr. 2011

*Generation Zombie: Essays on the Living Dead
in Modern Culture*. Edited by Stephanie Boluk and Wylie Lenz. 2011

*Race, Oppression and the Zombie: Essays on Cross-Cultural Appropriations
of the Caribbean Tradition*. Edited by Christopher M. Moreman
and Cory James Rushton. 2011

Zombies Are Us: Essays on the Humanity of the Walking Dead.
Edited by Christopher M. Moreman and Cory James Rushton. 2011

The Zombie Movie Encyclopedia, Volume 2: 2000–2010. Peter Dendle. 2012

Great Zombies in History. Edited by Joe Sergi. 2013 (graphic novel)

Unraveling Resident Evil: *Essays on the Complex Universe
of the Games and Films*. Edited by Nadine Farghaly. 2014

"We're All Infected": Essays on AMC's The Walking Dead
and the Fate of the Human. Edited by Dawn Keetley. 2014

Zombies and Sexuality: Essays on Desire and the Walking Dead.
Edited by Shaka McGlotten and Steve Jones. 2014

...But If a Zombie Apocalypse Did *Occur: Essays on Medical,
Military, Governmental, Ethical, Economic and Other Implications*.
Edited by Amy L. Thompson and Antonio S. Thompson. 2015

*How Zombies Conquered Popular Culture: The Multifarious Walking
Dead in the 21st Century*. Kyle William Bishop. 2015

How Zombies Conquered Popular Culture

*The Multifarious Walking
Dead in the 21st Century*

Kyle William Bishop

CONTRIBUTIONS TO ZOMBIE STUDIES

McFarland & Company, Inc., Publishers
Jefferson, North Carolina

ALSO BY KYLE WILLIAM BISHOP

American Zombie Gothic: The Rise and Fall (and Rise) of the Walking Dead in Popular Culture (McFarland, 2010)

LIBRARY OF CONGRESS CATALOGUING-IN-PUBLICATION DATA

Bishop, Kyle William, 1973–
    How zombies conquered popular culture : the multifarious walking
dead in the 21st century / Kyle William Bishop.
        p.   cm. — (Contributions to zombie studies)
    Includes bibliographical references and index.
    Includes filmography.

    ISBN 978-0-7864-9541-2 (softcover : acid free paper) ∞
    ISBN 978-1-4766-2208-8 (ebook)

    1. Zombies in motion pictures.   2. Zombies in literature.
3. Zombies in popular culture.   4. Popular culture—United States—
21st century.   I. Title.

PN1995.9.Z63B525 2015
398'.45—dc23   2015029994

BRITISH LIBRARY CATALOGUING DATA ARE AVAILABLE

Front cover art © 2014 Shannon Eberhard

Printed in the United States of America

McFarland & Company, Inc., Publishers
 Box 611, Jefferson, North Carolina 28640
  www.mcfarlandpub.com

For Rachel, Xander, and Sydney.

CONTENTS

Part Three: Broader Horizons

Acknowledgments

I began my first book, *American Zombie Gothic* (2010), as my PhD dissertation at the University of Arizona, and it was *much* easier to do the research, draft the chapters, and revise the manuscript with the help of a dedicated committee of faculty supporting and encouraging me at every turn. Writing a second book, largely by myself, has proven to be a much different task, but I thank my graduate school mentors for developing my research and writing skills so well: Charlie Bertsch, Susan White, Jerrold E. Hogle, and Carlos Gallego. My colleagues at Southern Utah University have also been incredibly supportive and helpful, listening to my brainstorms, helping me develop my ideas, and even reading over my drafts, including Charla Strosser, Todd Petersen, Charles Cuthbertson, Jessica Tvordi, and Lisa Arter, not to forget my research assistant and indexer, Melanie Jensen, and my brilliant cover artist, Shannon Eberhard. This book also wouldn't have come into being without the inspiration, support, and help of Jeffrey Jerome Cohen, Sarah Juliet Lauro, Markus Wessendorf, Jeffrey A. Weinstock, Kim Paffenroth, Rob Weiner, Megan O'Sullivan, Kelli Shermeyer, Dallin Bundy, and Angela Tenga. And I express much gratitude to the fine people at The Grind coffee shop, the best place in Cedar City to write.

Since many of the chapters of this book originated as public speeches and presentations, I also wish to thank Brent Fujioka, for inviting me to speak at Brown University in 2011; Antonio Dominguez Leiva, Samuel Archibald, and Bernard Perron, for asking me to be a keynote speaker at the First International Academic Conference on Zombies in Montreal the summer of 2012; Markus Wessendorf, again, for giving me the wonderful opportunity to travel to Honolulu in November 2012 to speak at the world premier of his mashup play *Uncle Vanya and Zombies*; Alberto N. García, for allowing me to talk about AMC's *The Walking Dead* (2010–) at the international and interdisciplinary "Identity and Emotions in Contemporary TV-Series" workshop at the University of Navarra in Pamplona in the fall of 2013; and Matthew

Nesvet and Laurel Recker for flying me to the University of California, Davis, to speak as part of their "Freudian Sips" Multidisciplinary Psychoanalytic Research Cluster in the fall of 2014. I also wish to recognize Alexandre O. Philippe, Kerry Roy, and Robert Muratore for coming to my home in Cedar City to interview me for *Doc of the Dead* (2014), as well as Jason "Jay of the Dead" Pyles, Joshua "Wolfman Josh" Ligairi, and Dave "Dr. Shock" Becker for dragging me into the world of podcasting, most consistently with their stellar "Horror Podcast Weekly" show. Additional thanks are also in order to the fantastic group of zombie scholars who have created a very supportive and productive community on Twitter: @VintageZombie, @DoctoroftheDead, @HorrorMovieCast, @jason_c_luna, @DVDinfatuation, @adamgolub, @boneyardbetty, @danofthedead82, @jeffreyjcohen, @Jessifer, @kelly_j_baker, @LawZombie, @monstersamerica, @Nicky_Zer0, @RickGodden, @ZombieResearch, and @zombiescholar, just to name a few!

Most importantly, I must thank my circle of intimates, without whom I wouldn't have had the drive or energy to complete this project: my parents, my son Xander, my daughter Sydney, and my very longsuffering and supportive wife Rachel. Her love of *The Walking Dead* is part of what keeps my love for the zombie fresh and new.

Some of the material in this book has appeared previously (often in abbreviated or dated versions) in a number of different publications. For example, I have been developing the introduction for a number of years; it began its life as one of the keynote addresses at the First International Academic Conference on Zombies, and I then developed it into the Tanner Distinguished Faculty Lecture at Southern Utah University in September 2012. A version of the introduction has been published in French as "L'émergence des *Zombie studies*. Comment les morts-vivants ont envahi l'Académie et pourquoi nous devrions nous en soucier" in the anthology *Z pour Zombies*, edited by Bernard Perron, Antonio Dominguez Leiva, and Samuel Archibald (2015: 31–44, © Les Presses de l'Université de Montréal). Much of Chapter 1 appears in a special issue of *Gothic Studies* as "The New American Zombie Gothic: Road Trips, Globalization, and the War on Terror," first published online 8 June 2015, DOI: http://dx.doi.org/10.7227/GS.0003 (2015, © Manchester University Press). Additionally, Chapter 2 was initially published as "Vacationing in *Zombieland*: The Classical Functions of the Modern Zombie Comedy" in the *Journal of the Fantastic in the Arts* (22.1 [2011]: 24–38, © International Association for the Fantastic in the Arts), and a shorter version of Chapter 4 was published as "Battling Monsters and Becoming Monstrous: Human Devolution in *The Walking Dead*" in the anthology *Monster Culture in the 21st Century: A Reader*, edited by Marina Levina and Diem-My T. Bui (New York: Bloomsbury 2013), 73–85.

PREFACE

When I first entertained the idea of the zombie, the walking dead, as a serious topic of academic study ten years ago, I had no idea if my first article on the non-literary origins of zombie cinema would have any traction in the professional scholarly community. After it was published in the *Journal of Popular Film and Television* in 2006,[1] I wasn't sure if I would be able to pitch the same subject successfully to the University of Arizona as a legitimate dissertation topic. After completing my PhD in American literature and film studies with, indeed, a focus on zombie cinema in 2009, I doubted I would be able to take the next step required of newly minted doctorates and find a press willing to publish my dissertation, which at that point I had developed into a manuscript on the cultural history and significance of the zombie narrative as part of the Gothic literary tradition in the United States. When McFarland readily published the book in 2010,[2] I began to think that, perhaps, zombie studies might—just *might*—pay off for me as a scholar—for a few years, at least. Now, looking back on the unusual and nontraditional academic path I have shambled along so successfully, I cannot help but feel surprise at the longevity of this rather bizarre phenomenon. As I have asserted on numerous occasions, I never thought the zombie narrative would continue to be popular—and viable—for this long. I have never been so pleased to be so wrong.

Today, zombie scholars need no longer hide in the shadows or struggle to come up with legitimizing euphemisms for their chosen scholastic passions; in fact, "zombie studies" can readily be found in college curricula, in academic publishing, and all across the Internet in both scholarly and journalistic circles. In February of 2014, Erica E. Phillips from *The Wall Street Journal* contacted me for a story she was writing on the rise of zombie studies in college and university curricula.[3] Thanks in a large part to the commercial success of narratives such as AMC's *The Walking Dead* television series (2010–), entrepreneurial faculty around the country have been using zombie studies as a way to (re)animate their otherwise zombie-like students. Arnold T. Blumberg was one of the first academics to offer such a course on zombie studies back in 2010 at the University of Baltimore as part of the school's new pop culture minor,[4] followed by Kelly Murphy's religion course at Central Michigan University titled "From Revelation to *The Walking Dead*."[5] In addition, Emily Hicks instructs her students in zombie culture at San Diego State University,[6] and Glenn R. Stutzky—with support from Keesa V. Muhammad, Christopher Irvin, and Hailey Mooney—teaches Michigan State University's fully online course SW290: Surviving the Coming Zombie Apocalypse—"Disasters, Catastrophes, and Human Behavior."[7] In fact, Phillips surveys a handful of high-profile zombie courses from such varied institutions as the University of Pennsylvania, George Mason University, Columbia College Chicago, Peru State College, the University of Texas at Tyler, and even Harvard University.[8]

Before McFarland published my first book on the American zombie Gothic cinematic tradition, only a few books dedicated exclusively to zombie studies were available on the market. Two of these were insightful surveys of films featuring zombies or zombie-like creatures, including Peter Dendle's *The Zombie Movie Encyclopedia* (2001) and Arnold T. Blumberg and Andrew Hershberger's *Zombiemania: 80 Movies to Die For* (2006), and Jamie Russell provided a critical overview of zombie history in his *Book of the Dead: The Complete History of Zombie Cinema* (2006). Shawn McIntosh and Marc Leverette produced the first collection of scholarly articles on the zombie phenomenon in 2008 with their landmark *Zombie Culture: Autopsies of the Living Dead*, followed by Deborah Christie and Sarah Juliet Lauro's collection *Better Off Dead: The Evolution of the Zombie as Post-Human* (2011), Stephanie Boluk and Wylie Lenz's anthology *Generation Zombie: Essays on the Living Dead in Modern Culture* (2011), and Christopher M. Moreman and Cory James Rushton's dual collections *Zombies Are Us: Essays on the Humanity of the Walking Dead* (2011) and *Race, Oppression and the Zombie: Essays on Cross-Cultural Appropriations of the Caribbean Tradition* (2011). Dendle has now published a second volume of his *Zombie Movie Encyclopedia* (2012), and both *Book of the Dead* (2014) and *Zombiemania* (2015) are reappearing in new, revised, and expanded editions to join the ranks of such volumes as Alain Silver and James Ursini's *The Zombie Film: From* White Zombie *to* World War Z (2014) and Ozzy Inguanzo's *Zombies on Film: The Definitive Story of Undead Cinema* (2014), not to mention the latest scholarly anthology, *The Zombie Renaissance in Popular Culture*, edited by Laura Hubner, Marcus Leaning, and Paul Manning (2015). In fact, enough academic books on zombie narrative and culture have now been published that McFarland has created an entire "Contributions to Zombie Studies" series (to which this book belongs).

But most of the works I have mentioned focus primarily on zombie cinema, as does my own initial book. This volume hopes to expand that reach, while limiting the discussion to texts appearing during the current Golden Age of the zombie, the so-called Renaissance of the monster and its narratives. While much has already been said about the walking dead—that essentially modern creature born from Haitian folk tradition and refined through the inventive efforts of George A. Romero and his followers—more critical, analytical, and scholarly work remains to be done. The zombie as we know it today is a monster that has developed over the past 100 years through adaptation, mutation, and fusion with other monstrous traditions, not to mention appropriation by other genres and media. As long as filmmakers, authors, computer game designers, television producers, playwrights, musicians, poets, and other artists continue to reinvent and redeploy the zombie figure, students will have fresh material to study and scholars will have more arguments to make. The walking dead will continue to teach us about our own repressed (and revealed) anxieties and tensions, and they will find new ways to continue to horrify and entertain the masses. Perhaps my more cynical declarations regarding the zombie craze have now been thoroughly refuted. Perhaps the zombie is really here to stay.

INTRODUCTION— A MULTIPLICITY OF ZOMBIES

How the Walking Dead Conquered Popular Culture

> The dead walk among us. Zombies, ghouls—no matter what their label—these somnambulists are the greatest threat to humanity itself. To call them predators and us prey would be inaccurate. They are a plague, and the human race their host.—Max Brooks, *The Zombie Survival Guide*

For the past decade, zombies and the narratives told around them have been more popular than ever, with films on both big and small screens; video, board, and card games; fiction, non-fiction, and even children's books; action figures, plush dolls, and other collectibles; and a host of timely metaphors to explain phenomena and theories in a variety of academic and scientific fields and disciplines. In fact, Sarah Juliet Lauro and Karen Embry observed five years ago that zombies were already being found everywhere, and they argue that this "ubiquity of the metaphor suggests the zombie's continued cultural currency."[1] In my attempts to explain this "continued cultural currency" throughout the ongoing "Zombie Renaissance," I have explored the fundamental nature of zombie cinema through not only its singular origins but also its relationship to post–9/11 cultural consciousness. Building on an essentially "New World" and relatively recent folkloric tradition, the zombie has evolved and matured into a universally recognizable figure, joining the hallowed ranks of other, more established supernatural monsters—but now perhaps transcending them, thanks in large part to their mutability in nature, kind, and application. Indeed, zombies and their associated apocalyptic landscapes seem to be appearing in the real-world—through the aftereffects of

5

terrorist attacks, natural disasters, drug crazes, and pandemics—resulting in survival manuals, training retreats, and even governmental apocalypse contingency plans. However, the contradictory nature of these various and changing zombies—dead but alive, conscious but lacking consciousness, animated but decaying, alive but infected—makes them the perfect figures to explain an apparently inexhaustible host of natural occurrences, social interactions, technological advances, psychological and physiological anomalies, economic structures and relationships, political dynamics, and more. In other words, modern zombies are now more than just fictional monsters that allow people to cathartically deal with the horrors of the post–9/11 era; they are "meaning machines"[2] that have become the "allegory of the moment," embraced not only by the entertainment industry but also by academic and professional disciplines beyond film and cultural studies as a valid subject of investigation and critical study.

Zombies, Zombies, Zombies

Society's current obsession with zombies should come as no surprise, as the walking dead are, in a certain sense, *real*. Rather than simply being born in the mind of an inventive Gothic novelist or developed over time on the page or the stage, the zombie has its noteworthy origins in what to most in the West would be considered folklore, but to the practitioners of the Vodou religion might be considered reality. Vampires, reanimated golems, and ghosts can be traced back to specific literary traditions, and even the werewolf has arguably just become a variation on Robert Louis Stevenson's *The Strange Case of Dr. Jekyll and Mr. Hyde* (1886). The zombie, on the other hand, comes from Haitian folklife, nonfiction accounts, and travel narratives of bodies "raised from the dead to labor in the fields,"[3] not from fiction. Appropriated by art, the zombie has now become an important *cultural* figure because of its powerful role as a multifaceted *allegorical* figure. All monsters should be read metaphorically, of course, as Jeffrey Jerome Cohen and W. Scott Poole both remind us,[4] but the zombie has (at least currently) the *most* mutability and potential for application. In fact, we now need to speak in terms of zom*bies*, not just *the* zombie anymore. The key to understanding the valuable significance of this "multiplicity of zombies," not to mention their current explosion in popularity, is to develop a workable—if reductive—taxonomy to understand the ways zombie allegories have appeared over the course of their development and refinement. With this taxonomy in mind, the reasons behind the multifarious appropriations of the zombie figure in so many artistic, academic, scientific, social, and cultural fields becomes clear—zombies can be whatever we *need* them to be, and their various natures, manifestations, and mutations lend themselves to explaining ideas and concepts efficiently that would otherwise be difficult to understand.

The first type of zombie to consider in this taxonomy is of course the "real" zombie, the "walking dead" monstrosity created by misappropriated Vodou ritual and magic—or, more likely, homeopathic pharmacology. This kind of zombie has been a terrifying part of Vodou culture, particularly that found in the post-colonial nation of Haiti, for over a hundred years now. According to ethnographers Hans W. Ackermann and Jeanine Gauthier, many West African and Congolese mythologies describe the *zombi* as a "corpse" or a "body without a soul."[5] This ancient belief was likely transformed when abducted slaves were exposed to the Christian concept of resurrection—a body returned from the grave—and the ideologies of colonial enslavement—bodies lacking freedom and autonomy. As a result of this cross-cultural fusion, Haitian zombies were born: victims of nefarious chemical assault, lacking conscious minds and, implicitly, their souls as well. Of course, these New World zombies aren't dead, flesh-eating monsters but rather the targets of rogue *bokors* who poison their prey and turn them into mindless slaves. Ethnobotanist Wade Davis claims these mystics use their knowledge of plants, poisons, and natural sedatives (specifically tetrodotoxin) to concoct a "zombie powder"—called *coup poudre*—that makes its victims appear clinically deceased.[6] After a quick burial and brief period of entombment, the oxygen-starved and thus brain-damaged victims are dug up and revived by the *bokor* for his own nefarious purposes or to be sold into slavery.

Thus the real-world zombie of Vodou folklife isn't a monster to be feared, but rather a tragic victim to be pitied. Instead of being used to populate massive armies of the undead, as would be sensationally depicted on the screen by Hollywood, these poor souls are taken from their families, sold to unscrupulous plantation owners, and forced to work the sugar fields in abject misery for the rest of their days. Such creatures were hardly of interest to horror movie producers, but they did receive the attention of anthropologists and ethnographers. Perhaps the first to write about theses pathetic zombies was William B. Seabrook in his 1929 travelogue *The Magic Island*. Seabrook describes the zombies he saw as plodding brutes, "like automatons ... [with] the eyes of a dead man, not blind, but staring, unfocused, unseeing. The whole face ... was vacant, as if there was nothing behind it."[7] Years later, in 1938, Zora Neale Hurston gave a more analytical account of the Haitian zombie. In *Tell My Horse*, Hurston narrates her encounter with the zombie named Felicia Felix-Mentor, who had a "blank face with ... dead eyes. The eyelids were white all around the eyes as if they had been burned with acid."[8]

Although these creatures are not necessarily *monsters*, they are nonetheless *monstrous*—the difference is that, in Haiti, one is not afraid *of* a zombie but rather of *becoming* one.

The second type of zombie to develop was directly adapted—albeit loosely and fictionally—from the first: the feckless victims of evil voodoo practitioners, especially white, *female* victims. Thanks to the popularity of Seabrook's largely unsubstantiated reports of Haiti as a backwards country of pagan magic and primitive superstition, the zombie that made its way to general U.S. audiences was one deeply (mis)informed by ignorance and imperialist racism. The first of many films to feature this kind of zombie is Victor Halperin's 1932 production *White Zombie*.[9] Clearly designed to take advantage of the popularity of Universal's *Dracula* (1931, directed by Tod Browning), Halperin's film is dark, brooding, and overtly Gothic, focusing primarily on the maniacal actions of an evil voodoo master and mesmerist, "Murder" Legendre, played with melodramatic relish by Bela Lugosi. Films such as *White Zombie* abuse Haitian folklore to manifest the greatest fear of a white, imperialist audience: that subservient, black "Others" would rise up and enslave their former oppressors. The true "monster" of these "voodoo zombie" films, including *King of the Zombies* (1941, directed by Jean Yarbrough) and Jacques Tourneur's *I Walked with a Zombie* (1943), among others, are not the shambling, clumsy zombies themselves but rather those who create them; in other words, as with the Vodou legends, these zombies are most frightening because of viewers' fear of enslavement rather than that of a violent death.

In addition to epitomizing colonialist slavery, Halperin's zombies also draw parallels between slaves and capitalist proletarian workers. As the first zombies to appear on the movie screen, Legendre's slow-moving, dim-witted, and essentially dumb creatures have established the conventional and expected "look" of the zombie. On the one hand, the dark-skinned zombies would have reminded viewers of black slaves and a recent, imperialist economic structure. On the other, however, Halperin's macabre cast would have no doubt emphasized for his audience the toiling working class or the hopelessly unemployed who shuffled almost as aimlessly in Depression-era bread and soup lines.[10] For viewers in the United States, the idea of being turned into literal slaves might have been far-fetched, but the thought of being enslaved by a tedious job, a bleak economy, or a helpless government was an immediate reality. This trope of losing one's independence to a greater power continued to manifest well into the post–World War II era, with science-fiction films such as *Invisible Invaders* (1959, directed by Edward L. Cahn), *The Earth Dies Screaming* (1964, directed by Terence Fisher), and even, to some extent, Don Siegel's *Invasion of the Body Snatchers* (1956). These Cold-War variants, while not zombie movies in the true sense, nonetheless build on Halperin's initial idea of enslavement, but with the added fear of invasion and domination.

Xenophobic fears of Communism set the stage for the third variant of zombie, the one that has come to dominate popular depictions of the monster today: a horde of cannibalistic, walking-dead ghouls, invented almost single handedly by George A. Romero with his 1968 film *Night of the Living Dead*.[11] In his low-budget attempt to adapt Richard Matheson's *I Am Legend* (1954) to the screen, Romero drew from a variety of literary and cinematic influences to create, perhaps inadvertently, the "modern zombie." As I discuss in my contribution to Christa Albrecht-Crane and Dennis Cutchins' *Adaptation Studies: New Beginnings* (2010), *Night of the Living Dead* is a clever amalgam of images and tropes from the early zombie films, popular alien invasion movies, rural siege narratives—notably Alfred Hitchcock's 1963 film *The Birds*—and vampire movies such as Ubaldo Ragona and Sidney Salkow own adaptation of *I Am Legend*, *The Last Man on Earth* (1964).[12] Most importantly, perhaps, Romero was inspired by another mythical fiend: the ghoul—an otherworldly creature from Arabian folklore that haunted graveyards and ate the flesh of human corpses. Like vampires, Romero's monsters feast on human victims, but they eat the whole body, not just the blood. To up the stakes even further, the monstrous condition is contagious: being killed by the ghouls of *Night of the Living Dead*—or even simply being bitten by one—means joining their ranks as one of them as well.

Rather than being converted to the army of walking dead by a maniacal voodoo mesmerist or invading aliens, then, Romero's victims become subject to "living death," a condition that strips them of both intelligence and natural life to make them infected, contagious, and horrifically violent killers. Suddenly everything about the zombie changed: the zombies themselves became the unequivocal monsters to be feared, "driven by their hunger rather than by a necromancer's will,"[13] becoming both slave and enslaver in one; and rather than having a group of humans fighting a single foe, as in *Dracula*, the scenario now became a multitude of "them" versus a dwindling number of "us."[14] As Romero redefined—or, perhaps more accurately, reinvented—the zombie forever, he helpfully provided viewers with a clear set of "rules" that would come to dominate most depictions of the zombie to follow. Using the media as a mouthpiece, *Night of the Living Dead* establishes these simple yet fundamental basics: recently dead humans have returned from the dead to attack and eat the living, anyone bitten by one of the creatures—or killed in any other way—becomes one of them, and the only way to destroy one of the monsters is by destroying its brain. Furthermore, the slow moving ghouls are only really dangerous *en masse* because, as Sheriff McClelland (George Kosana) famously states, "Yeah, they're dead. They're all messed up."

With Romero, then, the metaphorical force of the zombie expands into a broader analogy, one that addresses violence, death, mortality, cannibalism, invasion, and infection, not to mention sexism, racism, the collapse of the nuclear family, and even incest. Filmed in the midst of the Vietnam War, *Night of the Living Dead* forced its contemporary viewers to face the morbid realities of violent death: rotting corpses, dismembered bodies, and bloody bullet wounds.[15] Released without a rating, the film's violence was all the more horrifying not only because of its raw brutality—clawing hands and rending teeth with cannibalistic results—but also because it often occurs between family members. This familial barbarism can be read as a kind of symbolic incest, and it draws attention to the general disintegration of the traditional family structure of the 1950s. In fact, *Night of the Living Dead* depicts the literal siege of a family home, and the zombie plague results in a young couple dying in an explosion, a brother killing his sister, and a young girl feasting upon the flesh of her murdered parents. In addition, the supernatural monstrousness of the zombies is mirrored by the more realistic atrocities committed by the human characters, including violent acts against women, a domineering patriarchy, and a racially coded lynching.

Most fans and scholars consider the zenith of the 20th-centry zombie movie to be Romero's *Dawn of the Dead* (1978), the film that most overtly brought the central analogy of the "new" zombie to the fore: *they are us.* By shifting the action's focus from the farmhouse to the suburban shopping mall, Romero redirects his critical lens as well. The metaphor this time is less worried about war and civil discord as it is about economic instability and unchecked consumerism. Cohen argues that because zombies are "[c]reatures of pure consumption and drive, [they] are the logical products of capitalism."[16] Fittingly, then, the relentless "mall zombies" of *Dawn of the Dead* criticize humanity as mindless victims of their implacable drives and desires, people whose overwhelming need to shop and consume will motivate them even after death. Instead of suggesting that humanity has something to fear either from the zombies or about becoming part of their insatiable army, Romero's second zombie film frightens audiences by revealing how everyone is potentially already a kind of zombie in real life, mindless drones infected with irresponsible capitalistic desires. The zombies relentlessly clamoring to enter the shops of the Monroeville Mall are decidedly pathetic, once again cast in the role of victims, and, as the movie's heroes learn over the course of the film, anyone can join them in their tragic fate. Romero's movies—along with those produced by his imitators—can thus be read in a variety of ways, depending on one's prevailing concerns and interests.

The contagious, flesh-eating monster of the zombie invasion narrative enjoyed a measure of success as a diverse and flexible cultural metaphor in both the United States and Europe (most notably Italy with fare such as Lucio Fulci's *Zombi 2* [1979]) almost exclusively on the movie screen for over a decade, but in the 1980s, the monster suffered a decline in both popularity and usefulness as the genre shifted into its parody phase. The beginning of the decline came in 1983 with the release of Michael Jackson's epic *Thriller* music video, a film short (directed by John Landis) that features dancing and jiving corpses drawn from their graves. Rather than serving an allegorical purpose, Jackson's zombies are kitschy, exaggerated, and decidedly non-frightening. A showdown of sorts was brewing between the serious and the comedic, and it reached a tipping point in 1985 when Romero's third zombie movie, *Day of the Dead*—an insightful critique of the Cold War—was less prolific, popular, or profitable at the box office than Dan O'Bannon's revisionist, irreverent, and even silly *The Return of the Living Dead*. The brain-eating monsters of O'Bannon's "zomedy"—or zombie comedy—made $4.4 million the film's opening weekend compared to *Day of the Dead*'s $1.7 million.[17] After 1985, the traditional and "serious" zombie narratives all but disappeared from the scene, replaced by lighter fare such as *I Was a Teenage Zombie* (1987, directed by John Elias Michalakis), *Dead Heat* (1988, directed by Mark Goldblatt), and Peter Jackson's *Braindead* (1992, also known as *Dead Alive*). Instead of having something valuable to say about society, the cinematic zombie was relegated to mere schlock entertainment, and few scholars saw any reason to afford the creatures serious attention. The horrifying and useful zombie thus went into a period of incubation, sustained primarily by video games such as id Software's *Doom* (1993) and CapCom's Romero-inspired *Bio Hazard* (1996, directed by Shinji Mikami and Mitsuhisa Hosoki), since retitled *Resident Evil*.

However, like the walking dead themselves, monstrous and metaphorically pregnant zombies returned, reentering mainstream consciousness in the wake of September 11. Danny Boyle's *28 Days Later* (2002)—although featuring "infecteds" that are living, breathing humans who have simply been infected by a "rage virus"—reignited the zombie invasion narrative. Once again, an isolated band of disparate survivors are on the run from a seemingly endless horde of bloodthirsty cannibals, but this time the creatures move with lightning speed and infect their prey with their tainted bodily fluids in mere seconds. More importantly, Boyle's living zombies reinstated the allegorical power of the monster. Released at a time when the shocking images of a devastated New York City were still fresh on viewers' minds, *28 Days Later*'s apocalyptic sequence of Jim (Cillian Murphy) wandering aimlessly around the deserted streets of London, picking up scraps of useless paper money and pondering a vast street shrine with photos of the dead and missing, can clearly be read as a cathartic restatement of the horrors of natural disasters and terrorist attacks. As the film progresses, it also offers sober commentary on the risks associated with blood-borne viruses, such as AIDS, and the dangers of an excessively empowered military. By 2002, the zombie, it appeared, could once again be taken seriously as a source of both terror and horror.

Another key narrative in the burgeoning Zombie Renaissance was Paul W. S. Anderson's adaptation of the successful *Resident Evil* games, titled simply *Resident Evil* (2002). Like Boyle's film, *Resident Evil* appears to be more science fiction than horror, but its monsters are unequivocally walking dead zombies—although amazingly quick and powerful ones. Anderson's movie does offer an indictment against corporate greed and unethical scientific practices, but its relevance in helping get the zombie "back on its feet," as it were, comes primarily from making the monster both terrifying and popular again in the mainstream. *Resident Evil* raked in almost $18 million its opening weekend and went on to gross over $100 million worldwide.[18] Other producers and filmmakers quickly took notice, and it suddenly seemed as if any script with zombies in it was greenlighted and rushed into production. Over the next few years, major Hollywood studios were eager to produce and distribute a host of adaptations, sequels, and remakes, including Uwe Boll's video-game adaptation *House of the Dead* (2003), *Resident Evil: Apocalypse* (2004, directed by Alexander Witt), and Zack Snyder's *Dawn of the Dead* remake (2004), not to mention sophisticated zomedies such as Edgar Wright's *Shaun of the Dead* (2004), and even a brand-new Romero zombie film, *Land of the Dead* (2005). The zombie was suddenly and unarguable relevant again, and the creature at last had the financial support it needed to become a real box office star.

Over the course of the past ten years, the zombie as a metaphorical icon has multiplied and spread throughout popular culture in a manner not unlike an infectious pandemic, moving beyond film and video games to infest other forms of entertainment as well. Whereas the original zombie was almost exclusively limited to cinematic depictions, zombie books have recently made their appearance. Max Brooks lead the way with his successful *The Zombie Survival Guide* (2003)—a quasi-nonfiction piece that set the stage for zombie-themed survivalist preparation, training, and research—followed by his more traditional novel, *World War Z* (2006), and even Stephen King entered the fray with *Cell* in the same year. Zombie video games and graphic novels left the margins and went mainstream, with new additions, such as a host of *Resident Evil* sequels, *Left 4 Dead* (2008, directed by Mike Booth), Robert Kirkman's *The Walking Dead* comic series (2003–), and the irreverent comic mashup *Marvel Zombies* series (2005–). Before anyone knew to expect it, zombies could be found in card games, on iPhone apps, on the radio, in television shows, and all over the aisles at Toys R Us. In addition to proliferating across media, the zombie has also experienced rapid mutation. Some zombies remain dead, whereas others are alive; some only eat brains, whereas others eat the entire human body; some zombies merely grunt and moan, whereas others may have an eloquent command of the English language—and, of course, some are slow and others fast.[19] In fact, some zombies have even transcended their roles as monsters.

Many diehard fans of the zombie longed to root for these misunderstood creatures, wishing to elevate them from monstrous antagonists to sympathetic protagonists, and the fourth type of zombie was born. This transformation should come as no surprise; after all, Anne Rice did the same thing for the vampire back in the 1970s, and things have never been quite the same for that one-time frightening foe since. Of course, this latest change to the zombie started long before the current Renaissance. Romero himself introduced the idea of a "hero zombie" in *Day of the Dead* with the landmark character of Bub (Sherman Howard), a sympathetic figure who appears able to recall behaviors and mannerisms from his former, human existence. An even more sophisticated zombie character arises in *Land of the Dead* in the form of "Big Daddy" (Eugene Clark), the erstwhile gas station attendant who leads a zombie army against the humans of Fiddler's Green. Big Daddy seems to teach the other zombies to communicate, and he insists they overcome their zombie instincts to focus on a concerted task and to even use tools and weapons. And one of the most charming zombie protagonists in recent years is Fido (Billy Connolly), the unlikely hero and father figure in Andrew Currie's 2006 film of the same name. But each of these somewhat likeable creatures is still essentially dead, dumb, and less intelligent, sympathetic primarily because of their lingering and remembered humanity.

Other manifestations of the zombie protagonist alter the fundamental characteristics of the creatures even further—and, in my mind, more illogically—by giving them the power of speech and the ability to think and feel. This "Ricification" of the traditional zombie is a radical change from the mindless, silent horde originally envisioned by Romero, and even farther afield from the brain-damaged victims described in Haitian folklore. The conscious or so-called "agent zombie"[20] has its most influential origin in O'Bannon's

The Return of the Living Dead, particularly in the tragicomic duo of Frank (James Karen) and Freddy (Thom Mathews), who narrate the painful process of transforming into the walking dead. The other zombies can speak as well, uttering the now famous line of "Brains!" and the lesser known "Send ... more ... paramedics!" Not surprisingly, speaking, thinking, and feeling zombies have mostly been relegated to comedies, such as the web video *Zombie-American* (2005, directed by Nick Poppy) and the clever film *Wasting Away* (2007, directed by Matthew Kohnen),[21] as well as "zom-rom-com" novels, such as S.G. Browne's *Breathers: A Zombie's Lament* (2009) and Isaac Marion's *Warm Bodies* (2010). To depict a conscious zombie realistically in a serious narrative requires major alterations to the fundamental characteristics of the zombie, but Marc Price's micro-budget *Colin* (2008) does a good job of showing how a zombie could "star" in its own narrative by using a sympathetic, first-person POV and careful acting and directing.

Whether zombies can talk, think, feel, or remember their former lives, today's zombies are clearly more diverse than ever and thus more broadly useful for analogy in a variety of narratives across almost all media. One of the primary reasons the Zombie Renaissance was even possible was the world's collective fears and anxieties about terrorist attacks and global pandemics. Because zombies look like our former friends and loved ones, they represent the plain-clothed terrorist or the brainwashed extremist. Because zombies attack relentlessly in apocalyptic numbers, they signify an invading army, or, in the case of *Land of the Dead*, masses of illegal immigrants. Because zombies can infect anyone suddenly and incurably, they mirror our collective fears about anthrax, the bird flu, mad cow disease, and every other perceived infection. As with the films of the twentieth century, our new-era zombies allow us to continue our struggles with race, gender, sexual identity, religion, and class, not to mention ongoing critiques of failed political policies and a collapsing economy. Perhaps more importantly, as we allow ourselves to sympathize with these tragic monsters, we can use zombies and the stories told around them to explore our more philosophical questions about life and death or about our inability to live life to its fullest. Yes, Mr. Romero, zombies are us, but we are also always already them, which means they must no longer be confined to the limits of works of fiction.

The Mutable, Interdisciplinary Allegory

This mass proliferation of the zombie has now extended beyond the confines of mere entertainment culture, leading to the fifth type of zombie and bringing things full circle: real-world zombies. These are not the literal walking dead, of course, despite what certain imaginative members of the blogosphere would have us believe, but rather a passionate affectation of zombies and zombie scenarios in our daily lives and in a variety of disciplines, discourses, and fields. Experiencing a zombie holocaust vicariously through movies, books, and video games is simply not enough for some people; instead, they want to *live* the apocalypse first hand, perhaps because our collective fears of terrorist threats have made everyday life too much like survival horror anyway.[22] College campuses around the country are hosting zombie tag games, such as "Humans vs. Zombies,"[23] corporate paint-ball retreats have been replaced by zombie fantasy camps and survival courses,[24] and a new kind of "Run for Your Lives" obstacle course race includes staff dressed up as zombies to chase—and thus motivate—the runners.[25] The Sacramento River Train company even offers a special "Zombie Train" experience for the adventurous traveler—$35 to be a passenger; $50 if you want a gun![26] New survival handbooks,[27] training courses,[28] DIY kits, outfitter stores, and even cookbooks[29] have built upon the success of Brooks' book, and prepping for a real zombie apocalypse—or a realistic analog—has become a new kind of lifestyle. On the one hand, enthusiasts want to play the role of the survivors, proving to themselves and others they have what it takes to survive a real zombie apocalypse, but, on the other, many increasingly enjoy dressing up and acting the part of the walking dead as well. Zombie festivals, zombie raves, and zombie walks have gone mainstream, and people revel in the escapism that comes from trading one's concerns and responsibilities for the mindless lumbering of the zombie.[30] Zombies are now big business, and not just as part of the entertainment industry.

It should come as no surprise, then, that these mutable metaphors, these increasingly popular and diverse monsters that have moved from folklore to entertainment to lifestyle, are beginning to invade other academic disciplines and fields of social and scientific study as well. Zombies—or at least the idea of them—are being employed to explain mathematical variability, neuroscience, global economics, world history, and unusual biological, zoological, botanical, and astrological phenomena. A number of academic books are readily available on the market that deploy the zombie metaphor, including Henry A. Giroux's *Zombie Politics and Culture in the Age of Casino Capitalism* (2010), Chris Harman's *Zombie Capitalism: Global Crisis and the Relevance of Marx* (2010), John Quiggin's *Zombie Economics: How Dead Ideas Still Walk among Us* (2010), Daniel W. Drezner's *Theories of International Politics and Zombies* (2011), and Glen Whitman and James Dow's *Economics of the Undead: Zombies, Vampires, and the Dismal Science* (2014), not to mention a book about the entire multidisciplinary phenomenon itself, Andrew Whelan, Ruth Walker, and Christopher Moore's collection, *Zombies in the Academy: Living Death in Higher Education* (2013). A few years ago, Matt Mogk founded the online Zombie Research Society,[31] assembling a board of artists, academics, and scientists, which has been followed by similar websites, such as the Zombie Institute for Theoretical Studies.[32] As mentioned in the preface, a number of colleges and universities are now offering serious, legitimate instruction in "zombie studies" for academic credit, beginning with Arnold Blumberg's "Zombie 101" class at the University of Baltimore in 2010[33] and continuing through to the University of California Irvine's free online course titled "Society, Science, Survival: Lessons from AMC's *The Walking Dead*."[34] Zombies are not only big business, but also a big part of current scholarship, research, and education.

With zombies invading virtually every part of our social, cultural, and scientific existence, members of the academic and scientific community can finally come out of hiding and admit to their peers, administrators, and tenure committees that they are, indeed, zombie scholars. Why? Because zombies matter. Let me repeat that: Zombies. Matter. Although many still disparage "popular culture" as being too common or low brow, the truth is that anything with pervasive popularity needs to be taken seriously, and the current Zombie Renaissance is a textbook example of why literature, art, and even popular culture is so important to investigate, to study, and (hopefully) to understand. Tony Magistrale, in his influential *Abject Terrors* (2005), explains how the "art of terror, whether literary or celluloid, has always addressed our most pressing fears as a society and as individuals.... [Horror] is nothing less than a barometer for measuring an era's cultural anxieties."[35] In other words, when horror increases in popularity, we need to figure out why, because such works of art and culture indicate tensions and fears that may not be readily apparent otherwise. And the zombie represents the *horreur de la jour*, a versatile tabula rasa upon which to impress the darkest secrets of our collective souls.[36] Peter Dendle, the pioneer of modern zombie studies, reminds us that "the zombie holocausts vividly painted in movies and video games have tapped into a deep-seated anxiety about society, government, individual protection, and our increasing disconnectedness from subsistence skills,"[37] and understanding these anxieties will teach us much about many aspects of the modern world.

And so, the zombie, acting primarily as a multifarious metaphor for complicated phenomenon, can help us to understand the perplexing world around us. This approach has already been applied to the natural world, a world in which zombie fungi can take over the brains of ants and control their bodies,[38] in which zombie maple trees continue to live despite failing to grow,[39] and in which zombified caterpillars transmit their controlling virus by dying before molting.[40] The zombie metaphor can be used to understand bizarre astronomical occurrences, such as a communications satellite that has been turned into a zombie thanks to a massive solar flare,[41] dead white dwarf stars that somehow come back to life after a massive explosion,[42] or comets that return to view after appearing to "die."[43] The idea of the zombie can help us understand more about psychology,[44] brain chemistry,[45] and neuroscience[46]; provide a controversial form of motivation for drug addicts[47]; and illuminate new processes of cyber hacking[48] and nefarious digital viruses.[49] Zombie investments plague the oil industry[50] and zombie assemblies stall international political negotiations,[51] yet zombie math can help predict viral outbreaks and pandemics.[52] And even the federal government of the United States cannot escape the revealing power of the zombie meme, as it can be used to criticize international security,[53] banking practices,[54] and even health care legislation.[55] In fact, the Centers for Disease Control and Prevention have embraced a zombie worldview, dedicating a portion of their Office of Public Health Preparedness and Response to "Zombie Preparedness," providing the public with a blog, a series of public service posters, and a novella comic demonstrating what people should do during a zombie pandemic.[56] The zombie is more than just the movie monster of the month or the narrative trope of the moment— it has become a part of all kinds of serious academic scholarship and discourse, from biology to psychology to politics to economics to social studies, as well as a helpful social and cultural metaphor.

But why? I contend zombies are *the* great metaphorical monsters because they can be tailored and applied to almost any discipline or situation, and people see in zombies what they *need* to see. Zombies—be they exploring the horrors of slavery; depicting an apocalyptic, infectious invasion; or acting as metaphors for the latest scientific or cultural development—have clearly proven themselves as timely, popular, and relevant figures. As I wrote in my first book, because the stories told around zombies "so overtly and directly deal with the trauma associated with enslavement, infection, death, and decay, they operate as revealing lenses turned upon the heart of our social and cultural anxieties. Initially, zombies shocked audiences because of their unfamiliar appearance; today, they are even more shocking because of their familiarity."[57] Zombie narratives, games, and allegories allow us to confront the paranoia and anxieties we feel about infection, death, destruction, and the inexplicable mysteries of our cultural and natural world. We purge these anxieties through the catharsis of apocalyptic narratives, exorcise our destructive tendencies through violent video games, and verify our ingenuity and resourcefulness through survival scenarios and exercises. By participating in zombie walks, we (with cunning irony) raise money for food banks, and by giving our children plush zombie dolls and plastic toys, we prepare them to face the realities of mortality. We take advantage of the popularity and ubiquity of the zombie to explain the otherwise inexplicable, making complex ideas more comprehensible and disturbing phenomenon more palatable. And by finally admitting these creatures have become an unavoidable part of our art, literature, and culture, we can now dedicate a branch of serious academic study to zombies. The fact is that zombies matter, and I now think they are really here to stay.

Zombies Among Us

Since the publication of my 2010 book *American Zombie Gothic: The Rise and Fall (and Rise) of the Walking Dead in Popular Culture*, I have been afforded a number of opportunities to explore zombie cultural history and to perform close reading and analysis of a variety of zombie narratives in a variety of different genres, styles, and media. These critical investigations have manifested in public lectures, academic conferences, and publications in both scholarly journals and popular anthologies. My goal with this new monograph is to collect those essays, papers, and articles in one place, providing readers with a series of interrelated yet independent works that can be read or taught alone or in any sequence. While my first book explored how the zombie figure and its associated narratives developed over the course of the twentieth century, almost exclusively in the United States, I have since become more interested in the wider proliferation of these stories. In addition to the expected continuation of both mainstream and independent zombie films—including dramas and comedies—the zombie can now be found much more readily and frequently in narratives directed towards children and young adults, in comics and graphic novels, in short stories and literary novels, on television and the stage, and in video games. Additionally, like a pervasive pandemic, the zombie has made its way into multiple countries and cultures, and zombie studies must now more readily address international zombie narratives, such as John Ajvide Lindqvist's 2005 novel *Hanteringen av odöda* (translated into English as *Handling the Undead*, 2010) or Alejandro Brugués's 2011 Cuban film *Juan de los Muertos* (*Juan of the Dead*). And finally, because the zombie has finally established itself as part of the paranormal romance market, no comprehensive study of the contemporary zombie can ignore texts such as Adam Selzer's *I Kissed a Zombie, and I Liked It* (2010) or Daniel Waters's *Generation Dead* (2008) either.

I have grouped the chapters of this collection thematically rather than chronologically, beginning with a triptych that addresses the generic phases of the zombie narrative. Building on Cohen's observation that "[a]ny monster that captures the imagination long enough will inhabit three intimately related cultural registers simultaneously: horror, comedy, and children's media,"[58] the first section of this book will consider the horror of Marc Forster's 2013 film adaptation of *World War Z*, the comedic revisionism of Ruben Fleischer's *Zombieland* (2009), and Carrie Ryan's young adult zombie novel *The Forest of Hands and Teeth* (2010). Chapter 1 investigates the shift in the zombie Gothic narrative structure evinced over the past decade, a shift that redefines the horror of the zombie invasion in terms of optimistic movement and relocation rather than hopeless fortification and isolation. I also consider the transmutation of zombie films that once emphasized microcosmic, rural scenarios into a more global investigation of the broader social and cultural impact of a realistically depicted zombie apocalypse. Chapter 2 addresses the surprisingly classical nature of most zomedy films, focusing primarily on *Zombieland*. I argue zombie comedy films are essentially romantic adventures that pit unlikely heroes against supernatural foes simply so they might obtain the hand of a maiden "princess" and prove their "manly" worth. Chapter 3 develops my claim that zombie narratives for young adults—at least the serious, more frightening versions, such as *The Forest of Hands and Teeth*—can represent a teenager's greatest fears and perhaps greatest temptations: conformity, a domineering hive mentality, and the lack of requisite agency and decision-making responsibilities. These chapters explore three key generic variations in the zombie story across at least two prevalent disciplines.

The next section, "Beyond Film," departs from the traditional exploration of zombies on the screen and continues the investigation into literary zombies begun by Chapter 3. Chapter 4 offers a close reading of arguably the most successful zombie comic series, Kirkman's *The Walking Dead*. I argue how this ongoing narrative should be read as a morality tale about the dangers associated with fighting monster: one often becomes monstrous oneself. The protagonists of *The Walking Dead* must take desperate actions to survive in an increasingly devastating apocalyptic landscape, and most can only do this successfully by embracing violence, atavism, and antisocial behavior, and the series as a whole can thus be interpreted as a cultural indictment of recent aggressive U.S. foreign and domestic policies. Chapter 5 explores the cynical nostalgia of a post-9/11 world as represented in Colson Whitehead's literary zombie novel *Zone One* (2011). The chapter analyzes Whitehead's depiction of New York City as a zombified body, both in the novel—infected by viral "skel" and "straggler" zombies—and in real life—as a metropolitan city recovering from the violent trauma of a devastating terrorist attack. Chapter 6 focuses on what I consider performative zombie narratives, namely those found in some television serials and on the live stage. I examine the original play *Uncle Vanya and Zombies* (2012), written and directed by University of Hawai'i at Mānoa professor Markus Wessendorf, as an example of the interactive nature of the zombie in the Grand-Guignol tradition. The chapter also explores the parallels between zombies and contemporary reality television, as depicted by the Channel 4 miniseries *Dead Set* (2008, directed by Yann Demange) and Wessendorf's mash-up of Anton Chekhov's 1897 play, indicting the viewing audience in the voyeuristic nature of zombie narratives.

The final section of this book looks at "zombie variants"—or "Broader Horizons"—manifestations of the zombie that don't necessarily follow the established or proscribed expectations for the post–Romero zombie but instead push the monster into new and potentially exciting directions. Chapter 7 considers the interactive nature of zombie video games, specifically Neil Druckmann and Bruce Straley's 2013 game *The Last of Us*, to explore why that form of narrative may prove to be the most fertile ground for zombie development and variation. Because of the interactive nature of these kinds of games, the terror of the zombie narrative is enhanced, allowing players to experience their survivalist fantasies more realistically than through cinema alone. Furthermore, expansive video games allow for more character development, increase the level at which the audience identifies with those characters, and provide artists greater opportunities for interpretive license, creative development, and verisimilar depictions. Chapter 8 considers the host of "zombie lookalike" monsters that have cropped up in recent years, rebranding existing monsters from legend and folklore to take advantage of the current popularity of zombies. I focus my analysis primarily on Tommy Wirkola's 2009 film *Død snø* (*Dead Snow*), a story of Nazi *draugar* or *aptrgangr* that prove more dangerous than they should be because they are mistaken for Western zombies instead of Norwegian revenants. I argue writers, filmmakers, and game designers should be exploring the potential of all kinds of undead and supernatural monsters from a variety of cultures and traditions, and that these monsters should be able to stand on their own instead of being arbitrarily (mis)labeled as "zombies." Despite my personal reservations against thinking, feeling zombie protagonists, I offer Chapter 9 as my investigation—and admitted criticism—of zombie romances, focusing on Jonathan Levine's 2013 film *Warm Bodies*, adapted from Marion's novel. The chapter considers the similarities between the film and Shakespeare's *Romeo and Juliet*, as well as the *Twilight* series of books from Stephenie Meyer (2005–12). I argue against the risks such paranormal romances may pose for impressionable readers and viewers, as these narratives tend to champion passive female protagonists who fall in love with dominant and even dangerous "monstrous" boyfriends.

My goal with this collection is to provide readers of all stripes—academics as well as fans, scholars as well as lay readers—a sampling of the kinds of zombies, narratives, media, and arguments I have explored over the past few years, not as the end-all, be-all of zombie studies but rather as an access point for further discussion and discourse. Contrary to some of my naïve conclusions at the end of *American Zombie Gothic*, I think our collective love affair with the walking dead is far from over, and extensive scholarship on zombie movies, comics, books, plays, video games, and television shows—not to mention poetry, music, visual art, and other manifestations of the monster—has really just begun. While on the surface the zombie may appear to be a shallow and unsophisticated creature, it is actually a complex manifestation of what it means to be human—and posthuman, as Lauro and Embry effectively argue.[59] As the cultural contributions of the zombie continue to grow in both number and quality, more fans and scholars alike will give these shambling foes the attention they deserve. And, as a result, we will all hopefully learn more about what it means to exist in this mortal world of ours. The dead, ironically, have much to teach us about being alive.

Chapter 1

THE (NEW) CINEMATIC ZOMBIE
Road Trips, Globalization
and *World War Z*

"Movimiento es vida. Movimiento es vida."
—Gerry, *World War Z* (2013)

During the 20th century, most Gothic zombie invasion narratives on the screen, especially George A. Romero's first three canonical zombie films, centered on the relentless siege of a static, fortified location: a rural farmhouse, a suburban shopping mall, and an isolated military bunker. Rather than actively seeking help from the outside, the disparate survivors in these films concentrate their collective efforts on staying put, on staying *safe*. Now, as the zombie monster enjoys its current Renaissance in the twenty-first century, a noticeable shift in narrative structure has taken place, one that challenges the established Gothic conventions of fixed locations, hauntings, and uncanny revelations. In many of the post–9/11 zombie films, Gothic settings and themes have shifted from passive rural isolation and fortification to more active urban interaction and engagement. Instead of "staying put," the protagonists in many films—including Romero's three most recent zombie films, Edgar Wright's *Shaun of the Dead* (2004), and Ruben Fleischer's *Zombieland* (2009)—spend the majority of their narratives on extended "road trips," repeatedly locating and abandoning possible safe zones to seek some kind of utopian promised land or site of rescue and redemption.[1] This shift has resulted largely from the influence of zombie-themed video games and a new globalized Gothic aesthetic, as well as changes to post–9/11 U.S. foreign policy that include proactive international intervention.

Throughout the history of both Gothic literature and zombie cinema, monstrous symbols and metaphors have done important cultural work to reveal prevailing yet repressed social and cultural concerns and anxieties. In the past century, the Gothic zombie reacted to and illuminated fears regarding the shifting nuclear family, the violent impact of the Vietnam War, changes in the social roles played by both women and minorities, the rise of corporatization and consumerism in the United States, tensions resulting from the Cold War, and the development of new infectious diseases, to name just a few of these prevailing—and often repressed—concerns. Most of these anxieties were internalized by the citizens of the United States, seen largely as local problems or, at the least, international issues that manifested at the local level. With the violent attacks of September 11, 2001, the cultural consciousness of the United States has shifted from an internal, almost xenophobic narcissism to the reluctant realization that U.S. soil is *not* always safe, is *not* always an idealized "City upon a Hill."[2] The resultant "War on Terror"— along with increasingly frequent international natural disasters, political conflicts, and shifts in economic power structures—have pushed U.S. cultural consciousness, awareness, and engagement beyond the once hallowed borders of the country alone.

As the denizens of the United States are increasingly forced to see themselves as potentially vulnerable members of a global community, the very nature of the American Gothic has shifted to address new anxieties, new sites of horror, and new kinds of monsters. While Jerrold E. Hogle's rules of the Gothic and Freud's concept of the "uncanny" remain relevant today, Hogle's sense of the "antiquated or seemingly antiquated space"[3] has changed into a shifting and even mobile site of psychological trauma and real-world terror. In addition, the cinematic zombie Gothic narrative has begun to move from the domicile-centric tradition explored by Eric Savoy[4] to larger, more transitory scenarios. Now, the United States itself is the antiquated space, and the secret simultaneously hidden and revealed by Gothic monsters and other symbols is the illusion of peace and safety. This new American Gothic of the post–9/11 zombie movie is most dramatically manifested in the recent Hollywood film from Marc Forster, *World War Z*, a narrative that manifests what Glennis Byron calls the "globalgothic"[5] and rewrites traditional Gothic protocols to reflect both the influence of video game culture and the United States' new, proactive stance in the War on Terror. New cultural anxieties explore the risks of venturing forth into an unstable global community in search of a new standard of peace and safety, while questioning the ethics of such potentially intrusive and violent acts. The Gothic continues to reveal repressed anxieties and fears, but those fears have now taken on larger concerns and a much broader, international perspective.

The Twentieth-Century Gothic Zombie Film

As I argue at length in my book *American Zombie Gothic* (2010), most of the zombie films from the twentieth century function comfortably within the modal protocols of the Gothic literary tradition. Hogle establishes what may be the key "rules" of such fictions, including an antiquated setting, hidden secrets, a form of haunting, and an overt play between rational reality and the possibility of the supernatural.[6] He identifies the cultural work of such texts to be largely psychological in nature, focusing on the ways Gothic fiction "helps us address and disguise some of the most important desires, quandaries, and sources of anxiety, from the most internal and mental to the widely social and cultural, throughout the history of western culture."[7] The haunted settings and haunting figures of Gothic narratives, be they misread natural phenomenon or supernatural manifestations or monsters, function as uncanny representations of those things that have been repressed or hidden from conscious view and must now be revealed and addressed. Freud famously codified the "uncanny"—the *Unheimlich*—within the realm of psychoanalysis as "that species of the frightening that goes back to what was once well known and had long been familiar."[8] Uncanny images force that which has been repressed— the *Heimlich* or "secret"—to return to the conscious mind because they are simultaneously unfamiliar *and* familiar. The uncanny's dissonance with the regular world recalls and reveals that which had *once* been known, or at least known on a subconscious level.

Hogle's antiquated and uncanny settings occur throughout zombie films, especially those made by Romero.[9] These physical locations and settings "manifest disturbance and ambivalence in spatial terms,"[10] offering insight and commentary into both past and contemporary social shifts, tensions, and anxieties. *Night of the Living Dead* (1968), the film that essentially began the zombie invasion narrative subgenre, is particularly Gothic in form and content, taking place almost entirely in a lonely country farmhouse. The owners of the dwelling are dead, and the protagonists who hide within its walls are little more than strangers. In other words, the house fulfills a measure of antiquation, as it represents both the family that has passed on and the loss of safety the home once provided. The house is uncanny because a farmhouse should be a familiar location; yet as the survivors labor to fortify it against the marauding zombies, it becomes a kind of barracks, an unfamiliar transformation that draws attention to the gravity of the apocalyptic situation. Romero's second movie takes a similar approach with location, antiquating the suburban shopping mall by presenting it as empty and abandoned, yet strangely preserved. *Dawn of the Dead* (1978) does open with an extended helicopter journey, but the bulk of the film addresses the unfamiliar transformation of the shopping center, mirroring the fortification that takes place in *Night of the Living Dead*. *Day of the Dead* (1985), Romero's third zombie film, plays out almost exclusively in arguably the most antiquated of all his settings—an underground military bunker, a secret laboratory and warehouse. The apocalypse has implicitly been raging for some time in *Day of the Dead*, and the once modern bunker has taken on the dark and dreary appearance of a tomb, an uncanny transformation that calls forth the essential hopelessness of the protagonists' situation.

All three of these Gothic loci harbor secrets as well, secrets about interpersonal conflict, greed and consumption, and the military industrial complex. The farmhouse of *Night of the Living Dead* functions as a kind of petri dish for unstable human relationships, particularly those among different genders and races, and the film exposes many of the social tensions of the 1960s. Steven Bruhm argues the post–World War II Gothic registers the "impossibility of familial harmony,"[11] and in *Night of the Living Dead*, the traditional, nuclear family is literally under assault by both the zombies without the home and the dysfunctional relationships within, as a married couple bicker and argue, a brother kills his sister, and a daughter murders (and eats!) her parents. These tragic familial constructions support Fred Botting's assertion that "few families [exist] in Gothic fiction,"[12] particularly because such narratives explore the "transgression of the paternal metaphor."[13] Failed paternity manifests over the course of the film racially as well, as the inescapably black Ben (Duane Jones) verbally and physically abuses the catatonic white woman Barbra (Judith O'Dea) and fights with and eventually shoots the white patriarchal figure Harry Cooper (Karl Hardman). *Dawn of the Dead* famously shifts the focus of Romero's social criticism onto American greed and consumption. While initially a place of refuge and safety, the mall becomes a deathtrap for the film's protagonists because they, especially Stephen (David Emge), cannot leave the material goods of the shops behind, even when their lives are threatened. The uncanny mall calls forth the unhealthy obsession the living (and the dead) have with capitalist excess. Finally, in *Day of the Dead*, the military are presented as ruthless and megalomaniacal, willing to do whatever it takes to preserve their authority (and keep their secrets), even to the detriment of scientific advances and personal safety. Captain Rhodes (Joseph Pilato) reveals himself to be the most exaggerated caricature of a power-hungry despot, a reminder of the threats of the Cold War. The settings of Romero's films thus both conceal and reveal various social and cultural secrets repressed by contemporary society.

Hogle's understanding of the Gothic stems from his reading of the originating Gothic texts from England and Europe; of concern for my analysis of the American zombie Gothic tradition are those elements unique to the history of Gothic fiction in the United States. Savoy argues the formulaic plots of the European mode didn't simply translate an aristocratic genre to a democratic space but rather occurred through innovative energy and adaptation.[14] Of particular note are the experimental nature of American Gothic texts and their understandable focus on the "pervasive anxieties about the individual's capacity for common sense and self-control within the unstable social order of the new American republic."[15] Consequently, the American Gothic has traditionally been concerned with what it means to be part of a new country, one founded on democratic ideals, pragmatism, and, I contend, a rugged individuality that places the United States apart from other established governments. Additionally, Savoy classifies the uncanny figures of the American Gothic in terms of *prosopopoeia*, a personification of the haunting figure spoken of by Hogle that gives voice to the repressed and hidden "shadow" of the past.[16] In fact, Savoy declares this act of personifying the abstract to be the "master trope" of the American Gothic mode.[17] Giving a face to the Other allows allegorical personifications to be both uncanny and tangible.

Romero's films consistently feature democratic, pragmatic protagonists who come from the ranks of average, working-class citizens—a focus underscored by his casting of relatively unknown actors. These unlikely heroes make the most of their situations, improvising inventive and practical solutions without deploying any particular expertise or technical sophistication. *Night of the Living Dead* features almost bland, universal characters; they bring no particular occupational capability to the table, relying instead on hammers and scrounged nails to board up the farmhouse's doors and windows and improvising weapons and explosive devices to keep the zombies at bay. While Peter (Ken Foree) and Roger (Scott H. Reiniger) have expertise with firearms and weapons as members of a police SWAT force, the protagonists of *Dawn of the Dead* similarly rely on pragmatic improvisation, using whatever they can find in the confines of the shopping mall to fortify the structure, conceal the location of their hideout, and provide themselves with food, supplies, and entertainment. *Day of the Dead* does feature human characters that possess important skills and expertise, such as the soldiers and the crazed Dr. "Frankenstein" Logan (Richard Liberty), but the primary protagonists are simple, common folk. Sarah (Lori Cardille) is little more than a hardworking civilian struggling to understand the science of the zombie apocalypse while using weapons, technology, and her own wit to protect herself. None of these characters are particularly impressive, but they are unique and memorable individuals with whom the audience can easily identify and to whom they can relate.

Of course, perhaps the most important "characters" in zombie narratives are the uncanny monsters themselves, the allegorical creatures that personify or "give face" to the anxieties and concerns explored by each film. These zombies represent the antiquated world that once was, the "face of the tenants" that formerly inhabited the United States, and their uncanny appearance and behavior most effectively work to reveal the secrets that have otherwise been concealed and repressed. Decidedly supernatural, as reanimated human corpses, zombies are at once no one and everyone, largely anonymous "people" that nonetheless represent whatever type, individual, or trend is needed. With the focus on the failing traditional family in *Night of the Living Dead*, it comes as no surprise that two of the most frightening zombies were once known protagonists and family members. Karen (Kyra Schon) is decidedly uncanny as both a sweet, young girl and a bloodthirsty, trowel-wielding monster, and because zombie Johnny (Russell Streiner) still looks like Barbra's brother, the monster is able to penetrate the house's defenses. *Dawn of the Dead* similarly features once-known zombies, and after Stephen transforms, his lingering memory allows him to lead the other monsters up to the hidden apartment where the remaining protagonists are hiding. Stephen's greed lives on after his death, turned to a desire for human flesh and blood instead of clothes, jewelry, and guns. *Day of the Dead* features a particularly sympathetic zombie character, "Bub" (Sherman Howard), who struggles to reconcile his human past with his zombie present, driving the point home that we are all potential zombies already, atavistic monsters just barely repressed beneath the surface of a civilized facade. This kind of prosopopoeia personifies abstract conflicts through the immediacy of the zombie figures.

Whether intentional or not, the majority of the zombie invasion narratives produced on film during the twentieth century follow the modal protocols of traditional Gothic fiction quite closely. Even those U.S. movies not created by Romero follow his lead more often than exploring uncharted territory on their own, including the comedic hallmarks *Return of the Living Dead* (1985, directed by *Night of the Living Dead* cowriter Dan O'Bannon) and *Braindead* 1992, directed by Peter Jackson; also known as *Dead Alive*). In all of these examples, the narratives place their beleaguered protagonists in besieged, fixed locations where their struggles with both zombies and their fellow survivors gradually reveal various secrets concealed both consciously and unconsciously. Whereas international zombie films, most notably Lucio Fulci's *Zombi 2* (1979), explore the narrative possibilities of mobile protagonists and international locations, the U.S. cinematic tradition remained relatively static and uninspired during the twentieth century. However, video games such as Capcom's *Resident Evil* (1996) were beginning to challenge the traditional notion of the Gothic zombie narratives, taking players outside of the besieged mansion and suggesting a larger conflict and conspiracy. Now, in this new century, the zombie—"one of the central gothic figures of the twenty-first century"[18]—and the narratives associated with it are changing, and these shifts manifest larger developments in the Gothic mode as a whole, be it Justin D. Edwards and Agnieszka Soltysik Monnet's "Pop Goth," Botting's "Aftergothic," or Byron's "globalgothic."

The Twenty-First-Century Gothic Zombie Film

Edwards and Monnet identify much of modern, contemporary Gothic as "Pop Goth," or "an offshoot of Goth/ic ... arising out of a form of cultural production that has always been concerned with blurring the boundaries between the real and unreal, authentic and inauthentic, copy and counterfeit."[19] In this working definition, they evoke the claim of Hogle that all Gothic, even the foundational works of Horace Walpole, manifests the "ghost of the counterfeit," representations of things that are always already falsifications of the real world.[20] Botting points out that, traditionally, the Gothic engages with a past that is shaped "by the changing times in which it is composed,"[21] and most twentieth-century zombie invasion narratives illustrate these ideas, for while they may appear contemporary, they are primarily concerned with a lost past that has only recently changed. The twenty-first-century narratives, on the other hand, have begun to shift even further forward, using the "changing times" of an imagined Gothic future to offer insights into the present. Botting argues this "Aftergothic" is more concerned with a future "anxiously perceived as another place of destruction and decay, as ruined as the Gothic past,"[22] and Edwards and Monnet claim, "If the Gothic is haunted by the past, then Pop Goth makes the future its particular obsession."[23] Romero's latter three zombie films manifest these trends in the contemporary Gothic, exploring the problems of the present in terms of a frighteningly dysfunctional, dystopian future.

On many levels, Romero's twenty-first-century zombie films continue to operate within the traditions established by Gothic literature and his own initial cannon of movies, using antiquated physical spaces to explore key social and cultural fears and anxieties. Yet the nature of these locations has changed markedly, from secured sites of safety to almost unobtainable goals at the end of dangerous and largely unsuccessful journeys. In *Land of the Dead* (2005), the film's key location is the utopian apartment complex of "Fiddler's Green," a bastion of perceived hope that preserves the comforts of the "old world" for those rich enough to afford them. The leader Kaufman (Dennis Hopper) is more villainous than the movie's cunning zombies, and he uses his power and influence to separate the "haves" from the "have nots," the poor and impoverished who must struggle for survival in the slums surrounding the majestic high rise. Even though the film's human protagonists are kept outside of this location, forced to scavenge the ravaged countryside for supplies instead, the apartment building fulfills its Gothic role as an uncanny space that represents many of the problems plaguing contemporary society, specifically, unequal treatment of people because of money, social class, and power structures. Of course, the dream of Fiddler's Green is all an illusion, a counterfeiting not only of the old world in a post-zombie-apocalypse one, but also the very idea that the wealthy are better than everyone else. In the end, Kaufman's antiquated representation of pre-apocalyptic class disparity collapses against the onslaught of recently enlightened zombies and key betrayals by his own people.

The Gothic spaces of Romero's next two zombie films are even further removed from their narratives' respective protagonists, not looming above them the whole time but rather lying at the end of perilous road trips. The young protagonists of *Diary of the Dead* (2007) spend the majority of their film in an RV, a mobile version of *Night of the Living Dead*'s besieged farmhouse, but their real goal is the perceived safety of Ridley's (Philip Riccio) family mansion. When the group finally arrives, however, the house appears to be abandoned, with open gates and silent surveillance cameras. Ridley has arrived before them, and he, still dressed—fittingly—in his mummy costume from the movie shoot that took place at the beginning of the film, haunts the location with his tale of dumping his infected family and their employees into the swimming pool while harboring the secret of his own bite and infection. The past is well and truly dead at Ridley's mansion, and as more and more zombies compromise the high fences and security measures, the space takes on the uncanny cast of a majestic sepulcher. As with *Land of the Dead*, Romero's fifth zombie film reveals concerns about class disparity, but as the mansion is filled with CCTV cameras that can be safely monitored from a fortified panic room, the film also explores anxieties about surveillance, "Big Brother," and media culture in general. Indeed, as the entire film is presented through the subjective POV of the shaky "found footage" of Debra's (Michelle Morgan) video documentary, Romero's theme is hardly ambiguous.

Survival of the Dead (2009) presents a narrative that occurs parallel to

Diary of the Dead (the two groups of protagonists actually cross paths in the later film), and it similarly focuses on a journey to find an idealized, utopian location of peace and safety. The anti-heroic protagonists of Romero's sixth zombie movie, lead by the corrupt Sergeant Crockett (Alan Van Sprang), set their sights on an island off the coast of Delaware as the safest place for them to settled down and wait out the zombie apocalypse. Once they finally arrive, though, they find the island overrun by both zombies and two clans of feuding Irish-Americans. Plum Island is overtly antiquated because its heavily accented inhabitants adhere to the ways of the "old country" and live rural, agrarian lives. Furthermore, the antiquation manifests through the ancient feud that exists between the O'Flynn and Muldoon families. The island's juxtaposition of an apocalyptic future with an agrarian, colonial past makes the site uncanny, and the fight between the warring families can be read as a haunting that reveals anxieties about interpersonal conflict, violence, and even war. No one is safe on Plum Island, largely because no one was really safe there in the first place. After the patriarchs of the two clans gun each other down in cold blood, Crockett reluctantly leads his remaining two companions out to sea on a commandeered ferry boat; having found no place of safety, they must continue to look for one.

One of the key changes in the American zombie Gothic tradition— based on this survey of Romero's films, at least—is a redefining of the central, static location and the very nature of the narrative plot structure. Instead of focusing on defending the fortified sites of a farmhouse, a shopping mall, and a military bunker, Romero's later films are about seeking the safety of an apartment complex, a family mansion, and a remote island, but these locations end up being false ideals, sites of conflict and death rather than peace and safety. Botting makes the case that "[c]omputer games owe a debt to horror cinema,"[24] and I argue the contemporary Gothic, particularly recent zombie apocalypse narratives, owe much to the development of the video game in return.[25] Zombie-themed games, while initially following Romero's "besieged location" structure, as shown in the original *Resident Evil*, have developed into more elaborate narratives, usually requiring characters to get from one location to another, exploring a vast digital world in search of supplies, help, and eventual rescue and salvation (perhaps). Romero's twenty-first-century zombie films reflect this shift in structure, as the films focus increasingly on the journeys themselves and less on the actual destinations. On the one hand, such an approach keeps the genre fresh by varying the otherwise expected plot structure; on the other, it appeals to audiences who have had their expectation of the zombie invasion narrative determined by their beloved video games.

More importantly, though, the recent changes in American zombie

Gothic films must be explored in terms of post–9/11 national trauma and conflicts arising from the ongoing War on Terror, increasingly invasive technology, and social and racial disharmony. Bruhm discusses how the contemporary Gothic registers a "crisis in personal history," a crisis that constitutes a reaction to trauma; in fact, he declares the Gothic to be "a narrative of trauma."[26] While most Gothic narratives explore this sense of trauma, the zombie invasion narratives that have surfaced after September 11th are particularly influenced by and demonstrate a reaction to that shared national ordeal. *Land of the Dead* speaks directly to the aftereffects of the War on Terror, with Kaufman overtly referring to his human rival Cholo (John Leguizamo) as a terrorist and with the zombies being portrayed as an invading military force. Despite their electric fences, armed guards, and advanced technology, the colony of Fiddler's Green cannot protect itself from the onslaught of such a determined foe. While not overtly engaged with the language of terrorism, *Diary of the Dead* nonetheless addresses the trauma of a technological and digital world that disenfranchises its citizens, particularly through encroachments on personal privacy resulting from legislation such as the Patriot Act, and *Survival of the Dead* explores the futile dream of finding a place of familial and international peace and harmony in a world of social, cultural, and racial conflict, one in which warring ideologies refuse to find any common ground.

As with Romero's earlier films, living humans pose a greater threat to the protagonists of his twenty-first-century triad, often at the expense of the zombies themselves. Botting reminds us that "[c]orporate or military organizations are standard models of power in future fictions,"[27] and these two institutions become the key antagonistic forces in *Land of the Dead* and *Survival of the Dead* respectively. Kaufman acts more like a CEO and real estate baron than the leader of a post-apocalyptic human settlement, and his strongest motivation throughout the film is essentially (now worthless) money, a hollow obsession that results in his death. Crockett, in *Survival of the Dead*, was perhaps a hard working and ethical soldier once, but he uses his uniform, perceived authority, and government-issued weaponry to abuse and manipulate others, particularly in his quest for (similarly worthless) money and wealth. Indeed, his motivation, like Kaufman's, is greed, not personal safety or patriotic duty. These films manifest a not-so-repressed resentment toward and distrust of the giant corporations that seem to govern the United States today and the elected government that appears more invested in its officials' interests than those of the American people. Technology has also become one of the cultural anxieties most often explored by the contemporary Gothic,[28] and this fear lies at the heart of *Diary of the Dead*. As stated, this anxiety is more than just a distrust of invasive cameras, including fears about government surveillance, data mining, and the monitoring of Internet use—all in the name of national security and safety.

While the current American zombie Gothic mode remains tied to the traditions of the past, the films and their stories have shifted to reflect changes in national concerns and anxieties. As Botting rightly asserts, "over-familiarity will diminish a capacity to cross borders or produce terror or horror"[29]; therefore, like any subgenre, the zombie invasion narrative must also adapt and evolve to remain timely, relevant, and appealing to audiences old and new. With these changes, however, these movies continue to do important cultural work for viewers today. Through recent zombie invasion narratives, such as those produced by Romero and his imitators, the United States can "surviv[e] by proxy,"[30] confronting the traumas of 9/11, its fears of invasions and infestation, its mistrust of other races and nations, and, as I will illustrate through an analysis of *World War Z*, its ambiguous relationships with other countries and ethnic groups. However, because Romero's films, and those of most of his disciples, remain essentially Amerocentric in their settings, characters, plots, and concerns, they make little or no attempt to explore a "globalgothic" sensibility. *World War Z*, while nonetheless making notably stark departures from Max Brooks' 2006 source novel,[31] attempts this leap, depicting the story of the zombie apocalypse on a global level, following the journey of Gerry Lane (Brad Pitt) around the world as he struggles to find a way to defeat the zombie horde.

The Global Gothic Zombie Film: *World War Z*

The blockbuster movie *World War Z*, the highest-grossing zombie-themed film to date[32]—produced by and starring none other than international superstar Brad Pitt—epitomizes what Edwards and Monnet call the "mainstreaming of a Goth/ic aesthetic"[33] and, together with the AMC television series *The Walking Dead* (2010–), proves the "right kind" of zombie apocalypse has truly widespread appeal. Part of this reinvigoration of the subgenre for a larger audience, as discussed above, includes the abandonment of a fixed narrative location and the addition of a heroic journey or quest, but the next phase in the Gothic zombie film's development must also include an engagement with the global community. This expansion of the Gothic to include a global perspective and to engage with trans- and multinational stories, characters, and concerns is what Byron calls the "globalgothic," a new mode founded on the "emergence of cross-cultural and transnational gothics that called out for attention and which suggested that ... in the late twentieth and early twenty-first centuries gothic was actually progressing far beyond being fixed in terms of any one geographically circumscribed mode."[34] While this development of the Gothic is largely incompatible with Romero's body of work, even his recent movies, the idea of a globalgothic aesthetic resounds firmly with and is manifested through the structure, cast, and thematic content of *World War Z*, the most international and global American zombie Gothic film produced thus far.

Forster's big-budget, Hollywood-backed adaptation of Brooks' quasi-epistolary novel immediately transcends any audience expectations of a small-scale horror film, presenting itself variously as an action movie, a viral outbreak film, and an international thriller. *World War Z*'s departure from most of its zombie antecedents is perhaps best epitomized by the film's PG-13 rating, indicating the light-handed approach to violence and gore that potentially disappointed most hard-core horror fans. This more "family friendly" rating is shared by Jonathan Levine's *Warm Bodies*, also from 2013, indicating the future of the zombie on the big screen may be stories aimed at teenagers, women, and older demographics.[35] Additionally, the film's opening sequence marks it as something other than a traditional zombie movie; if anything, the tone, pacing, and action make it feel more like an alien invasion film such as Roland Emmerich's *Independence Day* (1996) or Steven Spielberg's *War of the Worlds* (2005). Indeed, the movie's core emphasis on a normal family struggling to remain safe and together in the midst of an inexplicable and unknown catastrophe is more reminiscent of Spielberg than Romero. The film's status as an action/adventure story is further confirmed by its exciting gun battles, multiple daring aeronautic escapes, harried flights through narrow city streets, and the dramatic crash of a commercial airliner filled with chomping zombies. Additionally, Forster's movie presents a potential dystopia, reflecting on the present through a science-fiction vision of the future, rather than a traditionally Gothic recreation of the past. Yet *World War Z* has multiple key sequences—dark, frightening, and suspenseful—that lodge it firmly in the camp of the new American zombie Gothic as well.

Whenever night falls or Gerry is isolated from others, *World War Z* takes on the aesthetic cast of a Gothic horror film. In the film's first act, Gerry's family spends the night hiding with a Spanish-speaking family in a Newark apartment building. The muted color pallet, Gerry's use of an old analogue radio to learn more about the crisis unfolding outside, and the need to improvise defenses against rabid, once-human monsters all nod to Romero's tradition. The halls of the apartment building feel antiquated enough, with flickering florescent lights, red emergency illumination, scrawled graffiti, and the absence of other humans. The building is uncanny and otherworldly, and the unfamiliarity of that which should be familiar adds to the movie's tension, suspense, and terror. Similarly, the South Korean military installation is presented in Gothic terms, instantly recalling the space of *Day of the Dead*, and with its harsh lighting and beleaguered team of cynical soldiers, the location can certainly be read as antiquated as well. More appropriate to the Gothic mode, though, is the holding cell that continues to harbor the charred corpses of the initial victims of the zombie outbreak. The room is literally a tomb, and it function as an uncanny reminder of the failure of both medical science and the military. While it's not clear if technology caused the zombie outbreak, it's clear the military isn't going to be able to stop it on its own, and the mystery of *World War Z* only builds through these spaces.

Other locations in the film are presented in antiquated and uncanny terms as well, and some of these provide viewers with more overt social and cultural commentary and criticism. For example, the UN aircraft carrier represents cutting-edge technology and modern-day military might, but the ship becomes an outpost for the remnants of a political system that has already become a thing of the past. The priorities of the carrier reveal a mistrust of the government and military in general, as their actions could be described as secret and self-interested, especially when Gerry's family are unceremoniously kicked off the vessel when those in power mistakenly believe Gerry dead and thus no longer useful. Despite Gerry's efforts and sacrifices, his government breaks its promise and sends his vulnerable family to a refugee camp in Nova Scotia. Additionally, Jerusalem, one of the most ancient cities in the world, has been surrounded by a massive, fortified wall, monitored by state-of-the-art helicopters and advanced weaponry. As in real life, this location represents the ongoing coexistence of the old and the new, the traditional and the technological. *World War Z*'s depiction of Jerusalem provides audiences with its most thinly veiled social commentary as well, as the jubilant singing of the Islamic refugees just inside the gates of the city's fortifications is what stirs the apocalypse of zombies outside to rally and swarm. An ancient feud, then, is linked to the fall of Jerusalem, and within its walls, the two warring ethnic groups end up dying together. *World War Z* emphasizes that organizations such as governments, the military, and even religions cannot be trusted, and the best course of action always lies with the individual.

All the spaces of *World War Z* are haunted as well, mostly by supernatural foes, exceedingly violent and desperate zombies that run fast and attack with inhuman strength. Rather than following Romero's lead, Forster goes the route of the modern zombie invasion narrative, in the vein of Danny Boyle's *28 Days Later* (2002) or Zach Snyder's *Dawn of the Dead* remake (2004). Yet while the monsters result from a biological infection as in the former film, the "Zeke" are established to be reanimated corpses, humans who are infected, die, and rise again all in twelve brief seconds. The monsters can only be destroyed by fire, and sometimes not even then. In other words, perhaps the primary antagonist of *World War Z* is Mother Nature herself, whom Dr. Fassbach (Elyes Gabel) calls the greatest of all serial killers. By couching things in both the supernatural traditions of the past and the scientific focus of speculative fiction, the zombies of *World War Z* are both terrifying beasts and pitiable victims, and the narrative can thus be presented in somewhat realist rather than purely fantastic terms. Since flesh-eating, walking-dead monsters are now so ubiquitously familiar to audiences, the zombies of *World War Z* "up the ante" considerably to make them newly uncanny. Thanks to the heavy application of CGI effects, these zombies swarm on a large scale like bees or ants, piling relentlessly upon one another to scale the massive walls of Jerusalem and flowing through its ancient streets like a flood of lost humanity. They are familiar yet unfamiliar, doubly uncanny for the characters and viewers alike.

I propose *World War Z* as the current zenith of the American zombie Gothic film's transition from a localized siege narrative to an international kind of "road trip" movie, a shift largely tied to the popularity of zombie-themed video games and the expectations and demands of viewers accustomed to such narratives, but also realizing Byron's idea that a globalized Gothic includes "increased mobility."[36] *World War Z* makes it clear early on why the traditional method of dealing with a zombie invasion is a flawed and outdated narrative model. Gerry explains, "I used to work in dangerous places, and people who moved survived and those who didn't.... Movimiento es vida. Movimiento es vida. [Movement is life]." Almost as if he has seen Romero's movies, Gerry knows the only thing hiding does is provide survivors a place to wait until they die. Solutions can only be found as a result of positive action and the search for salvation. Furthermore, many of *World War Z*'s dynamic action sequences feel a lot like a video game, from Gerry's frantic escape from Philadelphia in a stolen motorhome to the violent looting of a New Jersey grocery store to the harried escape from an overrun apartment building. And while the rescue of Gerry and his family from the roof of that building via helicopter is reminiscent of the ending of Romero's *Dawn of the Dead*, that moment marks the *beginning* of *World War Z*'s narrative, a story that starts with an uncertain journey rather than ending with one. For Gerry to fight the walking dead, he cannot rest in one place; instead, the film becomes a kind of globetrotting detective story, almost in the tradition of a Dan Brown novel. Gerry's goal isn't to hide but to seek a way to stop the spread of the zombie virus, and he follows each clue to the next in the manner of a carefully crafted video game.

The movement of the narrative takes Gerry to various countries and brings him into contact with a number of cultures, and *World War Z* thus sets itself apart from other films most notably in this globalization of the zombie invasion narrative. While the film does preference the efforts of the United States with its focus on an American protagonist, the majority of the film takes place away from U.S. soil in such disparate lands as South Korea, Israel, and Wales. The movie opens with a somewhat heavy-handed declaration that its focus will be much broader than the relative simplicity of one of Romero's films. The title credits are presented alongside a montage of footage showing people from all across the globe, commuting, working, and going about their normal lives. In addition, voice over narration, clips of real news programs, and documentary footage draw the viewer's attention to issues of global climate change, international pandemics, travel restrictions, civic unrest, and other kinds of worldwide conflict and crises. Of similar import is Gerry's former employment with the United Nations—not the United States government, the U.S. military, the FBI, or the CIA. After their rescue by the UN, Gerry's family is initially taken to the relative safety of the aircraft carrier, part of an international fleet of ships, military and government officials, and various specialists. The "war room" of the ship quickly establishes the essential fall of the United States government, the global impact of the zombie infection, and the need for everyone on the planet to band together, allowing *World War Z* to deliver on the promise of its title: this zombie war affects the entire globe.

Most of Romero's zombie movies feature female and African-American protagonists, and *World War Z* expands this tradition of diversity to an international level. The cast of Forster's film is decidedly multinational, and although the chief protagonist is admittedly a white, male, U.S. citizen, Gerry finds invaluable aid along the way from people of both genders and from a variety of countries and ethnic groups.[37] During their flight from New Jersey, for example, the Lanes are aided by a kind Latino family, and they are rescued from the doomed apartment building on the orders of a ranking UN official portrayed by the South African actor Fana Mokoena. Additionally, the scientist initially put in charge of finding the outbreak's "patient zero," Dr. Fassbach, is played by Gabel, a British-Indian actor, and the C130 pilot who flies the team to South Korea is portrayed by the French Grégory Fitoussi. The expert Gerry meets in Jerusalem is Jurgen Warmbrunn, played by Ludi Boeken, and Gerry gains a kind of bodyguard in Segen, played by Daniella Kertesz, both Israeli actors. And finally, the W. H. O. specialists and scientists are portrayed variously by the Scottish Peter Capaldi, the Italian Pierfrancesco Favino, the Ethiopian-Irish Ruth Negga, and the German Moritz Bleibtreu. While the majority of these actors are nonetheless light-skinned men, the film is certainly more ethnically and culturally diverse than most mainstream Hollywood productions, zombie themed or otherwise.

These diverse protagonists help Gerry complete his international journey, a quest that culminates at a World Health Organization installation in Cardiff, Wales. The final act of *World War Z* dramatically slows the pace of the action, shifting things generically from an action/adventure film to a more traditional Gothic thriller. The large W. H. O. facility is almost completely abandoned, apparently staffed by only four uninfected scientists, and the entire location is bathed in blue tones, low lighting, and stark shadows. The B-wing of the complex has been overrun by the infected, and the only way to access the kind of pathogens needed for Gerry's hypothetical solution to the zombie war is to infiltrate the eerie hallways. The sequence that follows, the one that concludes the film, feels more like a horror film than an action movie, with slower pacing, a nearly silent soundtrack, and numerous tense moments of suspense. Additionally, the zombies of the W. H. O. facility are not mere CGI cutouts but rather individuals acting through prosthetics and practical makeup, their cries and jerky movements evocative of birds of prey or even velociraptors. Admittedly, though, once the semi-dormant Zekes become aware of the presence of human flesh, the action speeds up dramatically, once again resembling a video game in its fast pacing and the need for the protagonists to run around the maze-like hallways in search of their predetermined goal.

The questing of the video game thus meets the tension of the siege narrative at the climax of *World War Z* when Gerry is locked inside a glass vault housing the world's most virulent and deadly plagues and bacteria. This sequence represents a fusion of the traditional zombie Gothic with the sensibilities and aesthetics of the new, as Gerry must use a coded keypad and just the right vial of pathogens to solve the "case" of the zombie war. Gerry sorts through the remnants of humanity's biological past, surrounded by diseases, bacteria, and viruses that were once plagues but have since been mastered, overcome, and cured. Only by bravely embracing that antiquated past, by infecting himself with an agent that was once deadly and incurable, can Gerry hope to face the present and realize a future—not only for himself and his family, but also for the entire human race. While an infected zombie "haunts" him from without, reminding him of his own fears of death and, perhaps more relevantly, failure, he is haunted from within the room by the infectious agents, both natural and synthesized, that underscore the fragility of human life. These microscopic organisms are perhaps not only responsible for the zombie plague, but they also represent the most deadly of all Mother Nature's killers, unseen but nonetheless merciless and effective. By confronting both hauntings, Gerry manages to survive: he infects himself, and that infection makes him an unsuitable host for the zombie plague, and the lone zombie scientist ignores him completely. This juxtaposition of the past with the future offers a solution to the zombie war, and curiously reflects the fusion of the old and new Gothic traditions as well.

Of course, *World War Z* must also be read in traditional Gothic terms as a manifestation of repressed trauma and concerns about the United States' place in an increasingly global international community, particularly in a post–9/11 environment. When *World War Z*'s various sequences are taken as a whole, they can be seen to reveal anxieties concerning both the possibility of another terrorist attack at home and the United States' aggressive efforts to seek out security threats abroad. The film's opening sequence on the streets of Philadelphia readily evokes the confusion and uncertainty of September 11, with low-flying helicopters, ambiguous news reports, the unexplained mobilization of the police, and, most evocatively, nearby explosions. The panic depicted is nerve-wracking and frightening, especially as the true nature of the threat remains unclear—like plain-clothed terrorists, the zombies of *World War Z* look like everyone else, at least initially. In the mayhem, one can hardly discern which people are fleeing for their lives and which are the monsters psychotically pursuing their prey. As the movie progresses, Gerry finds himself caught up in increasingly dangerous situations because of his insistence to get involved beyond the borders of the United States. His trip to South Korea results in the death of Dr. Fassbach, and Gerry learns one of the only nations successfully surviving the zombie apocalypse is North Korea, having ordered all of its citizens to have their teeth extracted to prevent further spread of the infection. His trip to Jerusalem is similarly frustrated when voracious zombies overrun the city and his UN-appointed airplane leaves him behind at the last moment. The international community of *World War Z* is portrayed as a frightening place, one that should be left alone or kept at a safe distance, at least initially.

However, evincing perhaps a new development in the contemporary Gothic, Forster's film ends on a hopeful and optimistic note, using a dystopian version of the future to offer viewers solutions to present-day crises and problems. The globalgothic of *World War Z* proposes a future in which representatives from the United States can work in harmony with those from other nations to solve global conflicts, depicting a world in which humanity unites despite national borders and ideological boundaries. In the film's attempt to address the shared national—and in fact international—trauma of September 11 and the subsequent War on Terror, this Gothic film proposes a panacea for the suffering and the wounded. Rather than fearing a foreign other, *World War Z* suggests the value of the global community and the need for all of humanity to come together. As Botting states, "gothic figures, always responsive to changing times, continue to serve as sites of projection and fantasy, metaphors of form and medium, screens of anxiety and desire operating at the limits of norm and meaning. While their appearance remains familiar their significance and value can shift, becoming increasingly attractive images of once negative states."[38] The negative perception of an unfamiliar and distrusted international community changes by the end of *World War Z*, as the film uses its uncanny monsters and Gothic structures and aesthetics to work through contemporary anxieties.

In addition to shifting the new American zombie Gothic mode from desperate and cynical siege narratives to tales of proactive journeys and dynamic international quests, films such as *World War Z* establish an unexpected optimism, and that optimism for a new world may be what is most repressed by current fears and anxieties. In essence, the film insists reconciliation with the past must take place to build a better future. As the virulent zombie plague is ultimately defeated thanks to the reintroduction of infectious agents from the past, so to must the world's problems be conquered through an acceptance of past failures and a repurposing of those relationships into something positive and affirming. In many ways, that's always been the point of the Gothic—a return of the repressed past to make a reconciled future possible. Gerry's sacrifices and willingness to risk everything, aided by a community of international politicians, soldiers, and scientists, makes a positive resolution to the narrative possible, emphasizing the value of true human globalization. While *World War Z* implies its ending is really only a beginning, the concluding montage of the film demonstrates the triumph of humanity. Rather than ending with the bleak ambiguity of Romero's six zombie movies, Forster's film concludes with the optimistic resolution of a *28 Days Later* or a *Shaun of the Dead*. And maybe that's the best shift in the Gothic we can hope for—a move from ambiguous hopelessness to an optimistic future and a reaffirmed sense of shared human experience and triumph.

Chapter 2

THE COMEDIC ZOMBIE

Zombieland and the Classical Functions of the Modern Zomedy

"It had to be a clown, and it had to be Wichita, for me to finally understand that some rules are made to be broken."
—Columbus, *Zombieland*

Two otherwise prolific and successful cinematic genres regularly fail to win the esteem of the so-called "serious" film critics, academics, and scholars: the film comedy and the horror movie. Of the eighty-six Best Picture awards given by the Academy of Motion Picture Arts and Sciences since 1928, for example, only six can be described as true comedies, and only one, Jonathan Demme's *The Silence of the Lambs* (1991), fits the bill of a horror film.[1] Comedies might be dismissed for being lowbrow, unsophisticated, or merely fodder for the masses, while horror movies may be seen as being anti-social, subversive, or even catalysts for real-world social unrest and violence. One should not be surprised to learn, then, that horror comedies are doubly stigmatized, even though, as Jeffrey Jerome Cohen points out, such films offer "a mode for at once expressing and containing monstrous anxiety."[2] For example, Ruben Fleischer's zombie comedy, *Zombieland* (2009), has been described by Manohla Dargis of *The New York Times* as "a minor diversion" that represents "an already overstuffed, undernourished subgenre."[3] In fact, despite recent investigations by the academic community,[4] the zombie comedy—or *zomedy*[5]—remains largely underappreciated by the cultural elite.

However, all developed genres enjoy a comedic or parody phase—be it the Western's *Blazing Saddles* (1974, directed by Mel Brooks) or the disaster film's *Airplane!* (1980, directed by Jim Abrahams, David Zucker, and Jerry Zucker)—and the horror movie is of course no exception; after all, because

41

the "discomfort that monsters elicit causes a bodily excitation that can be exorcised by a scream or a laugh there is not in the end a vast difference between horror and comedy."[6] Not surprisingly, then, Fleischer's zomedy caused something of a popular sensation, making $24 million its first weekend alone and eventually tripling its $23 million production cost in gross receipts.[7] In addition, *Zombieland* has earned a score of "90 percent fresh" among critics on the *Rotten Tomatoes*'s online "Tomatometer,"[8] and Clark Collis and Chris Nashawaty at *Entertainment Weekly* have declared, "Thanks to 'Zombieland,' what was once an entrail-strewn footnote to the horror genre is now mainstream."[9] But *Zombieland* has since proven itself to be one of the most popular films in the Zombie Renaissance canon, and it operates as part of a long-established tradition of zombie movies, screen comedies, and—as with so many zombie narratives in this new century—road films.[10] In fact, this unique tale represents the unlikely fusion of George A. Romero's *Dawn of the Dead* (1978) with Harold Ramis's *Vacation* (1983), particularly in the way *Zombieland* deals with familial tensions and social expectations. Because of this synthesis, Fleischer actually delves into largely uncharted territory with his zomedy, and *Zombieland* does much to add to this oft-maligned subgenre by openly embracing the classical conventions of the romantic adventure via a plot that is more about the hero's quest to establish a traditional family structure than it is about abject sight gags and gross-out humor.

The now canonical zombie invasion narrative, particularly those films produced by or made in imitation of Romero, traditionally offers audiences a rather bleak view of the apocalypse, one in which society's vital infrastructures are quickly destroyed by the unstoppable armies of the walking dead. Furthermore, as evidenced by Romero's early zombie movies, the primary target of such supernatural devastation is nothing less than the American nuclear family. In *Night of the Living Dead* (1968), for example, a young girl ends up devouring her bickering parents, and the film's female protagonist is ultimately murdered by her (formerly) teasing brother. Romero's *Dawn of the Dead*, although admittedly more lighthearted and sometimes comedic, can hardly be described as having a "happy ending" either. This hallmark film plays out as an almost mythic tragedy, for although the four survivors of the beleaguered Monroeville Mall manage to create a new human society and something of a surrogate family structure, that family is literally torn apart during the mayhem of the film's catastrophic conclusion.

Zombieland, on the other hand, provides viewers with a comedy in the classical Greek sense of the mode, a dramatic narrative in which "a young man wants a young woman" and whose "desire is resisted by some opposition."[11] For Columbus (Jesse Eisenberg), that opposition comes in the form of an intimidating, machismo society and uncaring parents—all now destroyed—and the life-threatening presence of the walking dead—which must *be* destroyed. Perhaps even more curious in light of the established protocols of the zombie subgenre, the four survivors of Fleischer's film are *not* killed, eaten, or transformed by the rampaging zombies; in fact, the movie concludes with not only a positive resolution, but also with the prospect of a happy marital union between Columbus and Wichita (Emma Stone). Thus, in an unexpected parallel to the dysfunctional Griswolds from *Vacation*, the unsuccessful family road trip to a California amusement park actually brings the conflicted and distrusting individuals closer together. Rather than being a schlocky, lowbrow knockoff, *Zombieland* cleverly challenges audience expectations and offers viewers a glimpse of how the zombie subgenre can function as a positive social force within both the comedy and horror traditions.

The Tradition of Tragedy in Zombie Cinema

In so many ways, the cinematic zombie narrative has always been about the social structure of the family—those both literal and symbolic. For example, the very first zombie film, Victor Halperin's *White Zombie* (1932), focuses its imperialistic plot on a young engaged couple. Neil (John Harron) and Madeleine (Madge Bellamy) have traveled to exotic Haiti for their happy nuptials, but their celebration is cut short when the menacing "Murder" Legendre (Bela Lugosi) enchants the young woman and turns her into his zombie slave. Jacques Tourneur's *I Walked with a Zombie* (1943) has a similar foundation: the selfless Betsy (Frances Dee) journeys to a remote Caribbean island to act as the nurse and caretaker for Jessica Holland (Christine Gordon), a beautiful woman whose improper love for her brother-in-law has driven her mother-in-law to turn her into a helpless zombie. Although the first of these two germinal films ends with a happy, if melodramatic, resolution, Tourneur's film ends tragically, and it has become the model (in tone if not in content) of most of the "serious" zombie movies that have followed, such as *King of the Zombies* (1941, directed by Jean Yarbrough), *Zombies of Mora Tau* (1957, directed by Edward L. Cahn), and *The Plague of the Zombies* (1966, directed by John Gilling)—and of course the series of films produced and directed by Romero.

While zombie movies may have been (except in the last ten years, of course) largely disregarded by the academic elite as unsophisticated works of narrative drama, these films are surprisingly classical in nature, particularly when one takes into account Northrop Frye's conception of fictional modes.

For example, one can best understand the "serious" zombie narratives in terms of the "*high mimetic* mode" of tragedy; that is, narratives for which the hero is "superior in degree to other men but not to his natural environment."[12] The primary male protagonists of both *Night of the Living Dead* and *Dawn of the Dead*, Ben (Duane Jones) and Stephen (David Emge) respectively, can be seen as tragic heroes in this sense, leaders who are nonetheless unable to overcome the (un)natural environments that (literally) besiege them. Furthermore, Frye emphasizes how the fundamental characteristic of tragic fiction is the isolation of the hero from the rest of society,[13] and in zombie narratives, this isolation comes about first because of the invading hordes of the walking dead and second when their human society—i.e., "family"—begins to crumble and disappear around them.

Frye characterizes tragedy as being concentrated on a "single individual," one who represents "the highest points in their human landscape,"[14] and although zombie films regularly feature ensemble casts of diverse character, *Night of the Living Dead* and *Dawn of the Dead* do focus audience identification upon such individual roles. In the first film, audiences are initially aligned with the vulnerable character of Barbra (Judith O'Dea), but her apparent helplessness marks her as a pathetic rather than a heroic character; Ben, on the other hand, enters the film abruptly, immediately taking charge and acting in the face of Barbra's overt inaction. Even as more characters enter the story, Ben remains the one in command, asserting his authority, persuading the others to follow his plans, and deftly—and often violently—quelling any challenges to his rule. In comparison, the character hierarchy of *Dawn of the Dead* is less rigidly delineated, as the four protagonists come to share roles of authority and leadership. However, Stephen, the helicopter pilot, is literally the "driver" of the group; like some apocalyptic Moses, he leads the rag-tag group of refugees out of zombie-ravaged Pittsburgh and finds them a "promised land" in the form of a suburban shopping mall. As the film progresses, he continues to assert his authority among the group, treating his girlfriend Francine (Gaylen Ross) more like property than an equal and insisting repeatedly—and with increasing irrationality—that the mall be possessed and defended at all costs.

As I will discuss shortly, the downfall of these (initially) heroic characters constitutes the core of the zombie film's tragic essence; however, these narratives are classically tragic for other reasons as well. According to Aristotle, the catharsis experienced via tragedy relies primarily upon the emotions of pity and fear.[15] In so-called "serious" zombie movies, the terror clearly manifests as a result of the zombies themselves, or, perhaps more specifically, from the taboo acts of violence, cannibalism, and incest performed by this supernatural horde. Pity, on the other hand, usually centers on female characters and children—the central figures of pathos in both low mimetic and domestic tragedies.[16] In *Night of the Living Dead*, as I have already intimated, Barbra devolves into an essentially pitiful character, a helpless victim who comes to die an ignominious death. Karen (Kyra Schon) represents an even more pathetically tragic character: she enters the film as a quasi-unconscious child who gradually succumbs to the zombie plague with barely a word of spoken dialogue. By 1978, Romero's female leads have become much stronger and more fully actualized, yet *Dawn of the Dead*'s Francine remains the clear focus of audience empathy and pity because of her basic inaction, her forced domesticity, and her uncertain pregnancy. The audience comes to fear for her most of all, and, although she manages to survive the carnage of the film, her future remains bleak and likely hopeless.

Regardless, all the protagonists in classic zombie narratives, the heroes and the pathetic supporting cast alike, suffer increasing isolation as their social networks—their real and surrogate families—devolve and collapse. In a marked contrast to dramatic comedy, which "works out the proper relations of its characters and prevents heroes from marrying their sisters or mothers," Frye emphasizes how "tragedy presents the disaster of Oedipus or the incest of Siegmund."[17] Zombie films in the Romero tradition fulfill this tragic protocol to the literal extreme. By the end of *Night of the Living Dead*, for example, Johnny (Russell Streiner) has attacked and morbidly embraced his sister Barbra, dragging her from the fortified farmhouse to her certain doom, and the dysfunctional married couple of Harry (Karl Hardman) and Helen (Marilyn Eastman) have been eaten by their zombified daughter Karen. The familial tragedy of *Dawn of the Dead* is, again, less overt, yet it appears nonetheless in the homosocial partnership of Peter (Ken Foree) and Roger (Scott H. Reiniger), one that culminates in the former euthanizing the infected latter with the penetrating force of a bullet, and in the increasingly emotionless relationship between Stephen and Francine.[18] By the end of both films, all of the previously established families, couples, and partnerships have been rent apart by the zombies and their unstoppable infection.

Ultimately, of course, these films, and those like them, are essentially and classically tragic because of the dramatic downfalls suffered by their flawed heroes. Frye stresses how in the tragic mode the hero "provokes enmity ... and the return of the avenger constitutes the catastrophe."[19] In both *Night of the Living Dead* and *Dawn of the Dead*, the enmity provoked by the tragic protagonists is linked to pride. Most tragic heroes possess *hybris*, "a proud, passionate, obsessed or soaring mind which brings about a morally intelligible downfall."[20] Ben's hybris comes from his impassioned obsession that he, and he alone, knows what to do; he repeatedly refuses to listen to Harry's (correct) insistence that the basement of the farmhouse is the only safe location, and he delays just such a retreat until all of his companions have been slain or converted into zombies. Stephen's obsession is perhaps even more tragic; although the protagonists of *Dawn of the Dead* could easily retreat from the overrun shopping mall in Stephen's commandeered helicopter, the pilot simply refuses to go—his obstinate attachment to the material possessions forces him to ignore the true peril of his situation. In both cases, these men are blinded by their own conceit, and their deaths constitute tragedy's inevitable catastrophe.[21] In other words, the catharsis of tragedy becomes didactic as well as terrible, for the Greeks and Romero alike.

Romero's first two zombie films exemplify the classically tragic functions of the subgenre, and the protocols they established have been imitated by most of the traditional zombie invasion narratives that have follow in their shambling footsteps, movies such as *Non si deve profanare il sonno dei morti* (1979, directed by Jorge Grau),[22] Lucio Fulci's *Zombi 2* (1979),[23] Romero's own *Day of the Dead* (1985), and Zack Snyder's *Dawn of the Dead* remake (2004), just to name a few. All of these films are overtly tragic for rather obvious reasons: the world as we know it has ceased to exist, the protagonists suffer numerous trials and hardships, and most (if not all) of the sympathetic characters end up dead, eaten, transformed into zombies, or abandoned by the plot to an uncertain future. Furthermore, these zombie movies are tragic according to Frye's sense of the drama because the heroes are driven out of society—both the society that was initially destroyed by the invading horde of the walking dead and the secondary family the survivors have formed in their disparate holds and refuges. Although the zombies are ultimately responsible for the eventual annihilation of this surrogate family—the "new" family unit of the zombie apocalypse—that annihilation usually comes about because of a key flaw in the tragic hero, be it pride, selfishness, greed, or a general lack of wisdom. The zomedies, in contrast, offer viewers all the shock, gore, and horror of the zombie tragedies, but their resolutions are markedly different: zomedies, true to their classical roots, end on a note of hope, promise, and stability in the form of a newly constituted family and/or marriage.

The Innovation of Comedy in Zombie Cinema

In stark contrast to the tragic zombie narratives discussed above, zomedies track plots and characters that are comedic not only because they are essentially humorous, but also because they follow, rather overtly, the defining qualities of the classical dramatic comedy. These archetypal protocols, as outlined by Frye, include a comedic hero, the promise of a romantic union, and the formation of a new society; in other words, the successful completion of a perilous quest. Not surprisingly, then, even though comedies begin as lighthearted and humorous (mis)adventures, they often cross into the realm of the romance: their plots actively pursue the happy creation of a heterosexual alliance. I therefore argue that the central defining feature of the screen zomedy is *not* the abject sight gags resulting from the excessive slaughter of various reanimated corpses—although they are plentiful, entertaining, and cathartic in their own way—but rather the re-creation of an almost utopian human society, one in which the previously ostracized hero has found purpose, stability, and social inclusion by establishing a traditional family structure. In *Zombieland*, this comedic triumph comes about appropriately enough through the quintessential American family road trip.

The zomedy certainly didn't begin with Fleischer's film; like its more serious precursors, the subgenre has a long and varied tradition. Zombies have made occasional appearances in comedic films ever since the Bob Hope vehicle *The Ghost Breakers* in 1940 (directed by George Marshall), but most of these early movies simply use reanimated corpses as bit characters or as local color. The first great (and financially profitable) zombie-centric comedy didn't really arrive until 1985 with Dan O'Bannon's *The Return of the Living Dead*, an irreverent and often silly film about a group of feckless blue-collar workers and deadbeat teenagers who vainly attempt to stave off an army of freshly risen zombies from the relative safety of a mortuary. As a formal comedy, the movie also follows a strong romantic quest; namely, the pursuit of a sweet young woman named Tina (Beverly Randolph) by the hardworking Freddy (Thom Mathews). Unfortunately for the development of the zomedy, this foundational film sticks to the tragic conclusion established by its grim predecessors: Freddy is turned (albeit slowly) into a brain-eating zombie, and Tina, along with the rest of the beleaguered survivors, perishes when the military vaporizes their failing refuge in a nuclear explosion.

More recent zomedies, such as Peter Jackson's *Braindead* (1992)[24] and Edgar Wrights' *Shaun of the Dead* (2004), provide viewers with zany, violent, ironic, and even poignant narratives that more actively achieve the goals of Frye's romantic mode. The basic story of *Braindead*, for instance, focuses on a meek and timid man named Lionel (Timothy Balme) who is thwarted in his courtship of Paquita (Diana Peñalver) by his domineering and dependent mother (Elizabeth Moody). Lionel's romantic quest is clear: he must grow up, stand up to his mother, and find the courage to pursue his relationship with the angelic Paquita. Unfortunately, things only get worse when an infected Sumatran rat-monkey bites "Mum" on the leg and transforms her into a mutant zombie creature. The infection soon spreads to others, providing Lionel with a host of trials and obstacles to overcome, and pratfalls, visual gags, and physical comedy abound—all combined morbidly with the prerequisite violence, blood, and gore of the zombie parent genre. However, unlike *The Return of the Living Dead*, which includes many of the same plot points and tropes, Jackson's film offers a hero who eventually rises to the occasion, defeating his overtly Oedipal mother and insuring a bright future with his true love.

Shaun of the Dead presents viewers with an even more nuanced script and higher production values, although its core narrative remains largely the same as *Braindead*'s: deadbeat Shaun (Simon Pegg) struggles to maintain a romantic relationship with Liz (Kate Ashfield) despite her protective roommates and his obnoxious best friend, Ed (Nick Frost). A number of obstacles stand between Shaun and marital bliss, and the arrival of the zombie apocalypse actually provides him with the means to rise to the stature of a hero. Like Joseph Campbell's famous *Hero with a Thousand Faces*, Shaun requires a supernatural call to adventure to push him out the door,[25] and he reluctantly begins a harrowing journey both physical and metaphysical to change his character and obtain his prize.[26] Thanks to the generic conventions of zombie cinema, all the people in Shaun and Liz's lives who stand between their happiness are eventually killed or turned into zombies, and the two finally have no reason *not* to move in together.[27] The modern zomedy, then, is as much about romance, the archetypal hero's journey, and happy endings as it is about humor and gore. *Zombieland* deftly builds on this tradition, but it pursues all three elements more fully and according to the classical mode, featuring the overt embracing of archetypical characterizations, an elaborate geographical journey, and a happy ending that keeps all the main protagonists alive as well.

Like its antecedents, *Zombieland* focuses on a motley group of unlikely protagonists as they struggle to survive the catastrophic results of an unexplained zombie plague. Nonetheless, Fleischer offers audiences a fresh and entertaining experience with his film, a comedic movie set in an apocalyptic world where the old society of the United States of America has been transformed into "the United States of Zombieland." Fleischer's film is even more classical and formal in its deployment of the modes of comedy and romance than either *Braindead* or even *Shaun of the Dead*, given that Frye describes the plot of a romantic drama in terms of a heroic adventure,[28] and *Zombieland* presents Columbus's quest as an American family road trip, a literal journey across the country through which the "everyman" hero fights to regain a sense of family and community. In other words, *Zombieland* not only provides viewers with a humorous cinematic experience, but it also takes them on the ancient journey of the comedic and romantic protagonist, a hero who overcomes increasingly daunting challenges and obstacles to elevate himself to the status of hero and, at least potentially, husband.

Of course, a key requirement of comedic drama is still humor, and *Zombieland* certainly delivers on this point. The film opens as a kind of training video for this new, apocalyptic society (not unlike Max Brooks' *The Zombie Survival Guide*, 2003), one in which only the smartest and best equipped can hope to survive. Columbus, speaking in voice-over, lists (and subsequently demonstrates) a number of essential "rules" that will insure survival against the zombies; including, "Cardio," "Double Tap," and, perhaps most importantly, "Don't Be a Hero." The situation itself is thus both fanciful and ludicrous—a world where zombie children attack a fleeing soccer mom, where a bride eats her husband at their wedding, and where even bathroom stalls provide no privacy or safety. In addition, the characters of the film are essentially humorous types: Columbus, an awkward college student who continually reinforces his social ineptitude through his Michael Cera–like hesitations and one-liners; Tallahassee (Woody Harrelson), an over-the-top caricature of a manly survivalist who only seeks the solace of an unblemished Twinkie; and Wichita, a rebellious and hard-edged woman who trusts no one because of her past experiences with betrayal. These three, along with the almost ubiquitous doe-eyed girl Little Rock (Abigail Breslin), constitute a rag-tag group of misfits who bicker and fight with each other almost more than they do with the continuous barrage of blood-thirsty zombies.

Like all great screen comedies, *Zombieland* embraces lower forms of humor as well, from verbal jokes and puns to clever pop-culture references to ultraviolent scenes of death and dismemberment. Columbus delivers a host of dry and self-deprecating observations, and Tallahassee offers quips that are equal parts irony and profanity. The two represent a relatively modern archetype of comedy: the mismatched partnership of a "buddy" picture such as *The Odd Couple* (1968, directed by Gene Saks) or even (perhaps more appropriately) Richard Donner's *Lethal Weapon* (1987). Funny references abound as well, particularly those that take pot shots at U.S. commercialism, Disneyland, and the Hollywood elite. In fact, the coup-de-grâce of *Zombieland*'s humor comes at the expense of Bill Murray—playing himself— whose home becomes a momentary refuge for the four travelers. Finally, the key to all zomedies' success lies in what has come to be called "splatstick" comedy. Originating primarily with Sam Raimi's *The Evil Dead* (1981),[29] splatstick exploits the frailty of the human body, exploring its abjection through extreme violence, physical pratfalls, and a tremendous amount of blood and gore. This aspect of *Zombieland* is epitomized by repeated references to the "Zombie Kill of the Week," Tallahassee's increasingly creative methods of dispatching the walking dead, and the group's progressively destructive abuse of everything around them.

Raw humor aside, *Zombieland* also fulfills the requisite expectations of its audience by closely adhering to the essential elements of the comedic mode; namely, the comedic hero, the romantic quest, and the establishment of a new society. According to Frye, comedies belong to the "*low mimetic mode*" because their heroes are "superior neither to other men nor to [their] environment"; in other words, "the hero is one of us."[30] Columbus fits this description to a T: before the zombie apocalypse, he was an isolated, lonely "loser," a socially inept college student who would spend days locked in his apartment playing video games by himself. And he was afraid of clowns. In his own description of his pre–Zombieland self, Columbus states, "Pride, nowhere. Dignity, long gone. Virginity, totally justifiable to speculate on." However, because Columbus narrates much of the film in the first person, the audience cannot help but identify with him and sympathize with his plight.[31] In fact, although he initially appears uninteresting and ordinary, viewers find Columbus socially attractive because of his wit, his cleverness, and his self-proclaimed quest for love and family.[32]

As he continues to ruminate on his past, Columbus shares his deepest desires with the viewing audience and establishes the trajectory of the film's plot. He explains, "My whole life, all I'd ever wanted was to find a girl and fall in love." This romantic quest lies at the heart of all comedic drama, namely, "an erotic intrigue between a young man and a young woman which is blocked by some kind of opposition, usually paternal, and resolved by a twist in the plot."[33] Before the zombie apocalypse, the primary opposition Columbus faced was his own shyness and his inability to compete in a macho, tough-guy world. His parents were little help either; Columbus describes them almost dismissively as "paranoid shut-ins." Yet even after the zombie plague, after the virtual destruction of such a restrictive social system, Columbus remains somewhat cowed in the face of romance. His first attempt to find love results in his "hot" neighbor, whom he only knows as "406" (Amber Heard), transforming into a zombie while hiding in his apartment. In other words, the plague itself represents yet another obstacle along Columbus' quest; however, he has little luck pursuing the alluring Wichita either, even when they share moments of safety. His own insecurities remain part of his problem, but Wichita's distrust of others forms another barrier to their union.

Finally, Tallahassee embodies the machismo society Columbus resents, and the one that continues to dog him even into the apocalypse. Tallahassee is tall, strong, and stylish. He drives a tricked-out Cadillac, wields various instruments of destruction with ease, and exudes an air of optimistic confidence. In many ways, Tallahassee represents the stereotypical hero of myths and legends; in fact, at one point Columbus looks up at his protector and almost lovingly declares, "You're incredible." Furthermore, *Zombieland* repeatedly ties Tallahassee to phallic symbolism and imagery: a bright yellow Humvee, a duffle bag full of shotguns and rifles, and even the spongy cake of his illusive Twinkies. His favorite war cry conjures up images of testosterone and masculinity: "Nut up or shut up." Next to such a virile companion, Columbus can do little more than recede into the background; he even introduces himself to Wichita as Tallahassee's "Sancho Panza." Although not a rival for Wichita's sexual affections, Tallahassee nonetheless proves a literal obstacle for Columbus as well. He interrupts the two just before they kiss, and the next morning, Columbus derisively calls Tallahassee a "cock blocker." Few colloquial phrases could better describe the role of the patriarchal obstacle in the classic romantic adventure.

By reading Columbus as a sexually frustrated and essentially impotent protagonist, one can thus see how *Zombieland* fits into the romantic as well as the comic tradition. Frye outlines the three main stages of the romantic quest as (1) a perilous journey, (2) a crucial and even deadly struggle, and (3) the discovery and recognition of the hero.[34] As already demonstrated, *Zombieland* tells a story that never really deviates from its perilous journey, and almost every turn results in a deadly struggle for survival. Columbus remains the central figure of this struggle, but before he can prove himself to be the true hero of the romantic adventure, he must complete his comedic quest. That is, Columbus stars in a romantic comedy, not a divine epic; his hero's journey will not result in his saving the world but rather in his creation of a whole *new* world, one in which he can find love, a family, and true happiness. Like most comic heroes, then, Columbus seeks to be incorporated into society,[35] and he does so by overcoming the obstacles standing between him and his potential bride, Wichita.

Essentially, each of *Zombieland*'s protagonists is on a similar romantic quest: they all are seeking a supportive familial structure. Columbus' goal at the beginning of the film is simply to return home; that is, he seeks his parents and the trappings of the past. Later, after learning of the burning of Columbus, Ohio, the hero shifts his focus to Wichita, seeing her as a potential mate and as a promise of his future. Just before Columbus steps out of the car to leave Wichita behind forever, he tells the audience, "It wasn't just because I had nowhere else to go. It was because, in that moment, it became clear. Wherever this girl was, that's where I wanted to be." In essence, then, Wichita's quest becomes Columbus', and they unite forces to pursue a similarly family-themed goal: a vacation at Pacific Playland. Later in the film, the audience learns Tallahassee has been following a similar quest as well. Rather than simply wandering happily across the post-apocalyptic countryside, Tallahasse is in fact a fundamentally tragic figure, a man who has also lost his family and who sees little hope for the future. While playing a board game with his new, surrogate family, he admits to having lost his son Buck to the zombie plague. For the first time in the film, this stoic and macho hero breaks down and cries, letting the façade of the old world fall away and allowing him to trust his new society. He therefore joins the quest to visit Pacific Playland for reasons similar to Columbus': he longs for a family, for a daughter to replace his lost son. In fact, while sojourning at Murray's house, Tallahassee teaches Little Rock to shoot at targets, and the experience clearly bonds them as the two begin to smile openly at one other.

The four travelers subsequently form something of an alliance, but they struggle to realize the promise of a unifying, surrogate family. Although each suffers from almost debilitating trust issues, their shared plight and desperation eventually drive them together; as Columbus says, "We were all orphans in Zombieland." In fact, as they enjoy a relatively safe drive west across largely deserted highways, they begin to talk, argue, and play games, just like a family on an extended road trip; Columbus even claims they are having fun for the first time any of them can remember. With a new family unit thus constituted, the only major obstacle remaining between Columbus and his dream of a family is Wichita's distrust of others. Like Columbus, she has a list of rules that have kept her and Little Rock safe, but her list was in place long before the zombie plague, and it consists of only two rules: "Trust no one; just you and me." This blind adherence to her past lifestyle ultimately destroys the loose familial alliance; like the flawed heroes of tragedy, Wichita allows her hybris to stand in the way of potential safety and security. Because of her obstinate loyalty to her now-antiquated rules of the old world, Wichita and Little Rock abandon and betray the men a third time, and they continue on to Pacific Playland on their own.

Yet Columbus refuses to let the prize of his quest escape him; undaunted, he finally rises to the occasion and actively pursues Wichita to the amusement park. For the first time in the movie, he goes on the offensive instead of merely playing it safe. Through this action, Columbus not only begins to act like a real hero, but he also sets into motion what Frye calls "the symbolic presentation of the point at which the undisplaced apocalyptic world and the cyclical world of nature come into alignment, and which we propose to call the point of epiphany."[36] At this moment of the journey, the hero manages to bring balance back into the universe, and, as a result, those around him see him for the true heroic figure he is. Furthermore, Frye points out how the most common settings for these epiphanic moments are "the mountain-top, the island, the tower, the lighthouse, and the ladder or staircase,"[37] and *Zombieland* once again lives up to the classical mode by placing the female protagonists in peril atop the "Blast Off," a towering amusement park ride that launches its restrained passengers straight into the air. Perhaps simply to resolve the romantic plot properly, Fleischer thus resorts to making Wichita and Little Rock uncharacteristic damsels in distress, and their vulnerability is only emphasized by the phallic nature of the ride that traps them in the midst of an encroaching mob of zombies. Regardless, this peril gives both men the purpose they have more or less lacked: Tallahassee is good at killing zombies, and Columbus now has a princess to rescue.

The climax of *Zombieland* thus becomes an archetypal showdown between a prince and a monster guarding a helpless woman in a tower. According to Frye, "the central form of quest-romance is the dragon-killing theme,"[38] and the last obstacle between Columbus and his bride—between them both and death, in fact—is not only a zombie, but also a *clown* zombie. Although Columbus has dispatched countless numbers of the walking dead before, this one represents his dragon, his ultimate challenge because it symbolizes his past, his childhood insecurities and failings. Even Columbus himself recognizes the significance: "It had to be a clown," he tells the audience, "and it had to be Wichita, for me to finally understand that some rules are made to be broken." The text of his long-standing Rule #17, "Don't Be a Hero," is physically transformed on the movie screen to read, "Be a Hero," and Columbus proceeds to beat the monster to death with a strongman hammer. Wichita safely descends from her tower, and only then does she perform the one ritual that goes against all her insecurities and all her rules about mistrust and independence: she tells Columbus her real name, Krista. That crumbling of the last obstacle leads Columbus to realize his life-long romantic goal: to tuck a woman's hair behind her ear and kiss her on the lips.

At the conclusion of *Zombieland*, then, Columbus achieves the dual resolution expected of the film's dramatic mode (but not necessarily of the film's cinematic subgenre): he finds love and he establishes a new society. Frye argues that the romantic hero must be seen as a harbinger of spring not only because of the fecundity his new marital union represents but also because "a new society crystallizes on the stage around the hero and his bride," a society in which the hero "naturally fits."[39] This time, the girls of *Zombieland don't* leave the men behind. Columbus looks at the two of them, waiting in an idling

SUV, and says to the viewing audience, "That's me realizing that those smart girls in that big black truck and that big guy in that snakeskin jacket ... they were the closet to something I'd always wanted but never really had. A family. I trusted them and they trusted me." Columbus has fulfilled his quest and achieved his dream—appropriately enough, in a family-themed amusement park[40]—and his small group of survivors is ready to found a new society together.

At the beginning of *Zombieland*, Columbus describes his desire for a girlfriend in terms of *family*, not merely in terms of sex or a marital union. In fact, he says, "maybe this girl could bring me home to her folks. And then I'd finally be a member of a cool, functional family." Although the term *functional* can hardly be applied to the newly constituted society formed by the romantic union of Columbus and Wichita and the father-child dyad of Tallahassee and Little Rock, the four are certainly and unarguably "cool." The film thus ends on a happy note; the future may still include roaming zombies and a post-apocalyptic wasteland, but at least these four people have found each other. They each have someone to love and to trust, and that paradigm represents a surprisingly conservative and traditional outlook on human society, a society in which the honorable young man end ups partnered with the attractive young woman, and in which the dedicated father adopts the lovable daughter. As a result of this overt embracing of the classical comedic and romantic structures, Fleischer's *Zombieland* elevates the subgenre to the status of art, perhaps not a film worthy of Oscar recognition, but certainly one that challenges the critics and advances the cause. In stark contrast to many recent zombie remakes and imitations, *Zombieland* demonstrates the potential complexity and innovation of the zomedy, and it represents one direction zombie narratives could take if they want to remain timely and relevant.

Chapter 3

THE YOUNG ADULT ZOMBIE
Teenage Anxiety
in *The Forest of Hands and Teeth*

"I look to the Forest, to the fence line, and I wonder about my mother and father. Is their life any easier now? Is there fear in the Unconsecrated? Is there loss and love and pain and longing? Wouldn't a life without so much agony be easier?"
—Mary, *The Forest of Hands and Teeth*

As zombie figures and the narratives featuring these walking dead monsters have become increasingly popular, they have naturally come to infiltrate all corners of contemporary culture. As fans of the zombie have become parents, they have naturally come to share something of their love for the walking dead with their children. And as zombie culture has become an increasingly profitable business, companies have naturally begun to market the walking dead to younger and younger consumers. The majority of these youthful manifestations are understandably harmless, comedic, and sometimes even cuddly, as few parents are really interested in terrifying their young offspring. After all, as Jeffery Jerome Cohen points out, "Because monsters make us uncomfortable we reduce their power by rendering them cute or otherwise abjecting them as infantile things, fears to be left behind as we assume our mature identities."[1] However, as children grow up and begin to face the challenging concerns and anxieties of adolescence, they likely discover an increasing need for the more horrific brand of zombies, true monsters that allow them to face both their overt and repressed fears while exorcising them through dramatic catharsis. Indeed, contemporary "young adult" culture is currently awash with increasingly "adult" narratives filled with monsters and monstrousness, from terrifying tales of atavistic survival to apocalyptic dystopian novels to more traditional zombie horror fiction.

Survivalism has been a popular subject for the imaginative authors of children's and young adult entertainment since the days of Daniel Defoe's *Robinson Crusoe* (1719), and the tropes of the subgenre only escalated in esteem and severity with novels such as Johann David Wyss's *The Swiss Family Robinson* (1812) and William Golding's *Lord of the Flies* (1954).[2] Apocalyptic and post-apocalyptic narratives for a more mature audience also increased in frequency and popularity during the same span of time, from Mary Shelley's *The Last Man* (1826) to George R. Stewart's *Earth Abides* (1949) to Richard Matheson's *I Am Legend* (1954).[3] Since the international trauma of September 11, 2001, extreme tales of survival and the apocalypse are more in vogue than ever, including Danny Boyle's *28 Days Later* (2002), Robert Kirkman's *The Walking Dead* comic series (2003–), and Cormac McCarthy's *The Road* (2006). With the ongoing sensation that is Suzanne Collins' *The Hunger Games* trilogy (2008–10), survivalist post-apocalyptic literature has firmly established its place in the young adult market as well. An increasing number of such books are enjoying similar success, including *The City of Ember* series (2003–08) by Jeanne DuPrau, the *Life as We Knew It* trilogy (2006–10) by Susan Beth Pfeffer, and *The Maze Runner* novels (2009–11) by James Dashner, indicating a new generation of readers now has life, death, and global destruction on the brain.

Carrie Ryan's contribution to the subgenre, her *Forest of Hands and Teeth* trilogy (2009–2011), is of particular interest to me, not only because they are zombie novels but also because they provide young adult readers an assembled narrative that is part *City of Ember*, part Walter M. Miller, Jr.'s *A Canticle for Leibowitz* (1960), and part George A. Romero's *Land of the Dead* (2005).[4] These disparate antecedents and influences have produced a triptych of novels that manifest the Millennial Generation's fear of isolation, false security, unreliable authority figures, invasion, infestation, destruction, and inevitable mortality—in addition to the adolescent reluctance to become a responsible adult. In this chapter, I use two established perspectives to theorize Ryan's novels: Aleen Pace Nilsen and Kenneth L. Donelson's essential textbook *Literature for Today's Young Adults* (2009) and Elizabeth Rosen's timely study *Apocalyptic Transformation: Apocalypse and the Postmodern Imagination* (2008). In addition, I draw from my own theories and body of work about zombie narratives to inform my analysis. Ryan's works, particularly the first novel in her series, reveal how post–9/11 teenagers are struggling to choose between taking charge of their own uncertain future and passively accepting peer pressure and an arrested adolescent development.

Zombies for Children and Young Adults

Children are naturally curious about the things their parents manifestly like, and so as zombies increase in popularity generally, younger generations are logically becoming active participants in the ongoing Renaissance as well. For this youthful crowd, a host of lighthearted and age-appropriate zombies and zombie variants are readily available for consumption. These versions are understandably less terrifying, mere infantile caricatures found as plush toys, trading cards, designer dolls, animated characters, and Lego set minifigures; in video games, iOS Apps, and board games; and on onesies, lunchboxes, T-shirts, and bed sheets. Zombies have been consciously marketed to children since at least 1998, in the direct-to-video movie *Scooby-Doo on Zombie Island* (directed by Hiroshi Aoyama, Kazumi Fukushima, and Jim Stenstrum), and they are currently finding an all-new audience via the grunting *Zombie High* character "Ghoulia Yelps." In fact, arguably the most popular and pervasive zombies in the world today are not the sinister, rotting foes of AMC's *The Walking Dead* (2010–) but rather the various incarnations of the monsters found in the *Plants vs. Zombies* video game (2009, designed by George Fan) and the nocturnal beasts roaming the digital realms of *Minecraft* (2009, designed by Markus "Notch" Persson), both of which are readily available as action figures, plush dolls, t-shirts, pajamas, or almost any toy or accessory imaginable. Entrepreneurs are certainly justified in recognizing this lucrative market; after all, for a host of reasons, just like their parents, children and young adults today really like flesh-eating, decomposing, contagious zombie monsters.

An early manifestation of the zombie invasion narrative as marketed towards a child audience appeared in 2006 as the "Once Bitten" episode of *SpongeBob SquarePants* (2006, directed by Stephen Hillenburg).[5] SpongeBob's pet snail Gary (both voiced by Tom Kenny) appears to come down with "mad snail disease," and in his rage he bites the beleaguered Squidward (Rodger Bumpass). A paranoid Patrick (Bill Fagerbakke) suggests, in addition to a long litany of disturbing symptoms, the bite of an infected snail will turn its victims into zombies. Understandably, panic quickly spreads throughout Bikini Bottom, a panic driven by Patrick's insistent misinformation made all the worse by the efforts of the local media. In reality, Gary's bite is largely harmless, but because everyone *believes* what they are told about becoming zombies, they decided they must act that way. The "infected" denizens riot and form a mob of slow-moving drones in their pursuit of the uninfected SpongeBob, their arms outstretched before them, scored with music clearly reminiscent of Romero's *Night of the Living Dead* (1968). Additionally, the unbitten "survivors" of Bikini Bottom fortify themselves in the Krusty Krab restaurant, continuing the episode's deliberate homage to the zombie cinema tradition. When the snail veterinarian finally shows up, he declares mad snail disease a myth, an urban legend, suggesting the town has in fact been infected by "mass hysteria" instead: Gary was simply being grouchy because of a wood splinter. The punch line occurs when Squidward shows up to work and becomes the *real* zombie—a minimum wage worker in the fast-food industry.

While this brief *SpongeBob SquarePants* episode hardly lives up to the horror and violence of a traditional zombie film marketed towards adults, it nonetheless demonstrates the conscious transference of the genre and its key storyline, plot points, and tropes to a narrative mode more appropriate for a younger audience. This redirection of source material has been implemented for middle-grade readers as well, as in David Lubar's *My Rotten Life* (2009), the first book in his "Nathan Abercrombie, Accidental Zombie" series. This initial novel, one that has clear appeal to the kind of bookish ten-year-olds who would most closely resemble the work's protagonist, introduces readers to Nathan Abercrombie, a stereotypical fifth grader—a reluctant member of the "Second Best" clique—who suffers from all the pre-pubescent angst associated with that age. After being deliberately and publicly rejected by Shawna Lanchester and barred from her elite Halloween party, Nathan ruminates, "We all knew the truth—in fifth grade, popularity was everything. As far as I could tell, part of popularity came from who you were, and part came from what you could do."[6] Unfortunately, Nathan can do very little, especially when it comes to athletics; however, after he receives an accidental overdose of "Hurt-Be-Gone, the world's first all-natural, totally safe emotion killer,"[7] he gradually begins to lose his physiological awareness of pain. Over the course of the short novel, Nathan becomes "half dead,"[8] losing his need for sleep, nourishment, and even oxygen. While understandably concerned about this shocking transformation, Nathan soon realizes his zombie body is capable of superhuman feats—he can swim underwater indefinitely, he doesn't lose his breath when running, and his muscles never tire because they don't need oxygen. Suddenly, "Second-Best" Nathan is winning the school track meet, and he begins to think, "Maybe being half dead wasn't all bad."[9]

Lubar's novel shifts from the terrifying to the terrific as Nathan realizes all the benefits that come from his unnatural transformation; yet the central role of the monstrous arguably grounds the book in the Gothic tradition. According to Roderick McGillis and his analysis of the Gothic in children's literature, "Adolescents are, perhaps, as intensely haunted or even more haunted than the rest of us. Their bodies as well as their social milieu are in flux, changing as they—both body and social group—morph ... into maturity."[10]

In the case of Nathan Abercrombie, the adolescent body is quite dramatically in flux, changing on a supernatural level in a way that likely manifests, at least on a symbolic level, a young reader's hopes (and thereby also fears) concerning puberty. On the one hand, Nathan's newfound athletic prowess allows him to fulfill his wildest dreams: he is seen publicly as a "winner," Shawna recants and invites him to her Halloween party, and he finally feels accepted by the popular kids. Yet, on the other hand, Nathan comes to realize his *true* friends are Mookie and Abigail, the similarly outcast "Second-Bests" who have stood by him from the beginning and helped him find a cure for his condition. Just before Nathan transforms completely into a zombie forever, Abigail's house catches on fire, with her trapped inside. Nathan consciously chooses to abandon the hard-won zombie cure, ripping the medicated bandages from his still living feet because, as a zombie, he can safely rush into the burning home and rescue his friend. In other words, Nathan becomes something of a superhero, a revisionist zombie figure ready to star in a series of similar adventures, but he does it all without forgetting who he really is and who his true friends really are.

In other words, even these otherwise benign children's stories—and I am considering just two examples from the many on the market today—are doing the serious work of Gothic literature. They use their allegorical scenarios and symbolic monsters to shed light on the real world, subtly providing youth with social commentary and insights into contemporary anxieties, on whatever level. They also exemplify the fascination all people have, even children, with the darker side of human nature. Anna Jackson, Karen Coats, and Roderick McGillis argue that "[r]ather than seeing the Gothic as an anomalous intrusion into their lives from some external and alien force, the children in many contemporary Gothic novels court their dark side, and own it as an aspect of the self."[11] The denizens of Bikini Bottom demonstrate the ease with which they accept Patrick's misinformation and willingly join a mindless horde of lawless vigilantes, and no one must force Nathan to embrace his monstrous potential because he recognizes how being a zombie ultimately enhances the best parts of himself. This appeal of the darker aspects of human experience has understandably spawned a number of zombie-themed and related books for young readers, including John Kloepfer's *The Zombie Chasers* (2010), the first book in a series by the same name; Fred Perry's *Zombie Kid Diaries* comics (2012–2013); and even *Night of the Zombie Goldfish* by Dr. Roach, the first of the "Monster Stories" series. Such proliferation demonstrates even grade school readers can benefit from the Gothic tales of zombies, even when they are blithe and humorous.

Of course, not all zombie-related narratives directed towards children are fun and lighthearted; after all, the young can find pleasure in fear just as grown-ups do. As Noël Carroll reminds us, "many people—so many, in fact, that we must concede that they are normal, at least in the statistical sense—do seek out horror fictions for the purpose of deriving pleasure from sights and descriptions that customarily repulse them."[12] Being frightened can be a fun, cathartic experience, and perhaps because the vampire has become *too* cute and cuddly, young people are actively seeking a monster they can fear. The zombie, especially the contagious, flesh-eating one, certainly fits that niche. While R. L. Stine, that veritable Stephen King for the young, originally delved into the zombie subgenre on a more upbeat level with his *Zombie School* (1999) and *Why I Quit Zombie School* (2011), his more recent *Zombie Town* (2012) pushes into a more traditionally terrifying sphere. Anna Smith claims, "Fear thrives on distorting the familiar,"[13] and Stine realizes this uncanny Freudian reality by staging his zombie tale in common, everyday locations. When Karen talks Mike into seeing the horror film *Zombie Town* one dark and rainy afternoon, they head to the local Cineplex; and while a movie theater is likely a very familiar location for most people, this one is strangely, uncannily empty. The movie begins, and the two enjoy their popcorn; but when the film breaks, they find themselves alone in the dark theater. To make the setting even more unnerving, they soon discover all the doors are locked and they are trapped inside the building—and they are not as alone as they had thought.

Even though the audience of *Zombie Town* consists of middle-grade readers, Stine willingly appropriates many of the sights, sounds, and conventions of a Romero zombie film in his attempt to genuinely frighten his young fans.[14] Stine, with his dozens upon dozens of successful horror titles for children, clearly understands as well as any author today that "fear or the pretence of fear has become a dominant mode of enjoyment in literature for young people," largely because these books provide "a space for safe fear."[15] However, *Zombie Town* cleverly takes the "safe place" of the movie theater—the place where zombie films are enjoyed—and turns that into the least safe site for the book's protagonists. Somehow, inexplicably and uncannily, the zombies from the film-within-the-book have broken free from their celluloid confines, and these monsters are *not* the cute-and-cuddly fare found in other products marketed towards children: "His *eye*! One eye was missing. And as the living corpse turned, I could see that half his face was missing, too. As if someone had ripped off the skin on his right side."[16] This abject, stinking monster begins to lurch after the two children, and soon ten more join it, groaning and staggering in their relentless pursuit. Mike and Karen flee, desperately seeking an adult—any other living human—for help, but they are totally alone.

They manage to escape the theatre, but even though Karen tries to explain the whole experience away as an elaborate PR stunt on behalf of *Zombie Town*'s marketing team, Mike notes that the entire town appears to be just as abandoned as the movie theater. "Nobody is around," he says, "No zombies. But no people, either."[17] While the monsters themselves are an understandably frightening component of Stine's book, the real terror comes from this sense of abandonment.

Many children, teenagers, and even young adults struggle with feelings of abandonment and fear the loss of their parents; yet, ironically, another source of tension comes from the presence of that very family they hope won't abandon them. This angsty push-pull that adolescents feel between their needing the support of their parents and their wanting to be left alone as independent human beings constitutes much of the uncanny work performed by Gothic literature for young readers. Indeed, Smith claims that "most often Gothic writing continues to be allied with sick or scary families and communities."[18] Mike and Karen are certainly confronted by a sick and scary community, as they find their once-familiar town suddenly overrun by marauding zombies, but when Mike finally makes it back to the perceived safety of his own home, he must face the real horror of his situation:

> I gaped at my dad. At his sunken eyes, his slack jaw. The green skin sagging from his face.
> My mom's eyes drooped from their sockets, hanging by veiny threads. Her lips were fat and swollen. A chunk of her hair lay in her lap. I could see some of her skull through the wide bald spot in her head....
> Zombies. All zombies.[19]

Mike's forced encounter with his monstrous parents forces young readers to confront one of their deepest fears and anxieties as well: that their parents will betray them, turn on them, or abandon them. Yet total abandonment might be preferable to Mike, for once they notice their living son, they rise from the couch and begin staggering after him. Mike's parents have literally become monsters and the home has become the least safe place of all for Mike.

As with adult readers, then, zombies afford children safe opportunities to confront and explore their greatest fears through the catharsis of literature. Not surprisingly, this form of therapeutic entertainment has begun to thrive in the lucrative young adult market as well. Naturally, many of these books have followed on the heels of Stephenie Meyer's insanely successful *Twilight* series and fall rather firmly in the subgenre of paranormal romance with their primary focus on teen angst. For example, *Generation Dead* by Daniel Waters (2008) recounts the adventures of Phoebe Kendall, who has fallen in love with Tommy, the leader of their high school's gang of disenfranchised "living impaired" students, and *You Are So Undead to Me* (2009) by Stacey Jay presents readers with a new version of *Buffy the Vampire Slayer* (1997–2003, created by Joss Whedon), for Megan Berry is the chosen "Zombie Settler" who must deal with the "semi-dead" when all she really wants to do is just go to the homecoming dance. Other young adult titles are more sober and frightening in their engagement with the zombie subgenre, such as Cherie Priest's *Boneshaker* (2009), a fanciful steampunk zombie novel set in an alternate version of Seattle; Jonathan Maberry's *Rot & Ruin* (2010), a tale of young zombie hunters in a post-apocalyptic world; and *Zom-B* (2012) by Darren Shan, the first in an extended series about a young man's efforts to survive a zombie apocalypse. Because the Gothic "unearths skeletons from the past and ... raises fears for the future,"[20] books such as these are perfect for readers struggling to negotiate the tricky transition they face between child and adult, and if they can be entertained while sorting through their anxieties, all the better.

The Post-Apocalyptic YA Wasteland

One of the reasons Ryan's young adult, post-apocalyptic, zombie survival series deserves special attention is because she has crafted a creative amalgam of three different, established modes. Like any postmodern, poststructuralist work, Ryan's trilogy represents the intersection, or assemblage, of seemingly disparate antecedents, sources, and influences that have been recombined and synthesized to create an innovative narrative, one that retains the flavors of the original texts while creating something new and original.[21] This creative process means *The Forest of Hands and Teeth* (2009), *The Dead-Tossed Waves* (2010), and *The Dark and Hollow Places* (2011) must be read in terms of adaptation; although the books are technically original works, their tropes, themes, plot structures, characters, devices, and symbols can be found in a host of previously authored young adult novels, post-apocalyptic tales, and zombie invasion narratives. Additionally, they must be considered as part of the Gothic literary tradition, for her books overtly engage with "unrestraint, transgression, and the overturning of normalcy."[22] I propose a critical reading and analysis of the initial, pivotal act of Ryan's first novel as a poignant manifestation of the post–9/11 generation's existential crisis and malaise. *The Forest of Hands and Teeth* represents a noteworthy addition to the adolescent zombie narrative tradition, one influenced by a variety of inspirational source modes.

Nilsen and Donelson have done perhaps the most definitive work on the character, nature, and value of young adult literature to date, and they provide teachers, students, scholars, and authors alike with a simple list of generic protocols that make YA literature what it is today. Their list of essential "characteristics" for the quintessential YA formula resonates with an accuracy similar to Joseph Campbell's classification of fantasy tropes and plot points,[23] including

1. a dominant, adolescent perspective;
2. a young protagonist who is allowed to solve problems and succeed on his or her own;
3. fast-paced plotting;
4. works that cross generic lines;
5. a broad ethnic and cultural focus, with characters of a variety of races and classes;
6. an optimistic resolution accomplished by an adolescent protagonist who successfully transitions into adulthood; and
7. an exploration of emotions and psychological states that resonate with a teenage audience.[24]

While characteristic number four addresses the entire body of YA literature as a diverse and adaptable genre, the remaining six characteristics are important because they surface in almost every successful narrative intended for young adult readers. Furthermore, many of these generic characteristics cross over with the requisite features of both post-apocalyptic and zombie narratives.

The apocalyptic narrative, unlike the contemporary genre of "YA lit," has a much older, if not ancient, pedigree, one rooted in mythology, folklore, and religious texts. On the one hand, as illustrated by the Book of Revelations in the New Testament, the *apocalypse* indicates a story, tale, or parable that *reveals* and makes something clear. Rosen offers us a slightly more sophisticated definition of the term *apocalypse*: "Apocalypse is a means by which to understand the world and one's place in it. It is an organizing principle imposed on an overwhelming, seemingly disordered universe."[25] Tales of the end of the world, then, do more than just entertain or frighten—they function as allegorical tales and revelatory devices that help audiences make sense of the chaotic and frustrating world around them. Such a view of apocalyptic literature makes the mode a perfect match for YA literature. Both types of stories feature characters facing difficult if not seemingly insurmountable challenges, and the journeys or quests taken by their protagonists hopefully lead to an increased understanding of their place in a harsh, chaotic world. In fact, many teenagers, both fictional characters in print and readers in real life, likely see their coming-of-age transition from child to adult in terms of the "end of the world"—or, at least, the end of the world as they know it.

Like many other successful YA novels, Ryan's *The Forest of Hands and Teeth* accomplishes this logical fusion of adolescent literature and the apocalyptic genre, but it also obviously includes the key defining features of the zombie invasion narrative—in the tradition of Romero's politically pregnant horror films, and not that of the lighthearted children's zombie literature I have discussed previously. As I lay out in *American Zombie Gothic*, the modern zombie narrative—that is, the horror subgenre established primarily by Romero's *Night of the Living Dead*—has a number of key features, qualities, and characteristics. Most obviously, such narratives are defined by the presence of walking dead corpses, human bodies that have somehow become ambulatory and which have an overwhelming drive to eat the flesh of any living human being they encounter. In addition, and perhaps most importantly, the condition of the modern zombie is contagious; they transmit their mindless state to their victims, converting others to their apocalyptic horde.[26] Zombies are thus essentially liminal creatures—dead yet somehow alive, humans yet unequivocally monsters—who have lost their consciousness and autonomy in favor of an all-consuming and instinctual drive, a drive that results in a kind of hive mind and monstrous community. This community almost always proves irresistible, as zombie narratives invariably move from initial infection to massive proliferation to the eventual collapse of society's infrastructure.[27]

Most zombie narratives also belong to the genre of apocalyptic fiction, as a zombie invasion almost always leads to the end of human civilization, and the literary market of late demonstrates that young adult readers are clearly demanding such tales tailored to their own unique set of interests and anxieties. This fusion is perhaps even more logical than that performed by post-apocalyptic YA literature, as the zombie figure itself brilliantly represents the adolescent condition, or, at the very least, a desirable alternative to the increasing responsibility expected of burgeoning adulthood. Inasmuch as the zombie is a liminal creature that stands on the margins of life and death, adolescents inhabit a similar space between childhood and adulthood. Because teenagers are increasingly confronted with demands to grow up, to act responsibly, and to make adult decisions, they can be tempted to give into collective peer pressure and continue in childish and irresponsible behavior. *The Forest of Hands and Teeth* explores this temptation to arrest teenage development in the border state of adolescence through the allegorical figures of the zombies—for who hasn't thought of teenagers today in terms of the walking dead?[28] However, because Ryan's chief protagonist Mary eventually decides to survive and continue into her uncertain future, the novel ultimately uses its monstrous (as opposed to sympathetic or romantic) zombies to show that young adults must eventually break from the apathetic crowd—to defeat the monster—and live their own lives, especially as the successful conclusion of the coming-of-age transition from child to adult.

From the very first pages of *The Forest of Hands and Teeth*, Ryan establishes her book not only as a YA novel but also as a post-apocalyptic one. As mentioned, Nilsen and Donelson's first rule of YA literature is a dominant adolescent perspective, one usually accomplished by narration in the first person that unavoidably emphasizes a young person's point of view.[29] Ryan's book is intimately narrated by Mary, who begins her tale with personal reflections and memories of her mother and her own innocent childhood.[30] These reflections indicate the narrator is a grown and mature woman, yet as the story unfolds, readers realize the perspective being recreated is that of a Mary who has yet to enter fully into adulthood. Her references to her parents and her older brother establish she is yet in adolescence; at the very least, Mary still lives with her mother, caring for her and tending to domestic chores as a responsible child rather than a young woman keeping her own house.[31] Mary's exposition thus establishes her as the book's protagonist, not only because of her first-person narration but also because she rapidly weaves the details of the conflicts and crises she faces, conflicts and crises directly and indirectly related to her struggles to come of age. This quick pace realizes another of Nilsen and Donelson's rules for YA literature,[32] for the pacing of the novel starts fast and never relents.

Perhaps the most important element of the story established by this quick pacing is that Mary's world has suffered a grievous and life-changing apocalypse. The first line of the book, "My mother used to tell me about the ocean," not only establishes the subjective point of view of the adolescent protagonist, but it also references a legendary place only known to her from an ancient photograph of her great-great-great-grandmother standing on some forgotten shore.[33] Clearly, the world in which the ocean was a tangible and attainable reality had been lost many generations prior to Mary's story because of some kind of massive cataclysm. The setting of *The Forest of Hands and Teeth* is one in which young people cannot imagine salt water, or bodies of water so large as to be "useless."[34] Over the course of the first chapter alone, Mary efficiently reveals additional details that establish her world as a post-apocalyptic one: her isolated village is surrounded by an endless and impenetrable forest, garrisoned from the world outside by a heavily fortified and guarded fence line.[35] Additionally, Mary's world is a strange and foreign one to most readers, one governed by restrictive rules of survival. Young adult readers might indeed identify readily with a world with limited mobility and a strict system of traditions and behaviors, seeing it as a reflection of their own, and the constant presence of life-threatening monsters outside Mary's village should come to act through the novel as valuable and multifarious metaphors for the adolescent condition.

Within this dense forest and with these mysterious monsters, Ryan codes her novel as both a Gothic story and an undeniable zombie narrative as well. Jackson, Coats, and McGillis point out the settings of Gothic tales often include dark forests and labyrinthine corridors,[36] which become uncanny because they turn the otherwise familiar into the decidedly unfamiliar. Additionally, of course, this frightening "Forest of Hands and Teeth" is infested by abominations labeled as the "Unconsecrated." These mindless, carnivorous, and contagious monstrosities manifest all of the most recognizable characteristics of the modern-day zombie, and Mary emphasizes how they pose a constant threat to the beleaguered villagers.[37] Not only has her father already been lost to the dangers of the forest—a fate associated with what Mary terms "turning,"[38] a reference that will resonate with fans of other established zombie narratives—but her brother also serves on a kind of local militia that patrols the village's shaky fortifications. The Unconsecrated are dangerous for at least two reasons: (1) because of their numbers, they could potentially breach the ancient chain-link fences and (2) members of the village who mourn the loss of their loved ones and see no point in continuing the struggle to survive alone might allow themselves to be bitten by the ravenous beasts. This latter risk is what makes these liminal creatures particularly dangerous; because the ranks of the Unconsecrated are made up of former residents of the village, many of the monsters wear recognizable faces. Additionally, in a practice not normally seen in zombie narratives, going to visit the ambulatory dead, unlike the sterile ritual performed at real-world gravesites, is risky business because the corpses are infectious, predatory, and painfully familiar.[39]

Because humanity stands on the brink of extinction in the face of an unstoppable zombie horde, Mary inhabits a world that has already experienced its apocalypse—an apocalypse the human race has only barely survived. Rosen outlines the traditional stages of the apocalypse, as presented by St. John of Patmos in the New Testament, as the "Great Tribulation," the Second Coming of Jesus Christ, the global battle of Armageddon, the divine "Last Judgment" of God, and the establishment of a paradisiacal New Jerusalem on Earth.[40] While the world described by Mary continues to experience great tribulation—as evidenced by the continued threat of the Unconsecrated on the other side of the chain-link fence—the battle of Armageddon has clearly not only already ended, but also ended badly for humanity. The denizens of Mary's village are hardly an organized army ready to combat their walking dead foes but rather a cowed and timid group that has been slowly collapsing under decades of siege. Mary speaks of this ancient conflict as the "Return,"[41] a time in the distant past when the dead ostensibly rose up and all but annihilated humanity. An antiquated past none of the villagers can even remember—or, if any of them *do* remember, they refuse to speak of it.

What Ryan leaves notably absent from her vision of the apocalypse is any return of Jesus Christ or the promise of a divine last judgment. Instead, she presents organized religion in a decidedly negative light, for Mary's village is ruled by a secretive group of nuns who conceal any knowledge of the past in the confines of the village's inaccessible cathedral. Although the structure was once a house of worship, the antiquated and decidedly Gothic monument houses "nuns" who are hardly servants of Christ as Ryan's readers would understand them. Mary gives no indication she is a particularly religious person, and her efforts at prayer later in the novel are affected at best.[42] Furthermore, at no point does anyone in the novel discuss Jesus, the atonement, salvation, or a concept of heaven. Yet Ryan does indicate her novel will address the idea of a New Jerusalem, the hope that a better place exists somewhere in the aftermath of mass destruction and suffering. The first sentence of *The Forest of Hands and Teeth* establishes this ideal—the ocean, a place that represents both Mary's past and foreshadows her hoped-for future. This legendary place, this nostalgic utopian ideal intimately associated with her own mother, becomes Mary's goal, a place she irrationally believes will offer her safety and freedom.

With dazzling economy, then, Ryan introduces her readers to Mary, her dystopian world, and her essentially Gothic challenges and conflicts, all of which fit nicely in the genres of YA lit, post-apocalyptic lit, and the zombie narrative. On the one hand, Mary's world is an adolescent and subjective one, and she is presented as a liminal character on the cusp of transitioning from a child to an adult. On the other, Mary lives in a post-apocalyptic world plagued by zombies—she knows nothing else, and the pre–Return world is little more than a distant myth. Unfortunately for Mary, however, she is almost immediately forced to make hard choices and begin the quest that will consume the rest of the novel. This catalyzing event—what Campbell would label the "Call to Adventure"[43]—is a kind of *second* apocalypse, a personal apocalypse that brings the adolescent life Mary knows to an end. As the novel begins, Mary's father has just recently been turned into a zombie and banished to the Forest; her mother, as a result, is dangerously depressed and reckless. Mary and her brother Jed have been watching her closely, afraid she will make the choice other widows have made before her—allowing herself to be infected in hopes of joining her husband in the Forest.[44] Predictably, and abiding by Nilsen and Donelson's second characteristic of YA lit,[45] the mourning mother must quickly exit the story so Mary can pursue her journey on her own.

However, the key to Mary's personal apocalypse and her resultant call to adventure actually lies in a dual challenge to her status as an adolescent. Readers learn Mary's telling and symbolic name not from her directly but from her contemporary Harry when he invites her to go to the Harvest Celebration with him, an offer that equates with a marriage proposal.[46] With this offer, Mary faces the coming-of-age transition from childhood to adulthood, from daughter to wife. June Cummins argues that female development represents a significant feature of the Gothic in literature for adolescents: "At crucial junctures, the Gothic is blended with elements of Horror or the Grotesque in a swirl of allusions that evoke age-old narrative traditions surrounding female development."[47] At the same time Mary is struggling to come to terms with her own liminality as a woman in transition, her mother, unsupervised by her children, allows herself to be infected by a zombie at the fence line. When Mary hears the warning siren sound, she immediately realizes what has happened. Since everyone in the village knows not to get too close to the fences, almost any infection from the Unconsecrated must be the result of a conscious choice—a kind of suicide.[48] As with anyone infected in the village, only two choices remain for Mary's mother: "Die a quick death and save her soul or go exist amongst the Unconsecrated."[49] Devastated, but perhaps recognizing her newfound responsibility as a developing adult, Mary decides, without consulting her brother, to respect her mother's choice—she tells the nuns to put her mother out into the Forest.[50] Before she succumbs to the zombie infection, however, Mary's mother imposes a simple quest upon her grieving daughter: "The ocean, Mary, the ocean!"[51] With Harry's proposal and her mother's death, the world Mary has known effectively comes to an end, and she faces a choice between finding a path to adulthood and obstinately remaining in her role of daughter, in whatever prolonged capacity.

Not surprisingly, Mary will come to chose the path laid out for her by her mother, and this journey through the maze of the Forest of Hands and Teeth in search of the legendary ocean thus begins in decidedly uncanny terms, terms couched not only in her transition from girl to woman but also in the disruptive changes to her family and her place in the larger community. In most Gothic children's literature, the characters obviously experience dramatic changes, but the motifs of the uncanny are particularly related to the characters' places within their own families.[52] With the death of both of their parents, Jed, the only son, has inherited everything for himself and his wife Beth, and neither wish to help or support Mary as part of their new family unit as she has already—technically—come of age.[53] In other words, Mary's story becomes one of a "lost or broken" family,[54] and she finds herself with only two viable options: grow up or give up. In the village, young women who have been put out by their families must transition into adulthood either by marrying a young man and joining *his* household or by becoming part of the Sisterhood as a celibate nun and accepting their strictly controlled lifestyle.[55] When Jed harshly reveals to Mary that Harry no longer wants her as his wife, perhaps due to the stigma of her mother's suicide,[56] Mary reluctantly presents herself at the Cathedral. Although her biological age should be enough for her to transition into womanhood, the inherently sexist social structures and established traditions of the village leave the helpless Mary at the mercy of the whims of two men—her brother and her erstwhile husband—both of whom act selfishly.

The Cathedral proves to be a decidedly Gothic location inside as well as out, one filled with repressed secrets of the past just waiting to be uncovered and revelations about the future—or one *possible* future—that force Mary to come to terms with herself. To Mary's shock and horror, Sister Tabitha leads her down a subterranean tunnel and forces her up through a hatch and into a small clearing in the Forest, one protected by a ring of fencing interrupted by a lone gate.[57] The object lesson quickly becomes clear: Mary's real choice isn't between marriage and the Sisterhood at all; it's between living as a human or existing as one of the Unconsecrated. As if echoing the hard lessons learned in other zombie narratives, Sister Tabitha explains, "There is always a choice, Mary.... It is what makes us human, what separates us from them."[58] As in most zombie narratives, the key factor boils down to human agency, and faced with such a frightening alternative, Mary verbally agrees to a bleak life of scripture study and lonely piety. She is forced into a period of mute contemplation, forbidden to speak, isolated from others, and coerced into studying scripture day and night—in many ways, Mary appears to have simply become a different kind of zombie, a servant or slave robbed of agency at the hands of a hegemonic force. Yet instead of studying the word of God, as a good nun of the Cathedral should, the inherently rebellious Mary finds herself staring out her window at night and thinking about the Unconsecrated, wondering if her mother is cold in the Forest.[59]

Mary's struggle to accomplish her transition and find an adult identity of her own is further complicated when Travis, Harry's brother, is admitted to the Cathedral with a grave injury. Mary cares for him and nurses him back to health, and, in classic romance-novel style, grows to love him.[60] Unfortunately, Travis is already pledged to marry Cass, Mary's best friend—enter the prerequisite love triangle—and this undeniable fact fills Mary with rage and longing. Grieving for the adult life she cannot have, Mary finds herself tempted by the existence of the Unconsecrated: "I look to the Forest, to the fence line, and I wonder about my mother and father. Is their life any easier now? Is there fear in the Unconsecrated? Is there loss and love and pain and longing? Wouldn't a life without so much agony be easier?"[61] Mary has realized life as a nun will rob her of her agency, but she also decides that life as anything other than Travis' wife would be no life at all either. Therefore, she ponders what it would be like to arrest her development forever by joining the mindless, unchanging zombie horde in the Forest—to become permanently liminal: not child nor adult, not living nor dead, a choice that would result in her no longer being required to choose.

Before Mary can take any rash and deadly action, a *third* kind of apocalypse—a localized, communal one—interrupts her life and thrusts her into the dangerous adventure her mother had foreseen for her. Coming as no surprise to fans of zombie narratives, the Unconsecrated soon breach the village's defenses, and in the chaos that follows, the majority of the community is killed and scattered. Mary must flee into the Forest down one of the two ancient and overgrown pathways, protected on either side by rusty fences, but with no sense of where she is going. Harry, Travis, Cass, and a boy named Jacob accompany her, along with her brother Jed and his wife, and this motley group of survivors spends the rest of the novel struggling to navigate the maze of pathways that wander almost randomly through the seemingly endless Forest—while struggling to negotiate their new roles in a new social structure as well. Along the way, Mary must deal with the difficulties of rugged survival and the heartache of a painful love triangle. Yet only after she is cut off from the repressive structure of the village and its monolithic Cathedral in this seemingly traumatic way can Mary begin to make hard choices and develop into a responsible adult. When faced with either death or conversion to the masses of the Unconsecrated, Mary ends up choosing life. Although she appears to lose everything else in the process, a now adult Mary completes her difficult quest by the end of the novel, realizing the New Jerusalem of the ocean and a new life of hope and promise.

The cultural work of young adult literature is perhaps most effectively accomplished not just through post-apocalyptic stories but also through Gothic *zombie* narratives in particular. If the chief concern of literature for children and young adults is exploring adolescent anxieties about becoming an adult, what better analogy than an apocalyptic change in existence brought about by a tempting coalition of mindless, non-autonomous zombies? McGillis posits the form and sensibility of the Gothic are so pervasive right now because, to put it simply, "we live in a scary world."[62] Apocalyptic literature comforts people whose lives are overwhelmed by social disruption,[63] such as those plaguing adults young and old alike right now, and Ryan, like other authors before her, cleverly manipulates the apocalyptic paradigm to use it as "the most effective vehicle for ... social critique."[64] In addition, Cohen emphasizes how monsters manifest cultural anxieties—after all, the word *monster* shares the same root as *demonstrate*, meaning a sign or figure that teaches through a revelatory depiction[65]—and zombies in particular, according to Peter Dendle, are poignant "barometers" of contemporary cultural fears and anxieties.[66] The current popularity of Gothic literature among young readers makes perfect sense when seen in these terms, and McGillis makes clear why this surge in these narratives coincides with the times in which we all now live:

> Of course human beings have always feared the rough beast and always lived in a scary world, but at certain times things get just a bit scarier; at the end of centuries, in times of war, in times of revolution, in times of rapid change. In such times, the Gothic finds purchase. It expresses fear even as it accepts fear as inevitable. The Gothic may express our helplessness in the face of global forces set on controlling the way we live. Or it may work to inure us to terrible things, to numb our reactions so that we take the daily tide of turmoil as natural.[67]

The unconsecrated zombies in Ryan's novels address teenage fears of both the inevitability of death and potentially traumatic realities of adulthood. In other words, adolescents dread both corporeal death and the end of their childhood, and they are likely tempted to simply give in to the immaturity of their resistant peers. However, as the course of *The Forest of Hands and Teeth* demonstrates, it's better to live and to make adult choices even when the results are an unsure and less-than-idyllic future. But that's life, not death.

Chapter 4

THE COMIC BOOK ZOMBIE
Human Devolution
in *The Walking Dead*

"You don't just come back from something like that.... You don't rip
a man apart—hold his insides in your hand—you can't go back to
being dear old dad after that. You're never the same. Not after what
you did."
—Abraham, *What We Become*

As I lay out in the introduction to this volume, most serious explorations
of the zombie invasion narrative during the twentieth century—that is, those
horror tales following the generic formula established by George A. Romero
with *Night of the Living Dead* (1968)—based their thematic essence on one
key premise: the monsters represent humanity.[1] Now in a new century, one
defined by social insecurities resulting from the September 11th terrorist
attacks and cultural anxieties arising from natural disasters and global pandemics, the zombie is once again being called upon by filmmakers, novelists,
comic book makers, and video game programmers alike to excise our collective
fears and doubts. In both cases, zombie narratives address not only the
expected monstrous behavior of the hordes of the walking dead, but also the
monstrous acts committed by the few humans struggling to survive a dangerous post-apocalyptic world. Yet whereas the zombie tales of the previous century primarily limited monstrous human behavior to characters clearly coded
as antagonists—such as the destructive and murderous biker gang of Romero's
Dawn of the Dead (1978) or the megalomaniacal Captain Rhodes (Joseph
Pilato) from the later *Day of the Dead* (1985)—a number of recent narratives
that make up the modern-day Zombie Renaissance—such as Romero's *Survival of the Dead* (2009) and Robert Kirkman's sprawling and intricately

developed comic book series *The Walking Dead* (2003–)—present the otherwise sympathetic *protagonists* as monstrous creatures. In other words, some recent zombie narratives have flipped the original allegory: humans can be truly monstrous on their own.

Although hints of this rhetorical inversion appeared in the very first zombie films, only a handful of the most recent zombie narratives have so aggressively asked audiences to question the definition of *monster*.[2] Following in the hallowed footsteps of *Frankenstein* (1818), in which Mary Shelley reveals the real villain of her novel to be the vain and single-minded Victor, many modern zombie tales demonstrate the otherwise heroic human characters to be the monstrous beings that should actually be feared. Upon closer consideration, this change in attitude towards once delineated Manichean dichotomies comes as no surprise. Thanks to a perceived shift in U.S. foreign policy and military practices following 9/11, one that advocated invasions of autonomous nations and the unrestrained use of "enhanced interrogation techniques" such as waterboarding to keep everyone "safe"—along with the continued use of remote-controlled drones to carry out "hits" on unsuspecting targets—the most important allegorical function of zombie narratives may now belong to the human protagonists instead of the metaphorically pregnant zombies. The most overt example of this kind of criticism, Kirkman's *The Walking Dead* comic series,[3] sheds a harsh light upon the potential devolution of humanity—that we have become chaotic creatures of selfishness, violence, and unchecked aggression who do more damage to ourselves and the world around us than any reanimated corpse ever could. In Kirkman's paradigm, zombies are less important than the human stories told around them, and such tales do important cultural work by providing audiences with ethical guideposts and a sober warning against atavistic barbarism.

Fighting Monsters and Becoming Monstrous

Of course, contemporary zombie invasion narratives still feature hordes of reanimated corpses against which the humans must struggle to survive; the monsters are the primary draw of the subgenre, after all. However, as Friedrich Nietzsche memorably writes in *Beyond Good and Evil* (1886), "Whoever battles with monsters had better see that it does not turn him into a monster,"[4] and this axiom has become the new standard for a number of post–9/11 zombie narratives. The so-called heroes of survival fiction must make difficult choices to ensure their continued existence, decisions that often mean protecting themselves and their allies at all cost. *The Walking Dead* epitomizes this potential "monstrozation" of humanity by featuring protagonists who combat both zombies and other humans with equal degrees of brutality. Kirkman's popular series follows the (mis)adventures of a motley group of people who struggle against zombies, other humans, and even each other to survive an ongoing global apocalypse. At the beginning of his epic story, the former deputy sheriff Rick Grimes heroically upheld the values of a civilized society. However, over the course of the series, Rick, along with his fellow protagonists, has been forced to make increasingly difficult decisions, and what is "right" has become supplanted by what is "necessary." Whether the United States has truly experienced a similar ideological shift is open to debate; however, the overt devolution demonstrated by *The Walking Dead*'s traumatized heroes can nonetheless be read as an indictment of the arguably aggressive stance U.S. politics and foreign policy have taken since 9/11—one in which efforts to make the world safe may in fact be replicating the very atrocities committed by the perceived enemy—and, perhaps more importantly, a condemnation of the populace that so complacently allowed such changes to occur in the first place.

Traditionally speaking, monster narratives in general, and zombie stories in particular, operate on clearly delineated parameters: monsters are monstrous and humans are humane. According to Kevin Alexander Boon, what makes a monster decidedly monstrous is its difference from the human, its unnaturalness.[5] Zombies in particular are monstrous, Boon explains, because they act "in direct opposition to the living."[6] As the "walking dead," Romero-style zombies flagrantly defy the established boundaries of living and dead, confronting audiences with dangerous bodies that challenge the natural order of things. Furthermore, as Jeffrey Jerome Cohen argues, such liminality is essential because monsters work as "disturbing hybrids whose externally incoherent bodies resist attempts to include them in any systematic structuration."[7] Monsters are thus "othered" due to their resistance of easy classification, and as such they more easily function as manifestations of frightening difference. In the past, hybrid creations such as vampires, werewolves, or aliens were used to represent members of the Jewish race, homosexuals, Communists, and virtually all forms of the non–White, non-heteronormative Other. The value of the monster thus lies in its role as a cultural *monstrum*, a metaphorical figure that "reveals" and "warns" of something else, something larger than itself.[8] Ironically, by using markedly coded differences from humans, monsters function as revealing and didactic critics of the very humanity from which they ostensibly appear to be distanced.

But what about monstrous humans? The human antagonists in zombie fiction have almost always been sources of physical threat and violence as well, starting with the voodoo "puppet masters" in the earliest films, most notably Bela Lugosi's sinister "Murder" Legendre in Victor Halperin's *White Zombie* (1932). Many of the earliest zombies to appear in comics follow this lead, especially those that use misrepresentations of Vodou practices as the cause of the zombification and show the zombies as the sympathetic victims of nefarious foes. Even though these early zombies are difficult to classify— they were "caught between the mildly influential voodoo slave shufflers of the '30s and the wildly redefining, insatiable Romero gut-munchers of the late '60s,"[9] after all—they share the status of walking dead, be they avenging revenants or feckless slaves. In Al Feldstein's "The Thing from the Grave" (1951), for example, the insanely jealous Bill murders James in an attempt to secure the love of Laura. But when Bill, realizing Laura will never love him, tries to kill *her*, James returns from the grave to save his true love. Bill's actions clearly code him as a human antagonist, and James—the zombie—is the real hero of the tale.[10] Many of the zombie stories told in the pre-"Comics Code" era represent such didactic morality tales about vengeful zombies,[11] but others present the horror of being turned into a zombie slave. In "I Am a Zombie" (1953), illustrated by Lin Streeter, Roger Hanks, now a zombie, recounts to readers the ghastly tale of his own transformation at the hands of Mother Harana into a *morto*, a "thing without a brain or will."[12] Yet Roger's story reveals he was once a greedy oil prospector who had violently assaulted Mother Harana in his attempt to evict her unlawfully from her home in the bayou. In other words, while Roger is presented as a victim, a human turned into a monster, the tale suggests he was rather monstrous to begin with, an idea I will return to shortly.

In the Romero tradition, human villains continue to be a substantial threat to beleaguered protagonists—a threat *in addition* to the zombies. *Dawn of the Dead*, to offer one of the most celebrated examples, pits Romero's four human survivors against not only an unstoppable horde of hungry zombies, but also racist SWAT members, undisciplined country militia, and a marauding biker gang. In the post-apocalyptic wasteland ravaged by the walking dead, everyone who isn't an ally—be they zombie or human—represents a very real threat. Because zombies are essentially slow moving, uncoordinated, and brain dead, they actually pose little danger to the careful human survivor, especially when encountered in small numbers; human antagonists, on the other hand, are far more insidious. Scott Kenemore enumerates the main differences between zombies and their feckless prey: "Humans—unlike composed, unflappable, focused zombies—fight with one another. They are jealous. They are manipulative. They care about things like other people not having sex with their wives."[13] Humans think, humans have emotions, and humans can plot against one another. In Romero's *Day of the Dead*, the most dangerous threat isn't a zombie at all but rather the sadomasochist Captain Rhodes, who sees everyone other than his military brothers as decidedly expendable. Romero's *Land of the Dead* (2005) takes the antagonistic shift even further, subordinating the role of the zombies to that of Kaufman (Dennis Hopper), the crazed captain of industry who has set himself up as a violently oppressive "king" in his palatial Fiddler's Green apartment complex. Throughout the tradition, then, zombie narratives have regularly shown villainous humans to be potentially monstrous.

In recent years, however, the human *protagonists* have taken on increasingly monstrous qualities as well, some of them horrifyingly so. What makes these "monstrous humans"[14] particularly disturbing and important are their decided *lack* of liminal difference and their being coded as those to whom the audience should relate. Romero's *Survival of the Dead*, for example, builds its narrative almost exclusively around unlikable, sociopathic main characters. The movie opens with a shot of Sarge Nicotine Crockett (Alan Van Sprang) in close up, who explains in impassive voiceover how the zombie apocalypse came about. This establishing presentation, along with Sprang's top billing in the credits, implies his role as the lead figure of the film, the protagonist with whom audience members are supposed to identify. Unfortunately, Crockett quickly proves to be a criminal and AWOL vigilante, the leader of a gang of self-described "lousy people" who routinely use their outward appearance as soldiers to take advantage of others. They kill humans and zombies with equal remorselessness, and they are motivated more by money than survival. Tomboy (Athena Karkanis), the gang's only female member and lone voice of sympathetic reason, sees the truth: "All the wrong people are dying. Seems like all we got left are assholes." The film's ostensible hero Crockett acts with increasing villainy throughout the movie, and none of the other characters he (and by extension, the audience) encounters are much better—pretty much *all* the humans in *Survival of the Dead* act monstrously, regardless of their status as antagonists or protagonists.

Many zombie narratives appearing in the wake of 9/11 use allegory to address not only general fears of a post-apocalyptic future, but also the new cultural fears and anxieties associated with the threat of terrorism. Danny Boyle's *28 Days Later* (2002), for example, graphically depicts the aftereffects of mass death and destruction, and *Land of the Dead* recreates the xenophobic paranoia people feel in the face of potential terrorists and illegal immigrants by using both zombies and disgruntled human survivors as their proxies. Narratives such as *Survival of the Dead* and Kirkman's *The Walking Dead*, however, demonstrate a new symbolic manifestation, one that reflects not cultural fears about what terrorists *might* do, but rather what the "good guys" *can* do against potential or suspected terrorists. In other words, that which we should most fear is not the monstrous Other but our monstrous *selves*. Steven Pokornowski reads Kirkman's series as a didactic morality tale warning against justified violent action, for, if left unchecked, "the broad sanction of violence begins to destroy precisely those lives that it set out to defend."[15] I believe this new kind of zombie story should be read as a direct reflection of the United States' dramatic actions taken in the wake of the September 11, 2001, terrorist attacks. Instead of passively waiting for Al-Qaeda operatives to attack a second time, the Bush Administration chose to take the fight to them by invading both Afghanistan and Iraq (the latter on rather specious intelligence). In addition, military policies were allegedly altered to limit the rights of the suspected terrorists being held at the controversial Guantanamo Bay detention camp and to authorize the use of waterboarding and other problematic interrogation methods. Each of these changes to existing U.S. policy and practice— changes that could be perceived as a more offensive, aggressive position than in the past—were promoted as protecting the American public from future terror plots, and they were readily and unquestioningly embraced by many of the frightened and paranoid public.

Such a perceived shift in political and military ideology, one implicitly endorsed by politicians and citizens alike, has since manifested in key post–9/11 zombie narratives. The resultant attitude, one that casts the protagonists of zombie stories in the problematic role of monstrous aggressors, is best illustrated in Kirkman's ongoing comic book series about Rick Grimes' efforts to keep himself, his family, and those around him alive through a zombie apocalypse—at all cost. In his introduction to the first trade collection of *The Walking Dead, Days Gone Bye* (2004), Kirkman argues that "good zombie movies show us how messed up we are,"[16] and it doesn't take long before readers of his epic realize he is actually talking about his "good guys" just as much as the zombies or even the human antagonists. Furthermore, Kirkman openly articulates the key purpose of his ongoing zombie comic: "I want to explore how people deal with extreme situations and how these events CHANGE them."[17] From the onset, then, Kirkman promises readers that Rick, his tragic hero and central protagonist, is going to *change*, and likely not in a good way: "[W]hen you look back on this book you won't even recognize [Rick]."[18] All the characters in *The Walking Dead* change over the course of the narrative, but none as dramatically as the one-time noble deputy. Because Kirkman's narrative question is "What happens to our humanity when we do inhumane things?,"[19] Rick's slow, tragic loss of humanity develops into the most important subject of the story, one that mirrors the moral and ethical decline of a fearful U.S. population desperately seeking an Other they may scapegoat and blame.

Kirkman's Comic Morality Tale

From the beginning of Kirkman's long-arc narrative, *The Walking Dead* engages with the barbaric transformations that befall its protagonists, especially those in positions of authority who will do whatever it takes to keep people "safe." Indeed, Pokornowski claims, "One of the primary preoccupations of *The Walking Dead* is precisely its exploration of the cost with which security is gained."[20] In *Days Gone Bye*, Rick and his best friend and fellow police officer Shane almost immediately develop an uncharacteristically antagonistic stance towards one another. They argue heatedly about leaving the perceived safety of Atlanta, and Shane ends up punching Rick in the face. A traumatized Lori, Rick's protective wife, astutely points out, "It's never going to be the same again. We're never going to be normal.... Just look at us."[21] Shane's increasingly erratic and dangerous behavior towards Rick comes to a crisis when he actually points a rifle at his former partner, but before he can act, Rick's son Carl shoots Shane through the neck, killing him instantly. After Shane's burial, Rick expresses his shock at what has happened and his fears concerning what it might mean for the rest of the survivors: "This shit we're in is not to be taken lightly. If it can change a man like Shane so drastically, we're in deeper shit that we thought."[22] The unexplained zombie apocalypse has clearly rewritten all of society's rules; as Kenemore observes, "For humans to survive ... they must become killers."[23] To keep the beleaguered masses safe, then, even the "good guys" are forced to kill, both zombies and humans alike.

Other characters soon follow Carl's lead and become slayers of living people. Two of the more shocking examples take place after the survivors have taken refuge in a largely abandoned prison. A misguidedly romantic Chris botches the suicide pact he has with Tyreese's daughter Julie, and when Tyreese finds his daughter dead, he loses all reason. In his rage, he chokes the life out of the penitent Chris, and then he waits for the boy to return as a zombie so he can kill him again.[24] Days later, Tyreese confesses to Rick what really happened:

> [Chris] was trying to commit suicide with [Julie] and as far as I'm concerned I just finished the job! And I enjoyed it. After all these months and the hell we've been through—it's almost the only thing I've enjoyed.

> I turned into an animal on him—I mutilated him over and
> over—I ripped him apart and watched him come back for more!
> ...
> I killed for the right reasons. I murdered him, yes—but it was
> justified.[25]

As far as readers know, Tyreese has been a normal, law-abiding citizen his whole life, but his fear for his own safety and desire for revenge color his perspectives on violence and murder. Despite his admittedly inhuman actions, Tyreese tries to rationalize his behavior by explaining it in terms of justice, and Rick's own devolution from deputy sheriff to cold-blooded killer begins when he finds himself in a similar situation. After the former-inmate Thomas murders two young girls and attacks Andrea with a knife, Rick, desperate to protect his flock, violently beats Thomas to a pulp with his bare hands. As the survivors argue about what to do with Thomas, Tyreese points out their new society lacks the rules necessary to keep order. Rick dictates his old-world philosophy: "You kill? You die."[26] Rick wants to maintain the legal system he had upheld in his former life, yet he orders Thomas' "lawful" execution with little thought of a trial, a decision that presciently mirrors actions by the Obama Administration to execute dangerous U.S. nationals such as Anwar al–Awlaki without due process.[27]

As Rick faces increasingly difficult circumstances, his journey from rational human being to monstrous killer only accelerates. Although Thomas has been safely "put down," Dexter leads an armed rebellion against Rick. Fortunately for the beleaguered survivors, Dexter leaves the doors to the armory—and the zombie-infested A-Block—wide open, and a desperate and chaotic battle against the walking dead interrupts the humans' standoff. As the extermination comes to a close, Rick coldly shoots Dexter in the head and tries to pass it off as an accident; however, as Pokornowski points out, the visual layout of the page, with a wide frame emphasizing Rick's gaze before a page turn reveals Dexter being shot, insinuates Rick's premeditation and thus guilt.[28] Although Tyreese, who (similarly) saw everything, thinks Rick ultimately did the right thing for the safety of the group, he points out how Rick's actions "kinda throws the whole 'you kill, you die' thing out the window."[29] Tyreese accuses Rick of having developed a bloodlust, thinking the former lawman now actually enjoys violence, but Rick insists, "Everything I did—*everything*—I did for the good of this group.... That's what makes me right."[30] Reluctantly, Rick realizes the old ways are gone, and the new society needs a new rule: "You kill—you live."[31] Rather than attempting to rebuild society, then, Rick sees the need for the survivors to become something far more savage. As could be said of the post–9/11 Bush Administration's creation of the Patriot Act and its increasingly aggressive military actions overseas, Rick claims the old laws won't protect them, but self-defensive action and preemptive violence will.[32]

Rick embraces his protective barbarism further when he realizes Martinez, the man who had helped Rick and the others escape from Woodbury, is actually a spy working for the sinister Governor. After Martinez disappears, Rick takes Dale's RV by himself and violently runs the traitor down. Blinded at the thought of the Governor and his men finding the prison sanctuary, Rick chokes Martinez to death. Later, when he confesses the slaying to Lori, Rick says,

> Killing him made me realize something—made me notice how much I've changed. I used to be a trained police officer—my job was to uphold the law. Now I feel more like a lawless savage—an animal. I killed a man today and I don't even care....
>
> I'd kill every single one of the people here if I thought it'd keep you safe. I know these people—I care for these people—but I know I'm capable of making that sacrifice....
>
> Does that make me evil?[33]

Rick clearly recognizes his frightening transformation, but, like Tyreese, he sees such drastic behavior as justified—he must protect his people by any means necessary. The otherwise peaceful and contrite Hershel is more willing to face what Rick must rationalize: "The good Lord's put us in a world where we gotta sin to survive."[34] As supporters of post–9/11 practice and policy might also say in defense of aggressive government action, terms such as *evil* and *sin* must be redefined in a world ruled by zombies (or threatened by terrorists), and "survival" takes precedence over such antiquated ideas such as "law and order" and "due process." Hershel, like many U.S. citizens, is a God-fearing man who nonetheless agrees to a monstrous course of action if it means keeping himself and his family safe.

Rick's atavistic behavior becomes most problematic when his actions shockingly come to resemble those of the zombies themselves. When a trio of savage highwaymen threatens to rape Carl, one of the assailants restrains Rick in a tight bear hug. With no gun or knife at his command, Rick resorts to his most primal and natural weapons: his teeth. In a series of unexpectedly violent panels, readers see Rick tear into his captor's neck, biting and rending the flesh as he viciously rips out the man's throat. The one-time agent of law and justice then descends upon Carl's attacker with a knife, tearing the man apart like an animal. When it's all over, Rick wonders out loud if he's even human any more, but asserts he's still willing to do *anything* to protect his son.[35] Kenemore sees this transformation primarily as a good thing, a necessity for survival: "Kirkman's humans—however ineluctably—come to the realization that to survive a zombie apocalypse, they must *become like zombies themselves*."[36] Kenemore is partially correct, for in this example particularly, Rick does become like a zombie—a mindless animal that uses its teeth to bite and savage its prey. However, unlike a zombie, Rick does more than just follow his instincts for survival. Much like a battle-weary soldier for whom the concept of "murder" has grown hazy in a psychologically exhausting war zone, Rick is starting to indulge in unnecessary barbarism, starting to *enjoy* the violence, just as Tyreese feared. Rather than using the zombie monster as a metaphor for human violence, then, Kirkman is baldly presenting the human as directly and unequivocally monstrous, a devolution that becomes more overt and shocking as *The Walking Dead*'s narrative progresses.

After Dale is captured and partially eaten by a roving gang of human cannibals, Rick and his inner circle become their most monstrous, going beyond the necessity of survival and self-preservation and wallowing in atavistic violence. Rick confidently confronts the six rogues and impassively orders Andrea to shoot the ear off one and the index finger of another. Despite the ringleader's promise that they'll go away and leave Rick's group alone, Dale's friends are clearly more interested in exacting revenge than in simply keeping themselves "safe." In fact, their designs even transcend social justice—they see execution as too good for the cannibals. Mercifully, Kirkman spares readers most of the details of the resulting torture, but such horrors are indicated by an arresting two-page image of Rick's impassionate and haggard stare, as well as a series of eight vertical panels depicting splattered blood, gory weapons, and a spitted campfire.[37] Only later, as Rick speaks aloud to himself over Dale's fresh grave, does he allow himself to reflect on the gravity of what he has done: "What we've done to survive ... sometimes I feel like we're no better than the dead ones. I can't stop thinking about what we did to the hunters. I know it's justifiable ... but I see them when I close my eyes.... Doing what we did, to living people ... after taking their weapons.... It haunts me."[38] Monsters such as zombies kill as part of their natural drive and instinct; Kirkman's monstrous humans, on the other hand, *chose* to perform their brutal acts. Rick has crossed a line, and he realizes he will forever run the risk of confusing justified self-defense with unnecessary sadism.

Because most of Rick's violence takes place outside of the panels, readers are allowed to maintain a sympathetic connection with him, however tenacious; the erstwhile lawyer Michonne's graphically depicted violence, on the other hand, runs the real risk of alienating her from the audience. After being captured by the Governor, Michonne is repeatedly raped and abused, both physically and psychologically. He breaks her in every sense of the word, and after Rick and Martinez rescue her, Michonne's thoughts are on revenge, not escape. She confronts the Governor in his apartment, and over the course of *nine* vividly illustrated pages, she has her unrestrained way with him, drilling holes in his shoulder with a power drill, pulling out his fingernails, amputating his right arm, plucking out his left eye, and violating him in even worse ways.[39] Her savage behavior, in a perceptible parallel to the Abu Ghraib prison scandal of 2004, goes far beyond that feebly justified by Rick—Michonne's "justice" escalates to brutal cruelty and vengeful torture. Rick's excuse for his monstrous behavior is, according to Brendan Riley, that "even savage actions are acceptable in order to protect the group, but that savagery must be tempered by necessity, and the living must recognize it as 'bad.'"[40] Michonne has no necessity behind her heinous crimes; she had been rescued and could have quietly escaped. Instead, her revenge transcends justifiable retaliation or lawful punishment—she even enjoys herself. And by allowing the audience to see all the gruesome details of Michonne's vengeance, Kirkman viscerally condemns vengeful behavior, such as the waterboarding of accused terrorists that was sanctioned by the Bush Administration.

Although Kirkman may appear to approve tacitly of Rick's more justified behavior, he ultimately condemns that form of unchecked violence and aggression as well, especially when a myopic vision of what is right or wrong interferes with the safety of a larger community. Rick and his companions devolve so much over the course of their struggles that by Volume 13: *Too Far Gone* (2010), they can hardly integrate back into a civilized social structure (as the title indicates). Although Rick is given the logical assignment of constable by Douglas, the former politician who leads a fortified survivalist camp just outside Washington D.C., Rick cannot quell his atavistic "fight or flight" impulses. One of his first acts as "keeper of the peace" is to defy the community's weapons ban, as he and Glenn sneak into the armory to outfit themselves secretly with firearms. To Rick's surprise, Andrea balks at the move, refusing to accept a gun in violation of the community's rules. Echoing proponents of the Second Amendment, Rick justifies his actions by telling her, "I don't like being unable to protect ourselves."[41] Of course, Rick's behavior is really more about power than it is about civil liberties or human rights: "I'm doing this so that it doesn't get screwed up. I don't trust these people not to ruin this place. It's too important. *I* won't let anything threaten this place and our lives here.... *I* have to make things work. *I* have to be ready for anything."[42] Once again, Rick's hubris raises its ugly head; his traumatic experiences surviving the zombie apocalypse have convinced him that *he* is always right and his power is best maintained and asserted through *violence*.

Not surprisingly, as things get more complicated in the otherwise idyllic community in Alexandria, Rick *does* resort to violence to maintain the status quo *he* has determined appropriate. Perhaps driven by his own barely repressed feelings of guilt and inadequacy as a husband and father, Rick focuses his ire and rage on Pete, a local man who has obviously been abusing his family. Even though Douglas tells Rick to drop the matter, as Pete is a much-needed doctor who would do the community little good were he exiled or locked up, Rick, true to form, takes matters into his own hands. In fact, Rick loses all restraint when he breaks into the doctor's home without anything resembling a warrant, assaulting Pete without provocation and throwing him through a plate glass window before threatening to kill him in front of his family. Rick's actions are so violent and at odds with one-time "civilized" social codes that even Michonne recognizes he's out of control; she cracks him in the head with a rock, disarms him, and admonishes Rick to take a good look at himself and what he has become. A triptych of comic panels aligns the reader with Rick's visual perspective, showing Douglas's stern gaze, an injured Pete and his horrified wife Jessie, and Andrea with a wide-eyed, shocked expression. After a reverse on Rick's own stunned face, the page turn reveals a long-shot of the entire scene, with Rick whispering to himself, "What have I *done*?"[43] Once again, Rick finds himself teetering on the brink, trying, this time unsuccessfully, to strike the right balance between fighting the monsters and becoming one of them.

Douglas recognizes the need for this careful balance; after all, such wisdom has been what has kept the Alexandria community safe and secure for so long. Surprisingly, Douglas asks Rick to keep his job as the community's constable precisely because the former lawman *is* willing to do whatever it takes to keep the larger group safe. Douglas's encouraging words sound remarkably similar to the ideology outlined in the U.S. Patriot Act, which "removed the major legal barriers that prevented the law enforcement, intelligence, and national defense communities from talking and coordinating their work to protect the American people and our national security. The government's prevention efforts should not be restricted by boxes on an organizational chart."[44] Indeed, Douglas explains to Rick a very similar version of the ends justifying the means, a point of view that seeks to circumvent "barriers" and "restrictions":

> The fact is, I can live with [your having a gun]. To have a head of security who is willing to break rules in order to keep our community safe ... I respect that. I see that you weren't concerned in any way with your own well-being, you cared more that Pete not hurt Jessie again. So by all means, break rules ... do what you feel needs to be done. I value your instincts. I rely on them. But please know this ... this community survives on a very fragile balance."[45]

In a post–9/11 world, being "safe" sometimes means breaking the rules—at least that's what the citizens of the United States have been told to believe. However, Kirkman's attitude towards such extreme preventative measures remains ambiguous throughout the course of *Too Far Gone*. Pete, enraged by his treatment at the hands of Rick, seeks vengeance, but he accidentally kills Douglas's wife Regina in the scuffle. Had Rick exiled, imprisoned, or even outright murdered Pete in the first place, lives would have been saved. Not surprisingly, then, Douglas gives Rick the go-ahead to execute Pete on the spot, with no trial, no jury, and no due process.

Rick's descent into destructive selfishness soon reaches its nadir, and the man who was once a noble and ethical lawman must finally come to terms with the monster he has become. With the death of Regina, Douglas collapses into grief and regret, leaving Rick essentially in charge of things in the Alexandria community; unfortunately, Rick continues to think of little beyond himself and Carl. When the relentless press of zombies finally breaches the defenses of the community, Rick decides it's time to cut his losses and run, abandoning the people whose protection should be his chief concern. Rick has entered into an insincere sexual relationship with Jessie, and he explains how a small group made up of just them and their sons would be more likely to survive. When Jessie implores Rick to think about the families and children he would be abandoning, Rick coldly responds, "I know, but what choice do we have? The thing to keep in mind ... about other people's children ... they're not *our* children."[46] After coating themselves with zombie blood and guts, Rick leads Carl, Jessie, and her son Ron into the mass of monsters surrounding his house. When the creatures overwhelm Ron, Jessie panics, and she grips tightly onto her son's hand with one of her own while holding equally fast to Carl's with her other. Jessie cries out for help, but Rick impassively uses his axe to sever Jessie's wrist, freeing Carl so they can safely escape the horde. As Rick explains to Denise, the community's doctor, later, "I did what I had to do.... There was no other choice."[47] Rick's single-minded selfishness and instinct to protect himself and his son at all costs has destroyed an entire family, a family that had trusted him with their safety, including a woman who had come to love him.

So much death and destruction, much of it directly attributable to Rick's choices and actions, finally helps him recognize a new solution to the problem of survival, a solution that doesn't rely on violence alone. During the chaos of the zombie assault, Douglas accidentally shots Carl through the eye, and after leaving Carl in the capable hands of Denise, Rick reengages the invading masses of zombies, taking out all his anger and frustration on the seemingly endless waves of walking dead foes, destroying them with wild abandon. His almost superhuman efforts rally the rest of the community, who come together to help him in the fight. Together, the group manages the unthinkable: they beat the horde back and reestablish the safety of the community's fortifications. With Carl's miraculous recovery and the success accomplished by the group working together as a unit, Rick sees the key to rebuilding civilization. "The things I did," he tells his inner circle, "the moves I made. I justified it by saying it was for the good of my family ... but really, I was overlooking the most important part of survival in this world. Community."[48] When Rick is out on a supply run, Nicholas convinces some of the original members of the Alexandria community to rebel against Rick, to overthrow him so they can get back to their safe way of life. Glenn accidentally wanders by and overhears the discussion, and he and Nicholas soon find themselves in a standoff, both with pistols drawn and cocked. Rick returns just in time, and he persuades Nicholas to drop his weapon. Yet instead of killing the mutineer, Rick tells Nicholas, and the gathering crowd, "The most important thing you have here, something I'd never realized until recently ... is people.... We don't want to kill you, Nicholas.... We *need* you."[49] Even though Rick confesses to Andrea later that he really wanted to kill the man, mostly because it would have been easier, it was time for him to forego violence, to change, to build a better life for everyone. A life founded on a community of living people, not death.

Will Rick continue to be a sober and kind leader who values community over violence? Only time will tell—things certainly *seem* to be going well for Rick's flock ever since the deposition of the sinister Negan, but *A New Beginning* (2014) contains hints that not all is right with the reformed maniac, as when Rick violently beats and upbraids a man who simply neglects his patrol duties.[50] Despite Rick's ultimately "good" intentions, his continued reliance on violence to solve problems, his often enthusiastic embracing of atavistic behavior, and his fundamentally selfish ideology place him in a sphere far removed from the kind of human comportment espoused by pre-apocalypse organized religion. Racked with guilt and tormented by his fears, the priest Gabriel had secretly approached Douglas soon after arriving at the Alexandria commune to warn him about Rick and his group: "These people who were with me are *not* good people. They've done things ... horrible things ... unspeakable things. They simply don't belong here."[51] Gabriel articulates Kirkman's warning about unchecked aggression and violence: Rick has perhaps been driven too far to the edge to ever be a compatible member of civilized society again. Do the complicit citizens of the United States face the same fate? Has the population's enthusiastic approval of aggressively violent policies toward suspected terrorists and their supporters turned honest, God-fearing, and law-abiding people into monsters in their own right? At Pete's funeral, Rick tries to explain his feelings to the community at large, coming clean with everyone concerning his actions and inadvertently addressing Gabriel's concerns as well: "The things I've done to survive inform who I am as a person. I am a man who will do things to protect my family. A lot of these things I've done ... I'm *not* proud of. Are these things *my fault*? I know I would not have done them were the situation different ... so how am I to blame?"[52] Indeed, can the results of things such as the invasion of others nations, the use of enhanced interrogation techniques, remote-controlled drone strikes, and the U.S. Patriot Act itself—any collateral damage suffered along the way—be seen as in terms of "blame" if it keeps people safe?

As *The Walking Dead* remains an incomplete and ongoing narrative, it's hard to speculate what Kirkman's ultimate resolution to these questions may be. Can one use monstrous means to accomplish noble outcomes? Is preemptive violence justified? Is it a matter of need, or simply of degree? Rick tries to explain the slaughter of the cannibals by telling Carl, "I do things ... a lot of bad things, to help you and all the other people in our group.... That's the world we live in now ... but Carl, you need to never forget ... when we do these things and we're good people ... they're still bad things.... You can never lose sight of that. If these things start becoming easy that's when it's all over. That's when we become bad people."[53] The problem with Rick's impassioned speech isn't that he's wrong—it's that it *has* become easy for him. After Rick's brutal assault and murder of Carl's attacker, a stunned Abraham soberly tells Rick, "You don't just come back from something like that.... You don't rip a man apart—hold his insides in your hand—you can't go back to being dear old dad after that. You're never the same. Not after what you did."[54] Abraham, the confessed murderer, seems to be the only protagonist in *The Walking Dead* who sees things for what they really are. As much as Rick might tell himself and those around him that his violence is justified, such actions irrevocably change him, pushing him ever further away from his origins as an upholder of the peace. Perhaps Abraham speaks directly for Kirkman here, articulating the thesis of the series—it's already too late; the United States and its citizenry cannot go back to the way things were before they chose to become monstrous.

The Walking Dead demonstrates an increased level of violence and monstrosity on the part of the human protagonists, but should we really be surprised by this development in the subgenre? After all, a dangerous, barbaric protagonist stood at the center of the very first zombie invasion narrative, *Night of the Living Dead*. In his desperate efforts to protect himself from a countryside full of zombies, Ben (Duane Jones) not only slaps the hysterical

Barbra (Judith O'Dea) into submission, but he also beats and shoots Harry (Karl Hardman) when the man disagrees with Ben's plans. The potential for human monstrosity, it appears, has always existed. But something *has* changed. These new stories manifest the world's increased tolerance for interpersonal violence, potentially unethical political policies, and a "kill before they kill us" attitude. In a chilling reflection of post–9/11 U.S. military and political actions, such vicious protagonists are direct analogs not only for contemporary national leaders, but also for a complicit and bloodthirsty citizenry. As with Rick's rag-tag group of calloused survivors, the monstrous actions of the U.S. have potentially transformed its people as well—into the very thing they were initially fighting against. For Kirkman, the zombies aren't metaphors for human failings; they are the catalyst that reveals the monstrous potential that has been exposed within us all. It's no longer the terror of what *might* happen to humanity under such incredible circumstances but rather the realization of the horror our world has *already* become that really scares us.

Chapter 5

THE LITERARY ZOMBIE
The Infected City
of Colson Whitehead's *Zone One*

Why they'd tried to fix this island in the first place, he did not see
now. Best to let the broken glass be broken glass, let it splinter into
smaller pieces and dust and scatter. Let the cracks between things
widen until they are no longer cracks but the new places for things.
That was where they were now. The world wasn't ending; it had
ended and now they were in the new place.
— Colson Whitehead, *Zone One*

As I have explored extensively elsewhere, the modern conception of the
walking dead zombie as a flesh-eating monster returned from the grave to
wreck havoc on the living has no literary antecedent comparable to the ghost,
the vampire, or even the werewolf.[1] While various renditions of the Vodou
zombie appeared in English works of fiction prior to the release of George
A. Romero's *Night of the Living Dead* (1968)—including, among others, G.
W. Hutter's influential "Salt Is Not for Slaves" (1931), Richard Goddard's *The
Whistling Ancestors* (1936), and Leslie Carroll's *You Can't Hang the Dead*
(1944)—short stories and novels following Romero's model of the ghoul
wouldn't appear until decades later.[2] In fact, most of the early non-fiction
and fictional accounts of the Vodou zombie weren't collected until 1985 in
Zombie!: Stories of the Walking Dead, edited by Peter Haining, and stories
featuring the modern zombie weren't anthologized until the *Book of the Dead*
in 1989, edited by John Skipp and Craig Spector. Subject to how one defines
the idea of "zombie," the apocalyptic zombie novel may have begun with
David Moody's *Autumn* (2001), Brian Keene's *The Rising* (2004), or Stephen
King's *Cell* (2006), but the first commercially successful novel that unequivocally grounds itself in Romero's tradition is Max Brooks' *World War Z: An*

Oral History of the Zombie War (2006). Today, hundreds of zombie stories and novels are available for purchase, many of them self-published, but few, if any, have garnered any attention as "serious" works of literature—until Colson Whitehead's *Zone One* (2011).

Whitehead's critically acclaimed "literary" zombie novel takes place years after a global zombie outbreak, and it includes all the shock, violence, and horror one would expect in a narrative operating under the auspices of such a narrowly defined subgenre. However, in a manner similar to Romero's canon of zombie cinema, Whitehead "represents such futurial haunting by intertwining the apocalyptic future with the apocalyptic present."[3] *Zone One* transcends pulp fiction by piercingly exploring the national trauma of September 11 through the depiction of New York City as an infected biological body. While it may be tempting to read all recent zombie narratives through the critical lens of 9/11, the central focus on New York City in *Zone One* necessitates this kind of allegorical comparison. That city, repeatedly a synecdoche for the United States of America, has experienced a traumatic incursion that has left its "body" both wounded and ailing. David Harvey points out the value of such body politic metaphors—ones that propose new ways to understand the people that collectively make up a city, state, or nation—writing that these allegories "presume that the city is in some sense an organic form of social life that originates through human action. The city grows, is sustained, or dies out ... [and] can assume different states, such as robust or wounded, healthy or sick, elegant or shamefully ugly."[4] In *Zone One*, New York City has been infected by the walking dead, "reanimated" from its previous life, and all hope for the future of the human race rests with a dedicated group of "sweepers" acting as antibodies, a serum, or radiation treatment designed to resurrect it, and, by extension, the human race as well.

While the zombies of *Zone One* offer readers an exciting new variant on the established tradition, Whitehead's New York City must, first and foremost, be read as an allegorical representation for the real-world Big Apple, a city that is similarly struggling, even today, to come back from a fundamentally damaging and life-altering "illness." The trauma of 9/11 injured the city, and, by extension, the entire nation, and the future of both has yet to be written. As Aaron DeRosa argues, "the threat of a cultural trauma ... rests not just in its suddenness, but in its ability to radically alter the trajectory of cultural institutions and social interaction across generations,"[5] and Whitehead presents a bleak and perhaps even cynical course of progress. Following the generic conventions of zombie films and other such narratives, Whitehead opts for a traditionally bleak and ambiguous resolution to his story, as the efforts of protagonist Mark Spitz[6] and the other human survivors prove futile. Like a human body infected with the zombie plague, New York City is too far-gone to save, and while the version of the metropolis in *Zone One* is ultimately brought back to a kind of life, it is the mindless, plodding life of a zombified body, animated, but without its own consciousness. Whitehead's novel thus criticizes (failed) attempts to "cure" the real New York City through propagandistic nostalgia and heavy-handed commercialization, demonstrating the "wounded city" can never be fully healed to be what it once was. The fate of a post-traumatic community cannot be found by romanticizing the past but only in leaping into an uncertain future.

New York City as Traumatized Body

Whitehead's apocalyptic zombie novel has been rightly praised for both its literary qualities and its efforts to expand and evolve an ever-changing subgenre. In fact, Andrew Hoberek declares *Zone One* to be the "greatest American novel of the twenty-first century,"[7] particularly in its elaborate plot structure and meticulously crafted sentences.[8] Indeed, Whitehead weaves a narratologically complex story of human resilience and persistence, the captivating tale of society's attempt to rebuild itself after a devastating cataclysm that fundamentally altered the normal course of human existence. Yet despite the novel's narrative complexity, its occasionally difficult sentence structures, and its somewhat esoteric focus on both individual and national trauma, *Zone One* is also, unavoidably, a zombie narrative. Charlie Jane Anders proposes the novel to be "one zombie story that nobody's ever told before"[9]; whereas most zombie narratives develop isolated tales of microcosmic engagements and personal contact and interaction—and *World War Z* takes a global look at the macrocosmic zombie apocalypse—*Zone One* fits somewhere in between: telling the story of a single metropolitan city. In Whitehead's novel, the world has already been overwhelmed by a plague that infects the human body, kills it, and reanimates it as either a ferocious, flesh-eating "skel" or a passive and docile "straggler." However, in addition to the infection of the biological human organism, Whitehead proposes buildings, cities, and even the United States itself to be "zombified bodies," social, cultural, and political human structures infected with the walking dead and "reanimated" into monstrous versions of their former selves. Building on the tradition of films such as Danny Boyle's *28 Days Later* (2002) and Romero's *Land of the Dead* (2005)— post-apocalyptic tales of London and Pittsburgh, respectively—*Zone One* depicts the efforts of the dwindling human race to "cure" one of these diseased bodies, namely New York City.

While apocalyptic and post-apocalyptic stories have become common-place, even ubiquitous, what makes *Zone One* so significant for the twenty-first century is this focus on New York City. DeRosa argues that while cultural information can be transmitted in a variety of ways, "narrative holds a priv-ileged position in the field of trauma,"[10] and in an interview with *Publishers Weekly*, Whitehead acknowledges the influence September 11 had on the con-struction of *Zone One*: "Since 9/11, I've had a heightened sense of insecurity and anxiety, and I think that definitely plays out, perhaps in particular in the way the characters have made their sort of insane accommodations to what's going on."[11] At one point near the end of the novel, Whitehead makes its kin-ship with 9/11 overt: during an ill-fated mission to cleanse Manhattan's sub-way tunnels of zombies, Mark Spitz realizes the next station had been the World Trade Center, and while "[t]hat was a long time ago ... he remem-bered."[12] Perhaps of greater resonance with readers is Mark Spitz's obsession with falling ash, the hallmark of the feckless dead. The reclamation teams incinerate the bodies of the dead, and the ash cloud thus produced clearly recalls the debris resulting from the fall of the twin towers:

> The ash did swirl in a radius around the incinerators, it landed as dandruff on their shoulders, and yes, perhaps a small percentage was conscripted by rain on its way down. Certainly the downdrafts and eddies created by high-rises, the suction currents and zephyrs generated by the smaller buildings, gusted the flakes in turbulent jets across downtown ... for Mark Spitz it was everywhere ... the dust of the dead.[13]

Such rich descriptions understandably evoke memories of the news footage disseminated on September 11, 2001, and stronger memories still for those who survived the attacks firsthand.

Whitehead's focus on New York City therefore operates both in terms of personal biography and post–9/11 cultural response, but the city is also a logical choice for the fictional reconstruction efforts depicted in the novel. New York City is like no other city in the world, and as far as the United States goes, "Manhattan was the biggest version of everywhere."[14] As efforts to rebuild Manhattan progress, a Ms. Macy from the provisional government visits Zone One with news that the next international summit will be held there. She explains to Mark Spitz that "New York City is the greatest city in the world. Imagine what all those heads of state and ambassadors will feel when they see what we've accomplished. You've accomplished. We brought this place back from the dead. The symbolism alone. If we can do that, we can do anything."[15] Furthermore, calling the reclamation location "Zone One" evokes the rhetoric of September 11's "Ground Zero" language, again recalling the real-world tragedy of September 11. New York City was unquestionably "wounded" by the terrorist attacks, as the collapse of the twin towers resulted in a disruption to urban processes, the creation of long-term problems, and far-reaching social, psychological, and symbolic damage.[16] In *Zone One*, as in real life, New York City has become "sick"; conceived allegorically as a biological entity, the city is as infected and transformed as any of the zombies that continue to haunt its abandoned buildings.

Harvey writes in the collection *Wounded Cities: Destruction and Reconstruction in a Globalized World* about the "wounding" of New York City as a result of the September 11 terrorist attacks in terms of a body politic, describing the construction of human communities in notably biological terms: "Cities are constituted out of the flows of energy, water, food, commodities, money, people and all the other necessities that sustain life. These flows must be maintained as must the capacity to expel wastes effectively so that populations do not die in their own excrement."[17] This "body" of a city, when "healthy," is "a humanly constructed resource system, a vast assemblage of heterogeneous physical artifacts and assets, produced through human work and ingenuity, ready for people to use for whatever purposes they wish."[18] While Harvey acknowledges the vulnerability of cities, as fallible forms of human organization, he emphasizes how resilient they truly are, "recovering fast from devastation, sometimes (though not always) in a 'better state' (however defined) than they were before."[19] *Zone One*, acting as a fictional analogue to 9/11, presents an extreme example of citywide devastation, and the novel, through Mark Spitz's experiences, posits difficult questions about the process of recovery and the ultimate "state" New York City will achieve if the efforts to rebuild are successful.

As with any biological organism, the life of a city is marked by periods of growth and decay, destruction and reconstruction. Harvey points out, "The capacity for contemporary cities to overcome all manner of tribulations must in part be attributed to the fact that cities, in their capitalistic form, are hyper-active sites of 'creative destruction.'"[20] That is, for a city to grow and progress, its old structures must be torn down, excised, to make room for the new. In terms of a body politic, the diseased or dysfunctional "organs" must be removed and new, healthy tissue must be regrown or "transplanted" in their places. In fact, any destructive event, be it natural or caused by nefarious human agency, can be transformed into something worthwhile, an act of destruction that ultimately leads to new growth and creative progress.[21] A "wounded city," however, suggests that "cities are susceptible to life-threatening damage in some way over and beyond the chronic habits of creative destruction that capitalism ordinarily produces."[22] Considering the traumatized borough of Manhattan in terms of this metaphorical organic body is helpful in understanding not only the city as presented in *Zone One* but also the real city post–9/11, upon which Whitehead is commenting. While Harvey calls the September 11 attacks the metaphorical equivalent of a "broken bone" for the body of New York City,[23] he raises the idea of a far more threatening condition, such as the spreading of cancer.[24] Whitehead's version of an ailing Manhattan is more on par with the latter, a cancer manifested by zombies and treated, with only limited success, by the determined human survivors.

Of course, the disease presented in *Zone One* greatly transcends the 9/11 terrorists attacks in both severity and scope, yet obvious parallels can be drawn between both the wounding of the synecdochical city and the concerted efforts to rebuild it. Some time after the initial zombie outbreak—Whitehead's "Last Night"—a provisional government forms as small survivalist groups and isolated communes prove powerless. Whitehead presents such centralized governance as necessary to the healing process, but in somewhat cynical term: "[with] the elite antsy to drop their pawns, and the pawns hungry for purpose after so long without instruction ... tentative bureaucracy rose from the amino-acid pool of madness, per its custom."[25] In Buffalo, of all places, the greatest surviving minds unite to design a process of "rewind[ing]" the catastrophe, of "rebooting" New York City first, and then the entire country.[26] The effort is designated the "American Phoenix,"[27] and those who buy into the utopian vision of a rebuilt, resurrected United States are known as *pheenies*.[28] Mark Spitz reflects on the value of having established leadership, something that replicated "the old governmental structures,"[29] and the primary focus becomes not the establishment of new cities or communities but the *rebuilding* of New York City. Mark Spitz's lieutenant explains the logic behind such a marshaling of personnel and other resources: "If you can bring back New York City, you can bring back the world. Clear out Zone One, then the next, up to Fourteenth Street, Thirty-fourth, Times Square on up.... We'll take it back, barricade by barricade."[30] The Lieutenant's rhetoric recalls then President George W. Bush's famous "bullhorn" speech at Ground Zero when talk of rebuilding the towers and reestablishing the economic health of New York City was still news.[31]

The novel's three narrative days focus on the efforts of American Phoenix, the military, and the civilian sweepers to purge the systematic grid of Zone One of all zombie infestation. To this end, Whitehead describes New York City as both a giant machine and as a living body, with the inhabiting humans codified in similar terms. As Mark Spitz recalls his childhood, he imagines himself in the city as "a mote cycling in the wheels of a giant clock. Millions of people tended to this magnificent contraption, they lived and sweated and toiled in it, serving the mechanism of metropolis and making it bigger, better, story by glorious story and idea by unlikely idea. How small he was, tumbling between the teeth."[32] In Mark Spitz's present, New York City is still something of a machine, but one that has largely broken down and must be repaired by the mechanistic labor of the sweepers who, acting upon the ideological vision of the American Phoenix project, are once again "making it bigger, better, story by glorious story." But now instead of constructing the city through creation they are *reconstructing* it through destruction. Harvey's idea of "creative destruction" manifest in *Zone One* via the violent efforts of the sweepers as they annihilate the living dead still populating the nearly empty buildings, the "ghosts in the machine."

More importantly, though, Whitehead's vision of New York City is that of a diseased body, an ailing construct suffering from its own form of infection that the government in Buffalo is desperately trying to resuscitate. Young Mark Spitz saw the buildings in particular in anthropomorphic terms, sky rises with "massive central-air units ... glistening like extruded guts" and tenements with "tar-paper pates" for roofs.[33] He perceived the "creative destruction" of these building for the sake of progress and modernization in particularly violent terms: "Behind the facades their insides were butchered, reconfigured, rewired according to the next era's new theories of utility.... In every neighborhood the imperfect in their fashion awaited the wrecking ball and their bones were melted down to help their replacements surpass them, steel into steel."[34] In fact, his description of the new buildings smacks decidedly like newly risen zombies: "The new buildings in wave upon wave drew themselves out of the rubble, shaking off the past like immigrants."[35] Even after the apocalypse, Whitehead's descriptions of Manhattan are peppered with biological imagery and the language of death, from the "cinder block intestine" of a high-rise stairwell,[36] to the "corpses of crashed cars" and the remarkably intact "skin" of New York City.[37] The use of a body politic resonates throughout *Zone One*, as the anthropomorphism of the city increases the narrative's pathos while continuing to echo similar post–9/11 rhetoric.

Zone One is populated by the raised dead humans and the living dead city alike, yet efforts at curing the former have come to a virtual halt by the time period depicted in the novel. While "[i]n the early days, the government required a stock of the recently infected and the thoroughly turned for experiments, to search for a cure, cook up a vaccine, or simply investigate the phenomenon 'in the name of science,'"[38] any thought of overturning the effects of the plague was considered a waste of time and effort by most because "[t]he plague so transformed the human body that no one still believed they could be restored"; the only thing to do with a skel is to put it down as quickly as possible.[39] Such a fatalistic attitude is *not* the case for the infected and plague-ridden cities of the United States, though, and certainly not for its greatest city. Establishing Zone One is the first, key step in the American Phoenix project, and the new U.S. military establishes "Fort Wonton" in the former Chinatown as the control center, a city in embryo that represents "the reanimated system."[40] The provisional government devises an aggressive course for Manhattan with notable parallels to cancer treatment: surgery followed by radiation therapy to get rid of both malignant and benign tumors alike. The hope of a revived—even resurrected—New York City means hope for the nation and, by extension, hope for the entire human race.

The first step in New York City's radical "treatment" is the establishment of a safe zone from which highly trained and heavily armed Marines can be dispatched to "excise" the largest clusters of the cancerous zombie horde. The violent, feral, and procreative form of the zombies are knows as "skels," and in terms of the body politic of Manhattan, they can be conceived as malignant tumors, monsters "capable of spreading by invasion and metastasis."[41] Whitehead describes the defining qualities of these aggressive terrors: "Most skels, they moved. They came to eat you—not all of you, but a nice chomp here or there, enough to pass on the plague. Cut off their feet, chop off their legs, and they'd gnash the air as they heaved themselves forward by their splintered fingernails, looking for some ankle action."[42] I once thought that zombies, being so fundamentally and essential visual monsters—rooted in abjection, horror, and physicality—would never "work" as well in writing as on they do on screen and in comics, but Whitehead proves me wrong. The first zombie encounter in *Zone One* presents the creatures through horrific and vivid language, manifesting a version of the walking dead that reads almost realistic, almost *possible*:

> After all this time, they were a thin membrane of meat stretched over bone. Their skirts were bunched on the floor, having slid off their shrunken hips long ago, and the dark jackets of their sensible dress suits were made darker still, and stiffened, by jagged arterial splashes and kernels of gore. Two of them had lost their high heels at some point during the long years of bumping around the room looking for an exit.[43]

These skels—recognizable as traditional, "Romero-esque" zombies—are relentless and, ironically, single minded, driven exclusively by the need to reproduce, to spread, and to fill every corner of the diseased body of the city.

Enter the Marines and their skel-ectomy efforts. After stoppering up the tunnels and blocking the bridges, choppers airlift concrete segments of the barricade into place to create the first "zone" of New York City's reclamation. Then the Marines are sent in to perform their "monstrous cull,"[44] rappelling from their helicopters onto streets and into intersections populated by the dead denizens of the city, where they "strafed, loosed fusillades, and mastered the head shots, spinal separators, and cranial detonations that diverted the dead to the sidewalk.... The red tears of tracers shrieked through the thoroughfares and stray bullets cratered the faces of banks, churches, condos, and franchises, every place of worship a city has to offer."[45] Eventually, the seemingly endless tide of the skels begins to ebb, and the blunt force of the Marines becomes more tactical and surgical in their strikes and sniping. Whitehead writes, "As the numbers of the creatures thinned, the soldiers no longer offered themselves as lures. They hunted, ambled, leisurely, easygoing flaneurs drifting where the streets took them. The soldiers were the arrowhead of a global campaign and they understood it each time they overcame the resistance in the trigger, felt good about it."[46] Although coded in decidedly violent terms, the marine assault on the living dead infestation is driven by a positive purpose and optimistic resolution.

After the Marines finish their large-scale removal of the more threatening skels, teams of less-well-trained and much less-well-equipped civilian sweepers are sent in to clean up any overlooked zombies, especially the primarily docile "stragglers." More akin to benign tumors, which do not invade or metastasize and "only grow locally,"[47] the stragglers "did not move, and that's what made them a suitable objective for civilian units. They were a succession of imponderable tableaux, the malfunctioning stragglers and the places they chose to haunt throughout the Zone and beyond. An army of mannequins, limbs adjusted by an inscrutable hand."[48] The stragglers are stuck in one "discrete and eternal moment" from the past,[49] standing still in the act of something they once did with enough frequency to drive them even after death, "Cemetery statuary, weeping angels and sooted cherubs, standing over their own graves."[50] As the Lieutenant explains, the stragglers are "all messed up,"[51] the one percent of the skels that are simply "mistakes."[52] Sometimes, the less reverential sweepers play with the immobile stragglers, manipulating their stiff bodies, drawing on their faces, even giving them wedgies: "They didn't flinch. They took it ... it was generally assumed that this behavior was a healthy outlet. Occupational therapy."[53] Hardly considered a threat, the stragglers are simply a poignant combination of living-dead statues and ghosts, "stragglers haunt[ing] what they knew,"[54] silent memories of the lost past.

The efforts of the sweepers in the body politic of *Zone One* can also be read as analogous to the radiation treatment that would follow excision surgery, an invasive course of action that attempts to destroy the damaged tissue while preserving the healthy cells. Mark Spitz belongs to one of these three-person teams—the foreboding "Omega" group—which constitute the lowest level of the newly reconstituted military-industrial complex, "[s]oldiers of the new circumstance" drawn from the ranks of "unemployable man-children, erstwhile cheerleaders, salesmen of luxury boats, gym teachers, food bloggers, patent clerks ... seemingly unsnuffable human cockroaches protected by carapaces of good luck."[55] They have only been dispatched into New York City at the apparent end of the game to target the remaining skels and stragglers with surgical precision. The sweepers are under strict orders not to do any more damage than necessary, to preserve the body while exterminating the infection. The government-issued "No-No Cards" remind sweepers to keep the destruction of property to a minimum, warning them "repeatedly about brutalizing, vandalizing, or even extending the odd negative vibe toward the properties whenever possible."[56] In fact, anti-looting regulations are quickly put into effect to preserve the treasures of Manhattan for the future (re)inhabitants, because "Buffalo wanted the city habitable for the new tenants,"[57] and "everyone—soldier and civilian and sweeper alike—were prohibited from foraging goods and materials belonging to anyone other than an official sponsor."[58] The sweepers aren't invested in change but rather preservation, paving the way for New York City's remission and the hope for a "cancer free" future.

Of course, as aficionados of the apocalyptic zombie narrative would expect, the efforts of American Phoenix to "cure" New York City fail, as the infestation of the skels proves too powerful. The body politic becomes not one of hopeful remission but of zombified reanimation. The skels, acting upon the city like the plague virus flowing in their own necrotic veins, bring the city back from the dead, but as a living corpse. The remaining shadows of humanity are eradicated, replaced by the mindless apathy of the skels. In the end, efforts to save New York City, to resurrect the dead city, fail because the dead begin to break the understood "rules" of their existence. Whereas news of inexplicable "kill fields," where masses of skels are found immobile and deanimated, initially give the dwindling survivors hope that the plague will eventual just die out on its own, the skels and stragglers in and around Zone One start behaving with an aggression that defies the preventative measures so carefully cultured by the American Phoenix movement. A straggler "mutinies" against the rules and attacks a sweeper, and if one rule-breaking anomaly exists, there are bound to be more.[59] Worse, the skels assaulting the concrete walls of Manhattan suddenly increase in number and drive: "The ocean had overtaken the streets, as if the news programs' global warming simulations had finally come to pass and the computer-generated swells mounted to drown the great metropolis. Except it was not water that flooded the grid but the dead."[60] As the subgenre dictates, the fortifications of *Zone One* are breached by the relentless swarm of the limitless dead horde, resulting in the (re)destruction of New York City. Despite efforts to the contrary, "The patient stabilized for a time but now the final seizures announced themselves, the diminishing spasms conveying the body's meat to room temperature."[61] And because the collapse of Manhattan isn't an isolated incident—contact is lost with the other camps across the country as well—the inevitable, terminal apocalypse becomes complete.

Zone One's Destructive Nostalgia

Like all good stories, post-apocalyptic narratives must have some kind of motivation for their driving action, perceptively obtainable goals that give the beleaguered characters hope for a better future. More often than not, this idealized future is couched in terms of an equally idealized version of the past. Repeatedly throughout *Zone One*, "the past" is romantically presented as what is "normal," the sought-for ideal,[62] and that version of a remembered history becomes a propagandized image of the *new* New York City—what it *was* and what it *must* be again. For the protagonists of Whitehead's novel, the bleak and dismal present is simply "a series of intervals differentiated from each other by the degree of dread they contained," and the future is "the clay in their hands."[63] The potential of this malleable future manifests nowhere as much as in the physical location (and metaphysical conception) of New York City. The wounded and infected city at the heart of *Zone One* thus functions as an example of what Pierre Nora calls *lieux de mémoire*, or sites of memory, places where "memory crystallizes and secretes itself ... at a particular historical moment, a turning point where consciousness of a break with the past is bound up with the sense that memory has been torn—but torn in such a way as to pose the problem of the embodiment of memory in certain sites where a sense of historical continuity persists."[64] *Zone One*'s apocalypse resulted in just this kind of break from the past, and the memories the survivors so desperately cling to are torn, fragmented, and unique to each individual. The challenge for the New World becomes as much about successfully embodying these memories together into the new (old) historical site of New York City as it is about overcoming the tide of walking dead that continue to infest it.

Whitehead's novel tells its story largely by telling other stories, making it a book about an apocalyptic future constructed from memories of the historical past. Unlike so many zombie narratives that begin just prior to or in the middle of an unexplained zombie outbreak, *Zone One* takes place years after the collapse of modern civilization, and it opens with a flashback instead; specifically, with protagonist Mark Spitz's fond memories of his innocent childhood visits to his Uncle Lloyd's apartment in downtown New York City. The novel is tellingly riddled with such flashbacks, as Mark Spitz repeatedly insists on ruminating upon the past—"how things used to be"[65]—as a way to deal with his horrifying present, all the while consciously refusing to consider his uncertain future. Like the other characters inhabiting *Zone One*, Mark Spitz must create his own *lieux de mémoire* to preserve his past, for because "there is no spontaneous memory ... we must deliberately create archives, maintain anniversaries, organize celebrations, pronounce eulogies, and notarize bills."[66] According to Nora, unless people are consciously vigilant about commemorating the past, history will simply sweep those memories away.[67] Through its repeated acts of commemorative memory, then, *Zone One* constructs its narrative present through its protagonists' efforts to memorialize their past lives and experiences. In other words, the very narrative structure of the book itself manifests its consuming interest in nostalgia, an obsession with the (lost) past that fuels a desire to recreate an idealized version of that past as the hoped-for future, a motivating force that drives so many apocalyptic narratives.

To survive the trauma of a zombie apocalypse—or any trauma, perhaps—people construct subjective *lieux de mémoire* for both comfort and security. Almost everyone in *Zone One* has their own personal brand of soothing nostalgia, reminders of the past that (hopefully) drive them to continue working towards a brighter future. Mark Spitz primarily has his narrative memories, a dense jumble of thoughts, images, and loose connections that turn the novel into a morass of non-chronological, stream-of-consciousness flashbacks, but, as we shall see, his memories are anything but idyllic. By way of contrast, his sweeper teammate Gary carries the past with him in open, obvious ways, from the dirt constantly under his fingernails—"the very grime of Gary's youth preserved as a token of home.... [That] was what he'd scraped off the past and carried with him"[68]—to his predilection to speak of himself in the first-person plural in honor of his deceased triplet brothers.[69] Kaitlyn, the team's de facto leader, also has her own unique nostalgia, clinging to the rules and regulations that remind her of her halcyon days as Secretary of the Student Council. She smuggles her "distinct bit of home ... in the errant conversational tidbit or dimpled inflection that made it possible to pretend the three of them had been whisked away from the dead city and were riding in her family minivan."[70] Because she vocalizes her memories in a casual, anachronistic fashion, "Kaitlyn and her stories of the past were another stencil to lay over the disaster, to remind them of the former shape of the world."[71] The three disparate sweepers may have very different personalities and struggle with their surroundings in different ways, but they all rely upon nostalgia to give them solace.

While his day-to-day efforts as a sweeper are implicitly driven by this kind of "memorial optimism," Mark Spitz's memories of the pre–Last Night New York City have nonetheless been infected with the language of death and dismemberment, as if the imagination of his childhood had somehow prophetically perceived the future apocalypse. Perhaps influenced by the monster movies he so frequently watched on television, Mark Spitz remembers "his parents' hands dead on his shoulders" in family photos, his uncle's wireless speakers "like spindly wraiths," and the same uncle's "mausoleum of remotes" inside his ottoman.[72] Furthermore, he poignantly recalls seeing the people in neighboring apartments as bodies fragmented and dismembered by windows, blinds, and half-open curtains: "Pieces of citizens were on display in the windows, arranged by a curator with a taste for non sequitur: the played pinstriped legs of an urban golfer putting into a colander; half a lady's torso, wrapped in a turquoise blazer, as glimpsed through a trapezoid; a fist trembling on a titanium desk."[73] Whereas the current Mark Sptiz attempts to escape his living nightmare as a sweeper by recalling the populated and vibrant New York City of his past, when he was a boy, he saw his future in horrific, apocalyptic terms:

> [T]he boy conjured an uninhabited city, where no one lived behind all those miles and miles of glass, no one caught up with loved ones in living rooms filled with tasteful and affirming catalog furniture, and all the elevators hung like broken puppets at the end of long cables. The city as ghost ship on the last ocean at the rim of the world. It was a gorgeous and intricate delusion, Manhattan, and from crooked angles on overcast days you saw it disintegrate, were forced to consider this tenuous creature in its true nature.[74]

Whereas Buffalo's American Phoenix propaganda machine struggles to contradict negative views of the present with promises of restoring a nostalgic vision of the past, Mark Spitz resists the party line; to him, the past always already held within it the necrotic potential he now confronts on a daily basis.

One key moment from the past bonds all the survivors, and while it's not a pleasant memory, it's something they all have in common: Last Night. Sharing "Last Night stories" becomes the new icebreaker because "[t]he stories were the same, whether Last Night enveloped them on Long Island or in Lancaster or Louisville. The close calls, the blind foraging, the accretion of loss."[75] Mark Spitz's tale is notably linked to an early childhood trauma, to the Freudian "primal scene" during which he walked in on his parents during an act of fellacio. Returning from a disappointing vacation to Atlantic City, a grown-but-living-in-the-basement Mark Spitz had returned home, oblivious to any news of the plague or awareness of the catastrophe already raging around him. Stopping by his parents' room to check in, he sees his mother once again hunched over his father, "gnawing away with ecstatic fervor on a flap of his intestine, which, in the crepuscular flicker of the television, adopted a phallic aspect."[76] Confronted by the horror of conjugal cannibalism before him, Mark Spitz's brain sends him reeling into the past "because of that tendency of the human mind, in periods of duress, to seek refuge in more peaceful times, such as a childhood experience, as a barricade against horror."[77] While both experiences could be labeled as traumatic—for notably different reasons, of course—Mark Spitz's Last Night experience illustrates how memories can help individuals deal with difficult confrontations. In Freudian terms, people handle the unfamiliar, even the traumatically unfamiliar, by seeking connections with things that are familiar, even if they are uncomfortably familiar.[78] This juxtaposition of the past with the present can be a psychological coping mechanism, as illustrated here and above, but it also manifests as a kind of psychosis all the survivors of the global apocalypse suffer, and suffer together.

Despite finding some measure of peace with their nostalgic memories, everyone who survived Last Night has been diagnosed with a condition cleverly designated as PASD, or Post-Apocalyptic Stress Disorder.[79] This psychological malady—literally a suffering brought about by the past—unites all the survivors in a unique commonality. As Hoberek says, "[T]rauma is the thing that makes everyone at once unique (because everyone's is different) and the same (because everyone has one)."[80] Everyone shares this potentially debilitating psychological trauma; survivor's guilt, the loss of so many friends and loved ones, and the unavoidable obsession with the way things "used to be" result in this version of Post-Traumatic Stress Disorder, the acronym for which telling sounds like "past" when pronounced.[81] In the wasteland of the zombie apocalypse, nostalgia actually becomes a kind of psychosis, and "a hundred percent of the world was mad."[82] Mark Spitz's PASD manifests most acutely when he considers the pathetic pre-apocalypse identities of the skels and stragglers. When trying to find an ID for one of his first kills, for example, Mark Spitz ends up "weeping, fingers curled into a nautilus across his face and snot seeping into his mouth, sweetly."[83] Rather than inspiring hope, which is the response to memory the American Phoenix plan hinges upon, nostalgia often has a paralyzing, debilitating effect. Zone One emphasizes how an attempted rebuilding can in fact fail to result in any kind of healing—truly returning to the past is, of course, impossible.

Harvey discusses how a nostalgic hopefulness was initially employed to "heal" post–9/11 New York City, an attempt to "reinstate all the old values" of consumerism and economics, to shop and travel "as if nothing had changed."[84] However, thanks in large part to the resultant recession, these efforts failed: social inequality become more emphatic, homelessness increased, class-bound privileges worsened, and the economy only got worse.[85] An attempt to rebuild the body politic that contributed to the city's failure or vulnerability in the first place cannot fix what is wrong *now*. Harvey suggests New York City can only be truly healed through a reconstitution of its body politic in more socially democratic terms, creating a "new" New York founded on the mobilization of the poor, a transformed bureaucracy, and political alliances between the middle class, professional organizations, and the private sector.[86] Indeed, Anders claims obstinate obsession with nostalgia—with the way thing were "before"—will only make thing worse: "[I]f you cling too hard to what you used to have, or the world you used to know, then you're akin to one of those mindless, frozen zombies.... Memories of the horrors that everybody's lived through keep dragging them down and making them act in irrational, unpredictable ways."[87] The zombies of *Zone One*, especially the stragglers, are arrested in time, relics of the lost past, and refusing to accept the present on its own terms can results in the same kind of paralysis.

Unfortunately, Mark Spitz cannot avoid his nostalgic obsessions, even seeing the rabid skels in terms of the past. When four zombies attack him at the beginning of the novel, he identifies them in terms of dated antecedents. He thinks of the first skel as "Marge" because her hairdo was an affectation of the actress Margaret Halstead, whose television show had been popular before the calamity of the zombie apocalypse[88]; another he thinks of as "Miss Alcott," his sixth-grade English teacher, mostly because of its "bushy eyebrows, the whisper of a mustache."[89] Nevertheless, when combating the dead, these nostalgic moments prove to be useful for Mark Spitz:

> He hadn't decided if conjuring an acquaintance or loved one into these creatures was an advantage or not.... [But] perhaps these recognitions ennobled his missions: He was performing an act of mercy.... [T]hey were somebody's family and they deserved release from their blood sentence. He was an angel of death ushering these things on their stalled journey from this sphere."[90]

Rather than thinking of his loathsome sweeper obligations as optimistic efforts that will create a brighter tomorrow, Mark Spitz sees himself as someone fulfilling the incomplete work of the past. The dead have lingered on unnaturally, and, in stark contrast to the propaganda coming out of Buffalo,

Mark Spitz finds solace in bringing the past to its natural conclusion, *not* in bringing it back, somehow, in a renewed, resurrected form.

Mark Spitz not only uses memories of the past to survive the present, he choses to focus on his nostalgic thoughts and stories because he simply refuses to consider an unknown and increasingly unlikely future. He mocks the "insipid slogan" of the reconstruction government "We Make Tomorrow," and he struggles actively to resist such thinking: "He had to get all that crap out of his head or else it would turn out bad for him."[91] Thoughts of the future are dangerous, as "hope" can result in a lapse in judgment, a dropping of one's guard. In this way, *Zone One* can be read as a condemnation of both the Bush administration's *and* the Obama administration's post–9/11 reconstruction rhetoric, the former for focusing too much on the past and the latter for looking too naively into the unwritten future. A sense of hope and a catalog of utopian dreams make for compelling political promises, but they can also misdirect the conversation from what matters most: the present:

> Mark Spitz believed he had successfully banished thoughts of the future. He wasn't like the rest of them.... You never heard Mark Spitz say "When this is all over" or "Once things get back to normal" or other sentiments of that brand, because he refused them. When it was all done, truly and finally done, you could talk about what you were going to do.... This is what he had learned: If you weren't concentrating on how to survive the next five minutes, you wouldn't survive them.[92]

Daydreams of his childhood, indulgent ruminations on the past, end up lowering Mark Spitz's guard, allowing the skels in the Human Resources office to get the best of him. But the gravity of the present reminds him of the dangers posed by both the past and the future: "There was no when-it-was over, no after. Only the next five minutes."[93] This sober realization saves Mark Spitz's life—once again—and we can all learn from its timely lesson.

Despite all their valiant efforts to resurrect New York City as the famed "City on a Hill,"[94] Mark Spitz's Omega team fails, fittingly on the same day Zone One expires for good. The team encounters a straggler who was once a fortune-teller, and the creature *does* indeed predict the future, through both an apparent mutation in its behavior and the death of the sweepers that come in contact with her. The fortune-teller's shop appears anomalous to Mark Spitz, part of a number of "holdout establishments" that "stuck to the block with their faded signage and ninety-nine-year leases, murmuring among themselves in a dying vernacular of nostalgia."[95] The shop itself is like a straggler,[96] a perplexing holdout from a bygone age surrounded by new, modern stores and businesses. Inside, the Omega team finds the proprietor sitting at her table, ready to read a fortune, to tell the future. With this tableau, Whitehead decisively links the future with the past, the fate of the human race with its nostalgic futility. Inasmuch as Whitehead anthropomorphized New York City as a zombified body throughout *Zone One*, here, at the end, he describes a zombie in terms of the city: "A hunk of the fortune-teller's neck beneath her right ear was absent. The exposed meat resembled torn-up pavement tinted crimson, a scabbed hollow of gaping gristle, tubes, and pipes: the city's skin ripped back."[97] Gary, true to form, decides to play with the straggler, taking off his gloves to affect a palm reading with the docile fortune-teller. Initially, he asks about the dead, coding the encounter again in terms of nostalgia, but then he does ask about the future; specifically, about the fate of Omega team. As if on cue, the straggler suddenly lurches to action, clamping down on Gary's hand and biting his thumb off.[98] In other words, the fortune-teller *does* answer Gary's question, predicting the future of team Omega by facilitating its destruction.

Zone One—and with it, New York City, the remnants of the United States of America, and perhaps the entire world—is ultimately destroyed by a past older than human nostalgia, a necrotic infection that represents the greatest truth of nature: mortality itself. As the ocean of skels breach the barricades, "[t]heir mouths could no longer manage speech yet they spoke nonetheless, saying what the city had always told its citizens, from the first settlers hundreds of years ago, to the shattered survivors of the garrison. What the plague had always told its hosts, from the first human being to have its blood invaded, to the latest victim out in the wasteland: I am going to eat you up."[99] The body of New York City cannot be cured, the disease that has corrupted its very bones has become entropy itself, an inevitable futurity that no amount of spun nostalgia or brute force could ever hope to defeat. Finally, at the end, Mark Spitz realizes,

> whatever the next thing was, it would not look like what came before.... Why they'd tried to fix this island in the first place, he did not see now. Best to let the broken glass be broken glass, let it splinter into smaller pieces and dust and scatter.... The world wasn't ending; it had ended and now they were in the new place. They could not recognize it because they had never seen it before.[100]

With the fall of *Zone One*'s New York City, a fall resulting from the futility of nostalgic reconstruction, Whitehead completes his polemic against current failed efforts to rebuild the wounded borough of Manhattan, ultimately advocating for a trajectory for reconstruction that lies in the future rather than the past. The old world is already gone, and a new one is already in place.

Hopefully, with the completion of One World Trade Center—a building of the future, rather than a reconstruction of those lost on 9/11—and with the National September 11 Memorial & Museum on the hallowed site of Ground Zero, the new New York City can move forward through a thoughtful engagement with both the future *and* the past.

Chapter 6

THE STAGE ZOMBIE
Dead Set, Uncle Vanya and Zombies, and the Reality-TV Monster

"Stop clapping! What is wrong with you fucking people! Where the hell is your humanity?"
—Karissa, *Uncle Vanya and Zombies*

Zombies are inherently dramatic and performative monsters—as evidenced by the popularity of zombie walks, zombie raves, and zombie performance art in general[1]—so live-action zombie narratives are a natural development of the subgenre in our current Zombie Renaissance. In fact, the fictional zombie first developed on the stage in Kenneth S. Webb's 1932 play *Zombie*, largely inspired by the popular travelogue *The Magic Island* (1929) by William Seabrook, and numerous adaptations of George A. Romero's *Night of the Living Dead* (1968) have appeared over the years.[2] Recently, the walking dead have once more stepped upon the boards, as in Markus Wessendorf's *Uncle Vanya and Zombies*, which premiered on November 9, 2012, at the Kennedy Theatre on the University of Hawai'i at Mānoa campus. This provocative fusion, inspired by such juxtapositional works as Seth Grahame-Smith's literary mash-up *Pride and Prejudice and Zombies* (2009) and the British television miniseries *Dead Set* (2008), created by Charlie Brooker and directed by Yann Demange,[3] not only fuses the classical drama of Anton Chekhov's 1898 play with Romero's modern conception of the zombie, but also offers a scathing indictment of contemporary reality television programs and the audiences that watch them.

The invasion of the reality TV game show by the walking dead actually makes perfect sense, particularly as zombie narratives have become increasingly diverse, violent, and multimodal. A similar trajectory towards monstrous behavior and consumptive selfishness has been developing in reality television for years as well. Robert Sheckley predicted this kind of dark future in 1958, one in which a televised game show comes to mirror the violent atrocities of the ancient Roman Coliseum. In "The Prize of Peril," first published in *The Magazine of Fantasy & Science Fiction*, contestant Jim Raeder's attempts to evade professional murderers in a high-stakes "thrill show" are broadcast all across the United States.[4] Stephen King—writing as his darker half, Richard Bachman—has also explored this idea of the dystopian game show in *The Long Walk* (1979), which depicts teenagers forced into a life-or-death endurance race, and in *The Running Man* (1982), in which Ben Richards resorts to murder and acts of terrorism to "win" his game show. While today's *Survivor* (1997–) and *Big Brother* (1999–) have hardly escalated to the level of brutality and violence present in narratives such as Suzanne Collins' *The Hunger Games* series (2008–2010), reality television contestants and viewers alike are certainly more focused, obsessive, and driven than those associated with the innocuous *Jeopardy* (1964–) or *Wheel of Fortune* (1975–). In many ways, the cutthroat behavior of reality show contestants—along with the rabidity of some fans—resembles the single-minded focus and drive of the classic cinematic zombie. To win a seasonal game show, contestants must lie, steal, seduce, and manipulate—and perhaps the only reason the contestants don't resort to physical violence are the clauses in their contracts stating they will be ejected from the show for such atavistic outbursts. The contestants aren't the only ones reduced to their more beastly, primitive natures, though; viewers of reality TV participate in a synoptic relationship with their shows, becoming perverse voyeurs who primarily find their entertainment through potentially unethical proxy and schadenfreude. Both the zombie invasion narrative and reality TV programming, then, are modern sites of public suffering, bodily torment, and indulgent spectacle.

Allegorical parallels between competition-based reality TV programs and the zombie invasion narrative manifest in both *Dead Set* and *Uncle Vanya and Zombies*. In these mash-up narratives, reality show contestants must combat, rather than simply compete with, each other to survive menacing onslaughts of ferocious zombies. As with all dramatic productions—reality TV in particular—these unusual narratives manifest Jean Baudrillard's ideas of hyperreality, simulation, and the simulacra. *Dead Set* features actors, real-life celebrities, and former reality show contestants playing contestants, fans, and even themselves in a parody of the British version of *Big Brother*. The simulation of the already-simulated occurs on even more levels in Wessendorf's theatre production, which dramatizes the studio taping of a fictional reality TV show in which actors pretend to be normal people turned into untrained actors staging a production of Chekhov's *Uncle Vanya* for a studio audience made up of the play's actual audience. As the lines dividing human and zombie become increasingly blurred in these simulations of "reality," the members of the viewing audience find themselves implicated as well. Instead of manifesting a mediated version of Michel Foucault's "panopticon," as happens in other reality TV shows, these zombie narratives realize a modern-day version of public humiliation, more akin to Foucault's "spectacle of the scaffold." In other words, both *Dead Set* and *Uncle Vanya and Zombies* portray the reality TV industry as a manifestation of the Grand-Guignol tradition through which society participates in Thomas Mathiesen's social structure of the synopticon.

Hyperrealism, the Panopticon and the Synoptic Nature of Reality TV

Over the past two decades, the phenomenon of reality television has been the subject of much critical attention and scrutiny, particularly from cultural theorists. Mark Andrejevic provides a standard definition of the genre, one in which the "characters" are not professional actors and the recorded action, for the most part, is unscripted.[5] However, Katie N. Johnson calls this "mimetic strategy" specious, pointing out how "[a]n examination of reality-based entertainment throws the entire notion of 'reality'—and the representation of reality, or mimesis—into question."[6] For example, those who participate in such programs *choose* to do so, for a variety of self-interested motives, and their actions are often steered by showrunners and producers seeking a larger narrative outcome. Furthermore, programs such as *The Real World* (1992–) and *Big Brother* must be distinguished from "verité programs," such as *COPS* (1989–), and other game shows in that "they are based not on the documentation of exceptional moments but on the surveillance of the rhythm of day-to-day life."[7] What most people mean when they refer to reality television, then, is an implicitly authentic look at other people doing what they naturally would in certain contrived situations and scenarios for the entertainment of the viewing public.

Both fictional and reality-based television programs attempt to recreate the real world, either through professional acting and careful scripting or via the unimpeded actions of non-actors making their own choices, but only the latter makes the promise of "reality" a key feature of its production and promotion. However, Johnson's challenge of this so-called "reality" labels it something closer to a "simulacrum."[8] Jean Baudrillard, in *Simulacra and Simulation* (1981), argues any attempted simulation is little more than "the generation by models of a real without an origin or reality: a hyperreal."[9] In other words, Baudrillard questions the very authenticity of that being simulated, claiming these simulacra attempt to simulate that which is always already an illusion of the real. Baudrillard proposes Disneyland as "a perfect model of all the entangled orders of simulacra ... a play of illusions and phantasms."[10] The entire construct of the famed theme park—from the parking lot to the carefully crafted animatronic figures—seeks to present an ideological version of the entire United States, a "miniature" version of a utopic country, "[e]mbalmed and pacified."[11] A carefully constructed simulation such as Disneyland can nonetheless harbor some truth, albeit concealed, about the world it attempts to recreate, and therein lies the nature of "hyperreality." Baudrillard explains the complex relationships among the simulacra, that which is ostensibly recreated, and the truth disguised by that attempted simulation: "It is no longer a question of a false representation of reality (ideology) but of concealing the fact that the real is no longer real, and thus of saving the reality principle."[12] The failure of a simulacrum to recreate the truth constitutes the hyperreal because we *believe* the authenticity of the simulacrum instead of facing the realities of what is being simulated. Simulation is thus about perception, not the truth.

Nonetheless, viewers of reality television programs *do* buy into such hyperreal simulations of the "real world," regardless of their authenticity, primarily because of their desire to observe the actions and behaviors of others secretly, or at least in the anonymous safety of their homes. The viewing audience of a reality TV show is, ostensibly, "accorded full access to the subject"; therefore, as Daniel Trottier observes, "surveillance emerges as one of the predominant themes" of such programming.[13] Not surprisingly, then, Johnson sees direct parallels between the resultant surveillance structure of reality television programs, particularly that used in *COPS* and *America's Most Wanted* (1988–2012), and Foucault's discussion of the panopticon in his influential *Discipline and Punish* (1975).[14] Foucault explores the broader applications of Jeremy Bentham's design for a prison that could supervise the behavior of its inmates through an architectural panopticon. With a single tower at the center of a circle of inward-facing cages, guards could observe the inmates without being seen themselves, thus ensuring disciplinary control.[15] Foucault's description of the observed prisoners certainly sounds like the modern-day reality television program, particularly those programs built around the "hidden camera" model. Indeed, Andrejevic explains how in *The Real World*, "not everything [the cast] are doing is taped and watched, but they have to live with the knowledge that their words and actions could, at any time, be recorded for broadcast."[16] A show that reveals illegal, deviant, or simply questionable behavior, be it *COPS* or *The Real World*, allows the viewer to participate in a kind of panoptic social governance, as "we, in the comfort of our living rooms, can gaze at broadcasted desperadoes on our television screens,"[17] choosing to condone or condemn that behavior through a mediated version of discipline and punishment.

If reality television programs are indeed founded on the structure of the panopticon, then Foucault is correct in his claim that modern society is no longer one built on the "spectacle," particularly that of public torture and execution, but rather one of "surveillance."[18] Yet Baudrillard sees the hyperreality of television as the *end* of the panoptic system, a "switch from the panoptic mechanism of surveillance ... to a system of deterrence, in which the distinction between the passive and the active is abolished."[19] Mathiesen also challenges Foucault's understanding of the panopticon in modern society, particularly his failure to address the role of the media. While Mathiesen concedes the increase of public surveillance in which the "few see the many," he questions if we have indeed developed away from situations in which the "many see the few."[20] In addition to the panopticism of CCTVs, reality crime programs, and Internet tracking, modern society also indulges in *synopticism*; we are now a society in which "a large number focuses on something in common which is condemned."[21] This new "viewer society" has increased in waves with the development of different media:

> The enormous popularity of [cinema] implied the gathering of large crowds of people in large film theatres, blatantly contradicting Foucault's thesis that in modern times we have moved away from the situation where the many see the few, away from synopticism....
> The basic synoptical character of the media was in a fundamental way enhanced by television. As television developed, millions, hundreds of millions, of people could see the few on the stage.[22]

Reality television programs—be they capturing criminals, broadcasting the efforts of game show contestants, or simply recording the daily activities of "ordinary" people—simply don't create a situation in which the few watch the many. Instead, such a structure of deterrence reverses Foucault's model and returns us to a system of public spectacle and even punishment, one in which the many are allowed to see, and potentially condemn, the actions of the few.

Reality television's hyperreality potentially allows the masses to learn from the mistakes of the few on display; however, such an interactive structure cannot help but implicate the viewing audience as well. The didactic purpose of true-crime programs such as *COPS* and *America's Most Wanted* is relatively clear, as viewers see those who violate the laws of the land being brought to justice, but even competition-based shows have a similar function because such games require their contestants "to make morally difficult decisions, and to engage in morally dubious activities."[23] Participants on such polarizing reality programs as *Big Brother* and *Temptation Island* (2001–03) serve a didactic function as their lying, manipulation of others, intolerant and racist comments, and philandering and unfaithful sexual behavior are regularly condemned by the viewing public, through both Internet posts and interactive audience voting systems. However, as Adrejevic points out, a reality TV show loses its best dramatic characters if the viewers vote the "villains" out.[24] As a result, audience members may rally around the more deplorable characters to keep the dramatic tension higher and the episodes more scandalous. Viewers thus cannot remain above the problematic nature of such programs, as the desire to satiate their (potentially perverse) voyeurism fuels the design of such shows and the behavior of the competing contestants.

Because reality TV is founded on the premise of the many observing the behavior of the few on display, Trottier claims such programs cultivate "a form of voyeuristic consumption among audiences."[25] This voyeurism can undermine any didactic value the programs contain, for, as William Egginton argues, "we usually watch reality TV not to witness those who win the contests, but to watch the human dramas that emerge around those who lose— those who are, in the infinitely repeated phrased [sic] coined in the show *Big Brother*, 'voted off.'"[26] Andrejevic suggests what troubles the critics of sensational reality TV programs such as *Temptation Island* is "the possibility that the portrayal of promiscuity as a form of entertainment will erode the moral fabric and that once viewers start taking pleasure in the emotional plight of 'real' people, true moral decay will set in."[27] In fact, Egginton claims reality TV shows "appeal to the worst in our nature,"[28] and he's not alone in this condemnation: critics of *Temptation Island* included both moral watchdogs and wary advertisers who saw the program as the beginning of the end of modern human society. Mark Honig, executive director of the Parents Television Council, said, "If we're putting this kind of thing on TV as a form of entertainment, we might as well throw Christians to the lions,"[29] and Gene DeWitt, chairman of the media buying service Optimedia declared, "The whole show is founded on a premise that is totally distasteful. The next step is the Roman Colosseum."[30] Of course, non-fatal versions of the Coliseum have existed as part of popular entertainment before now, and reality TV should be seen as simply the latest version of that established tradition.

Current trends in reality television can be viewed in terms of the Grand-Guignol tradition of theatrical horror, a kind of entertainment that pushes the boundaries of social propriety, investing itself in convincing verisimilitude and the exploitation of the human body. Despite complaints about the morally questionable behavior of cutthroat *Survivor* contestants, racist *Big Brother* houseguests, and promiscuous *Temptation Island* participants, viewers nonetheless tune in each week, perhaps enjoying the broadcasts all the more because of the transgressive content. But would such shows garner the same kind of viewership and attention if the content were simply simulated by professional actors? According to Andrejevic, "The audience response to reality shows including *Survivor*, *Big Brother*, and *The Real World* suggests that fans of the genre are drawn by the fact that the emotions of the cast members are real—that, for example, when a cast member is crying, he or she is not an actor playing someone who's crying but is *really* upset."[31] A semblance of reality is essential, be it the hyperreality of reality television's simulacra or the deft efforts of actors coupled with an audience's willing suspension of disbelief, but what links reality TV to the Grand-Guignol tradition is this schadenfreude, this voyeuristic pleasure in the perceived (and real) suffering of others. This intersection of voyeuristic reality TV, the body-horror of the Grand-Guignol, and the modern zombie narrative come together in the socially astute British miniseries *Dead Set*.

The Grand-Guignol Tradition, Reality TV and the Zombies of *Dead Set*

As stated above, Foucault claims the discipline and punishment of modern society are now enacted via surveillance instead of the public spectacle of torture and execution,[32] and while Baudrillard challenges the extent of the panoptic system, he nonetheless claims television is "no longer a spectacular medium."[33] I respectfully disagree with them both as the public exhibition and potential humiliation of reality show contestants can be read as a synoptic form of public spectacle and even torture. Furthermore, the spectacle of discipline and punishment continues alive and well through drama and fiction, particularly the theatre of horror, be it on stage, in movies, or on television. When the two collide—either literally or dramatically—we have a contemporary version of the Grand-Guignol theatre, one enacted on a large scale and encompassing real participants, realistic performers, and complicit audience members. Brooker's *Dead Set*, a relentlessly abject critique of reality TV, celebrity culture, and mindless audience voyeurism, cleverly blurs the lines between the real and the fictitious, the simulacra and that being simulated. By tapping intentionally into the hyperreality of a real television program and real celebrities playing themselves, *Dead Set* functions as a modern-day Grand-Guignol performance that paves the way for *Uncle Vanya and Zombies*.

Grand-Guignol theatre embraces both horror and comedy presented in a raw, naturalistic style, one that emphasizes in particular bodily trauma through special effects and abjection. Richard J. Hand and Michael Wilson explain that the phrase "'Grand-Guignol' has entered the language as a general term for the display of grotesque violence within performance media, but it originates in a specific theatre down an obscure alley in Paris."[34] Oscar Méténier opened the Grand-Guignol in 1897 as a venue to challenge moral orthodoxy and explore the scandal of naturalist theatre. Two years later, Max Maurey turned it into the famed "Theatre of Horror,"[35] dedicating time, effort, and expense to "creating effects that were as realistic as possible: whilst a victim may die a melodramatic death, the means by which they met that death were as naturalistic as possible."[36] In fact, performances at the Grand-Guignol avoided the supernatural completely, focusing instead on human psychology and explorations of human monstrosity, including instinct, mania, death, sex, and insanity, "exacerbated or compounded by grotesque coincidence or haunting irony."[37] Although the theatre used actors rather than real people, the plays presented the realities of the human condition, for good or ill, and did so via shocking verisimilitude, an approach that revealed the perverse voyeuristic desires of the viewing audience.

The Grand-Guignol tradition is thus one interested in two kinds of monstrosity: that simulated by the performers on the stage and that ultimately revealed through the reception of the audience. Noël Carroll offers an additional interpretation of such performances, claiming, "*Grand Guignol* requires sadists rather than monsters,"[38] yet that sadism is the very kind of monstrosity being explored in the dramatization of grotesque and cruel behavior. On the one hand, the producers of such theatrical fare are sadistic in their relentless efforts to recreate violence, torment, and abjection so realistically and convincingly.[39] On the other hand, the audience members must be seen in terms of sadism as well, for they not only revel in the extremes simulated on the stage, but they also create a market for such base entertainment. Such a perspective is essential to an understanding of both Brooker's *Dead Set* and Wessendorf's *Uncle Vanya and Zombies*. While both texts undoubtedly employ the supernatural—in the form of reanimated, flesh-eating corpses—the primary focus of both narratives is the monstrosity of the human condition.

The former attends to the violent, selfish, and sadistic behavior of the *Big Brother* housemates and producers, not to mention the rabid fans of the program, and the latter presents its fictional showrunners as selfish sadists while simultaneously implicating the audience in the unethical performance. Both texts also use substantial violence, bodily abuse, and extreme abjection to drive their points home, aligning them with the ideological and methodological traditions of the Grand-Guignol.

Brooker's *Dead Set* presents itself as a hyperreal simulacrum of reality TV, with a great deal of self-awareness and less-than-subtle commentary on the entire television industry. The miniseries begins like an actual episode of the British version of *Big Brother*, with Marcus Bentley's expected voice-over providing a quick overview of and introduction to the various houseguests. Joplin (Kevin Eldon) tellingly ruminates on television to the vapid Pippa (Kathleen McDermott), who barely listens: "I mean, you know, what *is* TV anyway? It's just a big, fat arrow pointing away from the problem, especially shows like this. It's like the—the lead in the water pipes that sent the Romans mad." After such a concise establishment of *Dead Set*'s primary theme, the action shifts behind the surveillance cameras, showing the production staff as they sort through various footage and monitor the live feeds. *Dead Set* is thus not presented to viewers simply *as Big Brother* but also as a television drama *about Big Brother*. Furthermore, by casting former contestants from the real *Big Brother* program—such as Season 6 runner-up Eugene Sully, Season 7 finalist Aisleyne Horgan-Wallace, and Season 8 winner Brian Belo—as themselves and presenter Davina McCall in her same role for *Dead Set*'s simulation of *Big Brother*, the entire production is hyperreal with a verisimilitude that blurs the lines between fact and fiction, between the real *Big Brother* TV program and the fictional world of *Dead Set*.

In addition to recreating the contestants and production system of *Big Brother*, *Dead Set* simulates the fan culture surrounding the program as well, a depiction that draws revealing parallels between fans and zombies. After Pippa has been evicted from the house and during Davina's interview with her, the crowds of fans shout, hold up signs, and jockey for position. One uninvited guest stumbles onto the scene, however—a man who has been bitten by a voracious zombie and is in the process of turning into just such a monster himself. As the spared houseguests celebrate, they begin to hear vague and distant screams from the fans outside. Unconcerned, Joplin tosses back a beer while observing, "That's the public for you, isn't it? They're animals." This indictment of fan culture continues later in the show: when Joplin and Veronica (Beth Cordingly) make noises at the fence line to distract the zombies, the monsters rush and mob them in a parody of the opening sequence. And when Marky (Warren Brown) stands on the roof of the *Big Brother* house shooting the zombies inside the studio's fences with a rifle, Veronica asks why they keep coming towards the house. Marky answers, "Some kind of primitive intuition, maybe? They feel the *need* to be near us. I mean, don't forget—this place used to be like a *church* to them." The zombies, once hungry for the celebrity of the *Big Brother* contestants, now hunger more literally for their flesh and blood. Like the "mall zombies" of Romero's *Dawn of the Dead* (1978), the fans of reality TV can be read as real-world zombies, creatures of consumption driven by base desires and a skewed sense of ownership.

Not surprisingly, *Dead Set* also addresses surveillance and panoptic culture, themes particularly resonant for British viewers who live with a preponderance of CCTV cameras. During the transitions between scenes, the show often intercuts images of such cameras, the apparatus of the reality television industry. Despite the carnage raging outside the *Big Brother* house—and implicitly across all of England as well—these devices continue to collect their footage, and the remaining members of the house go on as if nothing has happened. Although Space (Adam Deacon) notices the cameras in the house are no longer moving, no longer following the houseguests' every motion, no one else seems concerned that "Big Brother ain't watching us." But voyeuristic observation *does* continue, albeit not in the way intended or expected. For example, production assistant Kelly (Jaime Winstone) has survived the zombie assault on the studio, and after she finds her way into the hidden passages of the *Big Brother* house, she can see the remaining houseguests through the one-way windows. Similarly, the zombies in *Dead Set* often stare hungrily at the television monitors or bang against glass doors or windows in their attempts to get at the contestants—once again a parody of the greedy fans. In other words, the cameras continue to transmit the objects of desire, but not simply for the pleasures of observation.

The obsessive focus and drive of the competitors, and their inherent exhibitionist drives, manifest in *Dead Set* in the way the housemates cannot— or *will* not—accept the reality of what is happening outside. Once Kelly gets into the *Big Brother* house, the houseguests (naturally) assume she is a new contestant on the show, somehow ignoring the blood splatters on her clothes and the knife clutched in her hand. She halting tells them about the "outbreak" and how people are transforming into dead monsters, but Marky laughs her news off, guessing her story is just another ploy by the producers of the show to increase dramatic interest. As part of *Dead Set*'s postmodern sensibility, Marky quotes *Night of the Living Dead*—"They're coming to get you, Barbra!"—as he mocks and belittles Kelly. Yet when Marky moves to open the door to the backstage area, Kelly threatens to attack him with her knife.

Despite all the evidence and reason Kelly brings to bear, including her emotional outburst, all the houseguests can do is laugh, so caught up are they in their own perceptions of the world around them. Only when Kelly takes them onto the roof of the studio do they accept the unfolding apocalypse, so completely have the houseguests bought into the idea that things must be both *seen* and *seeable* for them to be "real."

Witnessing the chaos raging around them, the houseguests begin to process the gravity of their situation; yet while they are understandably concerned about their odds of survival, they are at least as concerned about the end of their period of celebrity. Gazing down at the rabid zombies that were once their adoring fans, all Veronica can ask is, "Does this mean we're not on telly anymore?" This incredulous question gets at the heart of another aspect of reality TV culture being targeted by *Dead Set*: the selfish and exhibitionist natures of the participants. The synoptic nature of reality television, and the voyeuristic desire that drives the reception of the industry, can only work when willing contestants put their bodies on display in their pursuit of celebrity status. The confluence of voyeurism and exhibitionism is most apparent in the spectacle of Veronica taking a shower. Joplin sneaks into the observation corridors of the house to spy on her for his own sexual gratification, but as he stares at her naked body, the audience of *Dead Set* is watching as well. They cannot condemn Joplin's invasive voyeurism without condemning their own participation in the hyperreal "peep show." Perhaps most importantly, Veronica *knows* Joplin is watching her, and she doesn't care—as a willing contestant on *Big Brother*, Veronica is an exhibitionist as much as Joplin (and the audience) is a voyeur. Like all reality TV participants, she *wants* people to see and thus visually consume her body.

As the remaining characters settle into the routine of survival, the structure and system of *Big Brother* becomes a real life-or-death struggle to "win." The show has become more than simply a game—instead of contestants being "voted out" of the house, their numbers now only diminish as they are killed. Patrick (Andy Nyman), the coarse and narcissistic producer and literal "big brother" of the show, comes out of hiding and joins the houseguests. Tellingly, he is cast as the antagonist of *Dead Set*, especially when he suggests they use Grayson's (Raj Ghatak) corpse as chum to distract the zombies for an escape from the studio. When Joplin agrees the plan warrants consideration, the survivors mirror behavior of contestants on the real *Big Brother*: polarized alliances form based on varying ideologies and ethical perspectives. The houseguests debate the merits and risks of Patrick's plan, and the showrunner is "outvoted"; however, when Patrick refuses to conform to the will of the others, Veronica advocates murdering him outright, a clear escalation of *Big*

Brother's eviction system. Instead, Patrick and Joplin manage to take Kelly hostage, and as they try to leave the house, the mash-up between *Big Brother* and a zombie narrative reaches its unavoidable conclusion. A panicking Joplin fumbles the gate and lets the horde of zombies into the studio grounds. The "fans" kill him outright, but Patrick is slowly and methodically dismembered and consumed by the zombies, cursing and yelling the entire time. Only Kelly, Veronica, and Marky make it back into the house, with Space retreating to the master control room. As with the real *Big Brother* show, the actions of the houseguests result in increasingly fewer contestants, but for very different reasons.

With the Grand-Guignol tradition going full tilt, *Dead Set* staggers to its predictably tragic conclusion, a conclusion brought about by the selfish and naturalistic desires and drives of both houseguests and zombie fans alike. The fast-moving monsters break their way into the control room and injure Space. Before the latter succumbs to his bites, however, he unlocks the confessional room for Kelly; but Veronica and Marky are violently killed when the zombies invade the main *Big Brother* house. With only the two of them remaining, Kelly talks with Space through the house's intercom system, declaring him, somewhat hollowly, to be the winner of the show, the last survivor of *Big Brother*. Of course, all Space has really won is imminent death and eventual conversion to the ranks of the walking dead, and perhaps that's part of Brooker's message concerning the outcome of any such reality TV competition. A defeated Kelly asks the dying Space to unlock the door so she can make a run for it, and he begrudgingly acquiesces. After a frenetic montage of zombie violence and chaos, *Dead Set* cuts to CCTV footage of the zombified members of the cast feasting on the dead. The audience recognizes the zombies as former individuals, and their reduction to greedy, hungry, and pathetic monstrosities is clear. The indictment of reality TV culminates in the final shot of *Dead Set*: a zombified Kelly staring up at a camera, her glassy-eyed stare transmitted on all the television monitors in the control room. Dozens of images of Kelly, staring hungrily out at the viewing audience. According to Brooker, then, everyone involved in the realty television industry resembles a zombie, be it the greedy producers, the selfish contestants, or the hungry fan base.

The Performative and Interactive Indictment of *Uncle Vanya and Zombies*

Wessendorf's *Uncle Vanya and Zombies* also capitalizes on the performative nature of the zombie, manifesting the hyperreal through its creative mash-up of classical theatre and exploitative reality television, coupled with blurred lines between the real and the fantastic. Yet whereas Brooker's *Dead Set* targets the entire reality TV system, Wessendorf's theatre production primarily critiques the scopophilic and synoptic audience of such programs, challenging viewers through a Grand-Guignol experience to reconsider their complicity with unethical reality television, voyeuristic exploitation, and a general lack of humane sensitivity. By reconceptualizing Chekhov's play as a live reality television game show, and presenting the audience of the play in the dramatic role of the simulated studio audience, Wessendorf uses spectacle to make his chief argument. As Foucault writes, the "spectacle of the scaffold" only affects the public if they see it with their own eyes because "they must be made afraid ... they must be the witnesses, the guarantors, of the punishment, and because they must to a certain extent take part in it."[40] While *Uncle Vanya and Zombies* begins as a parodic and farcical comedy about an absurdist post-apocalyptic game show, the simulated suffering of the feckless cast members—made all the more tangible through the play's hyperreality and the visceral effects of its Grand-Guignolesque staging—increases in severity and gravity as the play progresses. By the end of the performance, the audience recognizes the true horror taking place on the stage before them, and they too late realize they are a complicit part of that public humiliation and trauma.

When Wessendorf was asked in 2011 to come up with ideas for his next theatre production, he decided to pursue a mash-up narrative in the tradition of *Pride and Prejudice and Zombies*. At about that time, the Fukushima nuclear power plant disaster occurred, and he realized he wanted to "do something that related to that," which meant starting with "a play that would be classical but relate to environmental concern[s]."[41] Additionally, Wessendorf took note that

> zombies seemed to have moved from the margin to the mainstream by increasingly invading other genres and media, from graphic novels to literary fiction, from television shows to zombie walks.... Since I had been an ardent zombie fan during my teenage years in Germany during the late 1970s, my interest in the zombie genre was reawakened (or better: re-deadened). I was particularly curious about the sudden mass appeal of the living dead across generational, ethnic and class boundaries.[42]

Like any good theatre artist, then, Wessendorf tapped into the most powerful trends he could identify in his contemporary zeitgeist, and one of the strongest was undeniably the zombie figure, which he saw as a reaction to "globalization, economics, anxieties, global warming ... 9/11, the Iraq war, the 2008 recession ... [and the] Occupy Wall Street [movement]."[43] Knowing he wanted to produce his own contribution to the ongoing Zombie Renaissance that would be memorable for its spectacle as well as its cleverness—Wessendorf teaches performance studies, among other topics, and recognizes the performative aspect of zombies, especially zombie walks, which are essentially *community* performance[44]—the inventive director also turned to the Grand-Guignol tradition for further insight and inspiration.

One key technique from the Grand-Guignol employed by Wessendorf is the tradition of setting the mood and tone of the play before the show even begins. Maurey, like Méténier before him, took advantage of the neighborhood surrounding the Grand-Guignol by "extending the theatrical experience beyond the walls of the theatre building. The Grand-Guignol is perhaps unusual in its nineteenth- and early twentieth-century context for being a theatre for which the theatrical 'event' began before the audience entered the theatre."[45] In a similar fashion, Wessendorf makes sure his audience is primed for the "event" of *Uncle Vanya and Zombies* while still outside the theatre. About 30 minutes before each performance, the cast members playing the titular monsters begin to appear slowly, in full makeup, outside the Kennedy Theatre box office. Without breaking character, these zombies shuffle in mock pursuit of patrons buying their tickets, groan and call to each other, and even lumber after passing cars. While the zombies are decidedly creepy, most patrons react with wonder and delight, taking pictures and occasionally play-acting the role of potential victims. Once inside the theatre, and after the houselights have dimmed, the standard pre-performance warnings, requests, and disclaimers are broadcast over the sound system, but they have been altered to develop the verisimilitude of the production. References are made to "armed escorts," and the use of recording devices and flash photography are forbidden primarily because they might agitate the zombies on the stage. In another nod to the Grand-Guignol, patrons are encouraged to report any signs of fever and dizziness immediately, as medical staff are on standby.[46]

In addition to these visual and auditory efforts to affect a real-life post-apocalyptic television broadcast, the printed program further invites the audience to embrace the fantasy of the production. Although the program for the play declares on one side that "*Uncle Vanya and Zombies* by Anton Chekhov and Markus Wessendorf" is part of the Kennedy Theatre's 2012–2013 mainstage season, the reverse of the tri-fold sheet tells a different story:

> The Public Broadcasting Corporation Presents:
> at the Charles H. Koch Auditorium
> Theatre Masterpieces and Zombies
> Uncle Vanya and Zombies

The 6th Episode of "Theatre Masterpieces and
Zombies" Featuring Anton Chekhov's *Uncle Vanya*[47]

This double-sided program represents a hyperreal artifact, declaring the "real"
play on the one side and the "reality television program" of the play's fictitious
world on the other. In addition to listing the University of Hawai'i at Mānoa
student actors as "Show Hosts and Crew," "Contestants," "Guest on the Show,"
and "Zombies"—rather than the characters they will play—the "Producer's
Notes" establish the "real world" of the play's scenario. The recent meltdown
of a nuclear submarine has resulted in a radioactive cloud over Oahu, one
that began turning people into zombies. The military has since taken over
the island, establishing martial law and a quarantine. The notes also explain
the nature of the night's performance in terms of a corporate-backed realty
television competition:

> To raise funding for medical supplies and food for island residents,
> the Public Broadcasting Corporation (PBC) decided half a year
> ago to create a reality show "Theatre Masterpieces and Zombies"
> and to broadcast it live.... For most Oahu residents participating
> in, and winning, a "Theatre Masterpieces and Zombies" contest
> is the only chance to leave the island in the foreseeable future.[48]

The audience is thus invited to join in on the simulation, to embrace the concept of the play, and to acknowledge their role as tourists to Oahu sitting in
the studio audience for the live "Theatre Masterpieces and Zombies" broadcast. Indeed, as the lights dim and the announcements sound, members of
the audience cheer and call out and applaud with exuberance, accepting their
role and playing their assigned part.

The stage and set for *Uncle Vanya and Zombies* are also key components
to the production's verisimilitude. Hall and Wilson explain, "The Grand-
Guignol stage was naturalistic inasmuch as it was strictly proscenium, which
worked to its advantage in creating a 'four-walled' claustrophobia. In addition,
the proscenium stage was invaluable for the effective execution of many of
the special effects that the theatre developed."[49] The stage of Wessendorf's
production, while that of a large auditorium theatre, nonetheless subscribes
to the ideal of a strict proscenium, with limited depth and tight framing. The
set, which was designed by Donald Quilinquin, resembles a basic country
home, with a kitchen, a stairway up to a catwalk, a treadmill, and a large
couch. More importantly, the back of the set is large enough to conceal all
of the backstage area, and two "holding pens" surrounded by chain link fencing fill the sides of the stage. While thrust forward to engage more intimately
with the audience, an imposing structure nonetheless separates the two: a 20-
foot high "electric" fence. On the one hand, the fence is off-putting, as it

obscures every action on stage and separates the audience from the players. On the other, though, such a device greatly contributes to the illusion of the play, as the audience comes to believe that perhaps the fence is there for a reason, that perhaps this innocent college production is not as safe as one would assume. In Mathiesen's discussion of the "older institutions of spectacle," he describes the differences in context between then and now: "In the older context, 'sender' and 'receiver' were in each other's proximity, be it in the ancient theatre or the festivals and image-building of the Colosseum; in the modern media context, distance between the two may be great."[50] Yet synoptic theatre *can* continue to exist today, albeit usually in a simulated form. The "real-world" synopticon of television programs such as *Big Brother* are replicated and simulated with the immediacy of the "older institutions of spectacle" in Wessendorf's *Uncle Vanya and Zombies*.

The fictitious *Theatre Masterpieces and Zombies* television program consists of five "rounds," with breaks, interludes, and intermissions for the supposed "commercial breaks" required of a live television broadcast; Wessendorf's play, then, frames the broadcast with both a prelude to orient the audience and a sharply abrupt denouement to bring the performance to a close. The play proper begins with a smarmy host and show runner, Walt Gaines, and his flamboyant cohost, Cocoa Chandelier.[51] Much of their banter was developed through improvisation, and it's full of cheesy jokes, one liners, puns, and zombie humor. In the Grand-Guignol tradition, such interplay between comedy and drama is essential; Maurey recognized the value of this alternation for "[t]he contrast between the styles exaggerated both the horror and the comedy."[52] The opening vignette of *Uncle Vanya and Zombies* thus fulfills Agnès Pierron's description of the Grand-Guignol: "From the rising of the curtain, the comedy prepares the ground for the horror."[53] Cocoa next explains the three rules of the show—Rule 1: Don't drop a line; Rule 2: Don't drop character; Rule 3: Don't drop dead—and if the contestants break any of the rules, she can use her control panel to release zombies onto the stage. Walt then describes the prizes the contestants may win, such as a scholarship to an Ivy League college or a job with a prestigious Internet company. Of course, the audience already expects most of the so-called contestants to die— after all, the mash-up promises *zombies*, and zombies kill people. As Hall and Wilson emphasize, "In Grand-Guignol horror the issue is not *what* will happen, or even *who* it will happen to, but rather *when* and *how* it will happen when it finally *does* happen."[54] In *Uncle Vanya and Zombies*, this tension in the script changes somewhat, as the audience is reasonably sure they know *how* the various characters will die; however, as a kind of game show, the question remains until the very end *who* will survive.

Throughout the first half of the show (before intermission), the play's style often resembles slapstick comedy, and the audience participates gleefully in the torture of the contestants through panoptic spectacle and bodily trauma. At the beginning of Round 1, however, the play unfolds as a standard, amateur production of *Uncle Vanya*—albeit abridged and condensed. The contestants attempt to play everything straight, although things have clearly been adapted for the modern day, with contemporary references to politics and technology and with updated slang and profanity. Many of Chekhov's original lines are recast as humorous, both through Wessendorf's adaptation and because of the double meaning the "game show within the play" affords. For example, when Seth N. Lilley, playing Dr. Astrov, tells Amber Lehua Davison (the housekeeper Marina), "People are freaks, you know?," he gestures towards the cluster of zombies just offstage; and when Alex Rogals as Vanya refers to the isolated country home as a "safe house" for Professor Serebriakov to hide from the government, the term has an obvious second resonance for fans of zombie films. While Amber is clearly trying her best to be a good actress, both Seth and Alex deliver their lines with clear derision, and their body language shows they, as contestants, have no love for the game show that is putting their lives in such peril. Garett T. K. Taketa, who plays the professor, comes very close to breaking character when his anger at the situation boils over and he starts yelling and growling at the caged zombies. Tragically, he gets too close to the gate, and one manages to grab his foot and bite him on the ankle. Everyone is visibly upset about the injury, but despite the gravity of what has happened, they must continue with the play. In other words, *Uncle Vanya and Zombies* cleverly unfolds two parallel stories at once, and the actors carefully play the scene on both levels simultaneously, resulting in multiple ironic lines and double meanings.

The first interlude between rounds establishes the dual natures of the characters and, in a marked contrast to *Dead Set*, presents them as potentially sympathetic figures to the audience. With Garett left on stage in his infected condition, Walt and Cocoa recap what has happened for the studio audience, all the while delivering more vaudeville-style jokes and puns. Cocoa helpfully explains the two different kinds of zombies: the stagnant "loungers," docile creatures that simply hang about, and "lunchers," fast-moving and aggressive monsters that seek to feast on human flesh. Walt then begins the game show proper by introducing the eight "contestants," whom he insists are all "volunteers"—even though an armed guard escorts them onto the stage. Cocoa explains that if infected contestants continue in character until they "turn," their surviving family will enjoy a "housing upgrade," which clarifies why Garett will remain in the role of the professor even though he is dying.

Kyle Scholl, who plays Yelena, the professor's wife, rancorously complains about the "bullshit" of the rehearsal process and declares that the viewers are not shown the whole story on TV. The audience also learns that Alex is married to Karissa J. Murrell, who plays Sonya—and that she is pregnant. Cocoa reacts to the news by calling her a "zip pack" for the waiting zombies, once again reaffirming the kind of morbid humor that pervades the commentary from the hosts. Viewers find themselves torn between feeling horror on behalf of the contestants and laughing at them because of Cocoa's lightheartedness.

The carnage escalates quickly in the second round, with violent spectacle often intermixing uncomfortably with ironic humor. Most of the contestants are poor actors, largely because they cannot completely disguise their disdain for the game show or avoid getting distracted by the zombies. Karissa, however, really gets into her role, perhaps motivated more than the others because she's "acting for two." She passionately delivers a line about treating women with respect, causing her husband to laugh with bitter irony, and Cocoa uses their behavior as an excuse to release a "luncher" from the holding cage and onto the stage. The contestants pause in their performance to fight the stumbling zombie, but despite a heroic attempt to subdue it by Garett, the creature manages to attack Josephine Calvo, was had been playing Mrs. Voinitsky. As Alex and Seth try to continue on with the play, Kyle is bitten on the face, and Harold brutally assaults the zombie behind the bar, followed by Karissa's enthusiastic stomping. While the violence is thus only implied, being hidden from the myopic view of the audience, Karissa uses the obstruction of the bar and the misdirection of the action to apply stage blood to her shirt, and Kyle uses bandages from the first aid kit to mask her application of makeup to her face. The action continues, and while Alex sticks to his lines despite Kyle's injury, he does make sure she stays well away from him. His line "I wish you could see your face right now" is understandably met with laughter from the audience, but when Kyle says, "There's a demon of destruction in every one of you," a line supposed to be directed at Alex's Vanya, she turns towards the audience and includes them all in a sweep of her hand.

The first death of a contestant only increases the uncanny interplay between horror and comedy. Kyle helps Garett to the sofa, where the two attempt to perform a scene together, despite the fact that they are both slowly dying from their injuries. Garett's agonizing death deeply affects Kyle, but many of their lines can be read ironically; for example, Kyle says, "Just be patient. Five or six years and I'll be old too," and the audience laughs because they know she will be dead within the hour. Garrett collapses in a chair with his back to the hall, and as Karissa and Kyle minister to him (in actuality applying his zombie makeup), Alex delivers the ironic line, "This is turning into a comedy," earning another laugh from the audience. When the newborn monster rises and immediately stumbles into the electric fence, Harold Wong, who has been playing Waffles, realizes it's a "lounger" and won't be a problem. He hits the creature on the shoulder with a bottle, an act that provokes further laughter from the audience even though a man has just died. The show must go on, of course, and Alex and Kyle continue the play, sitting on the couch next to each other. Alex delivers another awkwardly humorous line— "Knowing there's someone in this house dying right next to me"—before Karissa tries in vain to tie Kyle up. She understandably fights back, and her line about being left alone, which is supposed to be directed in character to Vanya, ends up being fittingly directed at Karissa instead. Even though the characters have been attacked and one has died, the play is still primarily comedic.

During Round 3, more zombies infest the stage, but they largely steal scenes and function as comic relief, even when the action of the play takes a serious and tragic turn. The performance—or contest—resumes, but Seth goes out of his way to act poorly, singing and clapping in defiance of the script, and Cocoa releases another zombie onto the stage. Once again, Harold determines it to be a lounger, and he clocks it harmlessly on the head with a bottle for another easy laugh. In addition, Josephine finally returns from the set's back room, now fully zombified, but she is also merely a lounger, one that jerks about with a very comedic walk. Regardless, Karissa, who had just received a paper cut from stacking boxes, gets too close when she tries to help the poor creature navigate the set: the zombie vomits onto her hand, and her wound becomes instantly infected. As the contestants continue on with their lines, Harold prepares paper towel bandages and Seth helps fasten a tourniquet around Karissa's arm. In a rush of desperation, Karissa plunges her hand into the sink's garbage disposal and pulverizes her hand, using misdirection and the concealing power of the sink to apply the requisite makeup on her hand and arm. With three zombies wandering aimlessly around the set, the scene is hard to take seriously, and the audience regularly laughs through and over the spoken dialogue. Kyle returns on set and enters into a painful dialogue with Karissa. As the latter tries to deliver Chekhov's lines through the pain of her mangled hand—"Because I'm happy! I'm so happy!"—the former writhes painfully on the ground, gasping out her dialogue as she slowly dies: "I feel like dancing right now!" Despite Karissa's cries of pain and grief, the audience laughs as Harold drags Kyle's dead body off the stage.

After a brief intermission, during which the zombies continue to roam and groan across the stage, the second half of the show begins; but now the play is no longer as funny, becoming instead increasingly grotesque and tragic. Only gradually do the members of the audience realize their complicity in the horror, for *they* are the true sadists. As the violence and horror continue to escalate, audience reaction begins to shift from laughter to shock, manifesting the response to some reality television programs in which the participants appear to be suffering for real.[55] Additionally, Grand-Guignol productions regularly broke the fourth wall, with actors making eye contact with the audience. Such a performance decision invites the audience spiritually, if not physically onto the stage to participate in the horrific acts of the players.[56] In other words, as Hall and Wilson emphasize,

> The audience become accessories to the act and, most crucially, willing witnesses. It is an acknowledgement by the actor that the violence on stage is not an abstract violence that exists in some fantastic realm far away from our everyday lives, but is an action by a de Lordean 'monstre virtuel,' which we are all, at any given moment, but a step away from (whether as potential victims *or* potential killers). This serves to intensify the horror by suggesting that the audience itself is, at least partly, responsible for the violence enacted on stage.[57]

The reluctant actors of *Uncle Vanya and Zombies* regularly engage directly with the audience, and this confrontational attitude increases in the second half of the production. Such directorial choices emphasize the viewer's role as voyeurs, "willing witness-collaborator in the act[s] of violence"[58] perpetuated on the stage, even if those acts are knowingly simulated.

Round 4 of Wessendorf's production requires the remaining contestants to interact substantially with Kyle, who has turned into a particularly animated luncher during intermission. At first, Alex bravely delivers his lines to Kyle, while nonetheless running away from her, until Karissa and Harold can tie her down to a chair. Seth enters to perform an intimate scene with Kyle, and he undertakes the challenge despite the obvious dangers. The resulting exchanges are potentially humorous, as only one half of the dialogue can be delivered, with Kyle simply growling and even roaring in response. Seth even shows the bound Kyle his maps and explains his plans to replant the forest, presenting Chekov's environmental discourse on dangerous and unchecked consumption, a reading of the play made all the more poignant when juxtaposed with the all-consuming zombies populating the stage. Of course, Kyle eventually breaks free, and chaos ensues on stage. In a clever and comedic turn, however, Seth tricks the Kyle zombie onto the treadmill. He realizes with some glee that he can now deliver his lines to her safely, as the monster simply staggers perpetually towards him.[59] Unfortunately, Seth gets cocky as his dialogue about Yelena become increasingly ironic with double meaning, such as "Sink your claws in me!" and "You witch—you sexy little witch." In the end, the zombie escapes from the treadmill and attacks Seth before Harold can subdue it and Karissa can tie it down again.

By Round 5, more zombies than surviving human contestants inhabit the set, and, apparently eager to end things, Cocoa releases a "luncher" onto the stage right at the beginning. Alex, fueled by his glimpse of actually surviving the ordeal, delivers his half of a scene with the professor while rushing around the stage with zeal and vigor. Harold does his best to combat the new zombie with a bottle; however, he is not only eventually injured, but the creature also attacks and kills Amber. Cocoa flips a switch on her control panel, unlocking a cabinet in the kitchen with a hidden gun, and Alex quickly finds it. Although he contemplates shooting Walt through the electric fence, despite a guard pointing an assault rifle at him, Alex uses both bullets to take down the luncher instead. Harold, now terminally injured, delivers Waffles' farewell speech, made all the more ironic because he is literally dying, and says goodbye for good, especially after Amber rises as a zombie and chases him into one of the back rooms. Almost everyone on stage is dead, dying, or zombified, except Alex and Karissa. One final exchange is tragically ironic, as Alex declares, "This is all too much! All I want is a new *life*!," and the rapidly failing Seth profoundly replies, "Are you listening to yourself? A new life? Maybe a hundred years from now, people will realize how *stupid* we were, what a mess we made of our lives. You. Me. The only thing we can hope for is a little peace and quiet before we're finally *dead*!" Karissa then speaks passionately to Alex, saying, "I'm just as unhappy as you are, but I won't give into this fear, I've got to accept things the way that they are. You've got to do the same.... You have to go on living ... Uncle Vanya." Karissa, as Sonya, is clearly speaking directly to her husband here, encouraging him to finish the play and survive.

The dystopian game show comes to its dramatic conclusion with a promise of hope, one quickly dashed by the generic requirements of a zombie mash-up in the Grand-Guignol tradition. After Seth's death, Alex and Karissa climb to the catwalk and embrace in a passionate kiss, triumphant in their realization they are the only two contestants still alive. The happy couple is bathed in white light above the main set as the shambling zombies dance around in green light on the stage floor. The humans continue their final lines with casual disregard, even joy, as they think they have won and are completely safe on the catwalk. "We have to go on living!" says Karissa, ripe with double meaning. "We'll see a brand-new light, both shining and beautiful.... We'll look back on the pain we feel right now, we'll smile, and then we'll rest." How-

ever, instead of letting Alex and Karissa out of the enclosed stage, Cocoa
releases the entire holding pen of zombies onto the set. Alex charges into the
fray, sacrificing himself for Karissa. As she cries out in horror and grief, Alex's
dying words to her are "Finish it!" She delivers her last line, and Cocoa—
finally—opens the gate. As Walt tries to interview her, a shocked Karissa can
barely answer his questions.[60] Instead, she turns to the audience and screams
with fury, "Stop clapping! What is wrong with you fucking people! Where
the hell is your humanity? I don't understand—" before being sedated by the
armed security guard and dragged off stage. Walt and Cocoa wrap things up
clumsily and exit the hall, and over the cries and moans of the zombies on
stage, a claxon sounds and a booming voice instructs people to exit the theatre
immediately. Somewhat stunned by the abruptness of the violent ending and
Karissa's indicting words, the audience perhaps realizes that, "when it takes
on the role of the objective gaze, [it] simultaneously adopts the position of
the sadistic pervert, whose desire is complicit in the action from which it is
ostensibly removed."[61] *Uncle Vanya and Zombies* ultimately makes us recognize
our participation in a synoptic system that glorifies the torture (via humiliation if not bodily trauma) of the "victims" of reality television.

Since the very inception of the zombie, this walking dead monster has
been used by playwrights, filmmakers, novelists, television producers, and
videogame programmers alike as a multifarious metaphor, a highly flexible
and open-ended signifier that can covertly critique various aspects of contemporary society. The zombie—and, perhaps more importantly, the stories
told around them and because of them—gives life, as it were, to the most
pressing and at time suppressed cultural anxieties while simultaneously,
like *King Lear*'s cunning clown, saying the truths no one else seems permitted
to articulate. Brooker's *Dead Set* and Wessendorf's *Uncle Vanya and Zombies*
both deploy the zombie in their shared criticism of modern media culture,
a culture of surveillance, voyeurism, exhibitionism, and exploitation that
reinstates the archaic public spectacle under the guise of entertainment.
While not literal reality television programs, both *Dead Set* and *Uncle Vanya
and Zombies* present a hyperreality that is perhaps *more* "real," more true to
society despite their use of actors, sets, and scripts. *Dead Set* turns the glad-
iatorial combat of *Big Brother* into a literal struggle for life and death, and
Uncle Vanya and Zombies offers us a chilling view of the future, one in which
mortal conflicts become the standard for wholesome entertainment. Both
texts turn their accusatory gaze onto the audience as well, implicating them
as part of the synoptic Grand-Guignol of reality television. The exploitation
of others in the name of entertainment can only take place if a market exists
for such fare, and the more the viewing public demands innovation, escalation,

and the open violation of social taboos, the more likely the entertainment industry will be empowered to cross over lines of propriety. As we seek out our own forms of entertainment, we must chose wisely what future we want, and hopefully we'll choose one that keeps us from becoming zombies ourselves.

Chapter 7

THE VIDEO GAME ZOMBIE:
The Last of Us and the Digital Evolution
of the Walking Dead

"They see using sound.... Like bats. If you hear one clicking, you
gotta hide. That's how they spot you."
—Tess, *The Last of Us*

I write in *American Zombie Gothic* that the non-traditional narrative
form of the video game acted as an "incubator" that preserved the zombie
subgenre during the 1990s until it reemerged, revitalized and stronger, in the
cinema of the twenty-first century.[1] However, Tanya Krzywinska's work on
zombie video games has convinced me that something like "petri dish" would
have been a more apt analogy, as the game-playing realm is where some of the
most exciting recent zombie development and evolution have occurred, resulting in a "third generation" of zombies, one "born of the digital era."[2] Beginning primarily with Capcom's *Resident Evil* (1996),[3] iconic films such as
George A. Romero's *Night of the Living Dead* (1968) and *Dawn of the Dead*
(1978) inspired video game designers and gave rise to what is now commonly
called "survival horror," a subgenre of gaming that asks players to overcome
waves of menacing monsters while pursuing a redemptive goal, all within a
notably moody and disconcerting environment. In recent years, however, the
competitive innovation of the video game industry has invented original and
unexpected variations of zombie monsters and the narratives constructed
around them, paving the way for new developments in the more traditional
media of film and television.

Current zombie video games explore and develop original, more terrifying variants of the walking dead monster, and their increasing verisimilitude
places gamers in more threatening and thrilling settings and scenarios. This

emphasis on realism demonstrates one direction in which zombie narratives could evolve if they are going to survive as a subgenre and manifests the desires of gamers and zombie fans alike to experience more plausible plague and apocalypse scenarios. *The Last of Us* (2013), created by Neil Druckmann and Bruce Straley for Naughty Dog, is a prime example of this new and dynamic zombie narrative, one featuring monsters whose very existence has close ties to the natural world. In addition to suturing gamers into a terrifying immersive experience based on verisimilar scenarios and paralyzing vulnerability, the apocalyptic creatures featured in this award-winning game represent a possible real-world manifestation of the zombie, a fantastic variation of the entomopathogenic fungus *Ophiocordyceps unilateralis*, whose spores infiltrate the brains of ants, take control of their motor functions, and force them to facilitate the fungus' reproductive cycle. A close look at the storyline, gameplay, and foes of *The Last of Us* demonstrates that while zombie films have understandably influenced video games, zombie video games are now proving more adept to explore, develop, and evolve this still dynamic supernatural monster and its yet-to-be-exhausted narrative subgenre.

Video Games: Keeping the Zombie Alive

Zombies make for ideal movie monsters because, among other things, they have an abject physical appearance and they can be destroyed in a myriad of inventive ways. Matthew J. Weise claims the modern zombie's origins in cinema arose because the creatures are synonymous with "spectacular displays of gore and viscera,"[4] a fact to which any viewer of Romero's films can readily attest. Thanks to Romero's imaginative adaptation of Richard Matheson's *I Am Legend* (1954), we now recognize zombies as relentlessly driven foes, once-humans who have lost their agency to death or infection and are driven to attack, kill, eat, and further infect living human beings. These monsters are decidedly abject, often sporting open wounds and the signs of active corporeal decomposition, and they rend and tear their tragic victims with penetrating clawed hands and hungry, gnashing teeth. Zombies almost always come in waves and hordes, affording eager fans of the subgenre almost limitless opportunities to see the monsters beaten, shot, beheaded, dismembered, crushed, and otherwise destroyed over and over again. While this version of the cinematic zombie enjoyed a measure of commercial success in the 1970s and early '80s with films such as *Dawn of the Dead*, Lucio Fulci's *Zombi 2* (1979), and Romero's *Day of the Dead* (1985), the popular tide soon shifted notably towards comedies and parodies, including Dan O'Bannon's *The Return of the*

Living Dead (1985), John Elias Michalakis' *I Was a Teenage Zombie* (1987), and Peter Jackson's *Braindead* (1992, also known as *Dead Alive*). During this period, the zombie-as-monster might have been laid permanently to rest if not for the innovations taking place in the video game industry, innovations that successfully transferred Romero-style apocalyptic narratives "from the cinema to the living room."[5]

The qualities that make zombies so effective in cinema make them perfectly suited for video games as well, perhaps even more so. While "modern zombie films very much set the tone—the set of iconic traits—for later zombie fiction in other media,"[6] the interactivity of the video game allows players to transcend their status as passive viewers. Krzywinska illustrates how the zombie represents "the ideal enemy: they are strong, relentless, and already dead; they look spectacularly horrific; and they invite the player to blow them away without guilt or a second thought."[7] The often excessive and abject violence that appears in zombie-themed video games can be indulged without remorse, guilt, or any conflicting emotions—the fiends may look human, but they are unequivocally monsters; they may act alive, but they are already dead.[8] Such video games thus not only take advantage of the gory visual spectacle of the zombie as defiled monster and ambulatory corpse, but they also provide gamers with guilt-free and cathartic targets of aggression and violence. Indeed, pioneering zombie scholar Jamie Russell argues that Capcom's "*Resident Evil* single-handedly established the template for a new genre of videogame quickly dubbed 'survival horror' by industry commentators. Armed with a single gun [at least initially] and a limited amount of ammunition players of *Resident Evil* are plunged into a game in which simple survival takes precedence over conventional ideas of winning."[9] With this new kind of game, the zombie was able to remain a relevant vehicle for terror and fear despite the comedic depictions showing up around the same time on the big screen. This preservation of the subgenre—what Russell has called "The *Resident Evil* Effect"[10]—provided the zombie a milieu in which not only to survive but also to thrive.

Building upon the style and structure of earlier games that featured zombie foes—including ICOM Simulations' *Uninvited* (1986), Ubisoft's *Zombi* (1986, created by Yannick Cadin and S. L. Coemelck), and most notably Infogrames' *Alone in the Dark* (1992)[11]—the original *Resident Evil*, written by Kenichi Iwao and Yasuyuki Saga and directed by Shinji Mikami and Mitsuhisa Hosoki, presents the living dead as the main threat to beleaguered gamers who must carefully negotiate a cinematically rendered 3D-environment. Fusing Romero's science fiction and survival horror with the government conspiracy theory elements from Chris Carter's *The X-Files* (1993–2002),[12]

Resident Evil traps players in a mysterious mansion filled with flesh-eating zombies and asks them to solve riddles and manipulate their environment to survive. The monsters clearly recall the ghouls from *Night of the Living Dead* and *Zombi 2*: they are clumsy and slow, they overpower their victims by embracing or surrounding them, and they eat the flesh of their kills. However, although the zombie condition is described in the game as viral, gamers can be injured without becoming infected or transforming—the various medical kits and disinfectant sprays hidden throughout the mansion appear to overcome the deleterious effects of the zombie bite. Furthermore, the infection is not limited to humans; gamers must confront zombie dogs, zombie crows, zombie snakes, zombie frogmen, and even zombie sharks. Yet despite these variations on the established cinematic formula, the antagonists represent dangerous monsters that must be violently dispatched or, at the very least, deftly avoided.

The presence of zombies isn't the only noteworthy link between *Resident Evil* and the zombie cinematic tradition; a tense narrative of struggle and survival drives the game. As Weise explains, "Unlike most previous games featuring zombies, *Resident Evil* explicitly presented itself as a zombie survival narrative.... The impression left by *Resident Evil* at every turn was that it *was* a modern zombie movie, and *you* were the protagonist."[13] Indeed, Mikami saw the game as a way to improve on disappointing films such as *Zombie 2*, stating in a 1996 interview with *GamePro* magazine, "I thought it would be cool to make my own horror movie, but we went one better by making a videogame that captures the same sense of terror. I want *Resident Evil* to give the player the feeling that he's [sic] the main character in a horror movie."[14] Mikami's interactive zombie movie tracks, at least initially, the storyline of *Night of the Living Dead*: a deadly threat forces a group of humans to the perceived safety of a remote house, which they must defend to survive the night until rescue arrives. Gareth Schott observes how both narratives are stories of spatial negotiation; they tell their stories "through the experience of traveling through a real, or imagined physical space."[15] The protagonists of Romero's film must search the abandoned farmhouse for weapons and the raw materials for fortification, often being surprised or menaced by what they find in the various rooms, in the basement, and besieging them from outside. However, the mansion of *Resident Evil* represents a richer space, with many varied locations, most of which can only be accessed after certain items are discovered or puzzles solved. This maze-like quality of the mansion presents "players with a myriad of equivalent-looking rooms and corridors, some of which contain beneficial items for advancement while others contain dangerous adversaries."[16] Not only is the limiting narrative space of a film such as

Night of the Living Dead expanded in the digital environment of the video game—an expansion that substantially increases the narrative opportunities of the potentially tired zombie storyline—but those engaging with the narrative also have the ability to do their own exploring and to make their own decisions.

Resident Evil also brings a pervasive sense of vulnerability to the video game, once again drawing upon the horror tropes established in Romero-style zombie films. According to Weise, *Resident Evil's* "biggest contribution to gaming aesthetics was difficulty design, making players feel vulnerable by making zombies dangerous in ways they were in films and hadn't traditionally been in videogames."[17] Mikami explains how the game's difficulty changed the way players had to navigate the game space to survive: "Not all enemies can be defeated easily, so you sometimes have to run away rather than fight."[18] Because eager gamers can't simply dispatch all the monstrous threats by rushing into each new room with their guns blazing, players of *Resident Evil* must negotiate the Gothic spaces of the mansion, devise plans, and conserve their supplies. Unlike other first-person shooter video games, in which players are afforded increasingly powerful weapons and almost limitless ammunition reserves, *Resident Evil* only provides players with minimal supplies and no super-human capabilities. As a result, the players of survival horror must keep their heads,[19] prioritizing preparation and planning over firepower and reflexes.[20] Especially during the initial act of *Resident Evil*, gamers only have access to an ineffectual pistol and last-resort melee weapons; instead of destroying every zombie threat, they must sprint haphazardly through rooms and along hallways or delay certain encounters until they procure more potent firepower. The "fixed camera" aesthetic—one that admittedly results in more cinematic views of the shadow-filled spaces—limits player visibility, allowing monsters to lurch unexpectedly onto the screen or attack unwary players from behind. As in zombie films, the heroes of *Resident Evil* can die all too easily, and oftentimes they don't have the abilities or resources necessary to save themselves.

Weise calls *Resident Evil* the "zombie ur-text of videogames,"[21] and it marks just the beginning of a flood of similar games that continue to replicate the themes, stories, and aesthetics of zombie films with increasing fidelity as technology becomes more sophisticated. One of these recent video games also draws heavily from Romero's oeuvre, this time *Dawn of the Dead*: Capcom's *Dead Rising* (2008), written by Makoto Ikehara and directed by Yoshinori Kawano. As *Resident Evil* recreates the confined spaces of an isolated domicile, *Dead Rising* exploits the expansive excesses of the suburban shopping mall. While the gleeful destruction of zombies remains a key feature of the subgenre, "The chief aim of the game is ... to explore as much as possible, find out what you can, whilst staying alive and returning to the helipad within the designated timeframe."[22] Other notable zombie video games in recent years that build on cinematic inspiration for rich storylines include both Turtle Rock Studios and Valve Corporation's *Left 4 Dead* (2008, designed by Mike Booth) and Techland and Deep Silver's *Dead Island* (2011), both of which require survivalist exploration and the ability to withstand wave after wave of zombie attacks, the former doing so in a cooperative fashion particularly reminiscent of Romero's ensemble casts of protagonists. As Weise asserts, "Romero-style zombies influenced countless games that followed [*Resident Evil*], and gave the figure a mass-media foothold it hadn't enjoyed since the 70s."[23] The current Zombie Renaissance clearly owes its existence as much to these video games as to films, and the direction of adaptive influence and creative development has been shifting increasingly in this new direction.

The Last of Us: Paying Tribute to Zombie Cinema

While zombie video games continue to draw from their cinematic equivalents for inspiration, the competitive nature of the market and the increasing demands from gamers for greater levels of verisimilitude and more intense emotional experiences affords the medium the ability to transcend its source material and to push zombie storytelling in new and innovative directions. Krzywinska reminds us that "the video game industry ensures continued interest in its products ... through the added facilities and increasing graphical fidelity provided by new developments in game technologies,"[24] and these kinds of innovations have certainly helped maintain the ongoing popularity of zombie narratives. Game spaces have expanded beyond the confines of a single structure or small groups of connected buildings, and stories have grander goals than simply a *deus ex machina* rescue or prolonged survival. Digital characters have also developed—largely through the use of motion capture technology, photorealistic graphics, and professional voice acting— from pixilated human approximations into three-dimensional, naturalistic figures. The video games additionally have the power to make gamers feel even more vulnerable and susceptible to infection, harm, or death, as subjective viewpoints, simulated sensory perception, compelling sound effects, and vibrating controllers more thoroughly suture gamers to their avatars than is possible in film. Finally, new, more plausible depictions of the zombies are leading to storylines that suggest an apocalyptic possibility instead of merely an outlandish horror or sci-fi scenario requiring high levels of suspension of disbelief. Among a host of recent games, *The Last of Us* represents a high point in recent zombie video game design and development, providing gamers with a verisimilar zombie adventure while charting a new direction for zombie cinema, television, and literature.

Of course, like all zombie video games, *The Last of Us* owes a tremendous debt to the cinematic zombie tradition, and it presents itself, as did *Resident Evil* before it, in terms of an interactive movie starring the player as the chief protagonist. For the prologue section of the game, a new player is dropped abruptly into the lives of two unknown characters: Joel (Troy Baker), a scruffy-faced white male protagonist (so in vogue nowadays), who comes home late from work to find his young daughter Sarah (Hana Hayes) asleep on the sofa. The gamer can do nothing but watch the cinematic story play out on the screen as the two have a brief exchange to establish Joel's gruffness and Sarah's tender-heartedness. She then falls asleep peacefully, and Joel carries her off to bed. After a gentle fade cut, a frantic phone call from Sarah's uncle, who is desperately trying to reach Joel, wakes her in the middle of the night, but the phone cuts out almost immediately. Something is clearly wrong, and, as with most films representative of this specialized subgenre, the audience can only guess what is really going on. At this point, the gamer is given limited control over Sarah, who navigates the empty house, uncovering telltale clues to the larger narrative—clues that will resonate with fans of apocalyptic films in general and zombie narratives in particular. Besides the phone cutting out unexpectedly, Sarah finds a newspaper in the bathroom declaring "Admittance Spikes at Area Hospitals: 300 percent Increase Due to Mysterious Infection." Further headlines include "FDA Expands List of Contaminated Crops" and "Police: Crazed Woman Killed Husband, 3 Others." The apocalyptic storyline is established efficiently, fulfilling the player's horizon of expectation for the subgenre.

The generic coding escalates quickly. When Sarah makes it into her father's empty bedroom, a broadcast on the television reports how people are exhibiting signs of increased aggression before the feed suddenly ends. At the same time, explosions can be seen outside the bedroom window. Once downstairs, the gamer can have Sarah watch a series of police cars, sirens wailing, rush past the window, and her automated cries for her father become more desperate. Once Sarah is directed to the home office, gameplay suspends again for cinematic narration and a shift in audience perception and identification. Joel rushes into the room from the patio, warns Sarah of the neighbors acting "sick," and extracts a handgun from the desk. With little warning, a man breaks through the sliding glass door and lunges at Joel, who shoots him— all the player can do is watch this sequence; no other options are available.

The sudden attack, Joel's violent self-preservation, the blood on his arms and clothing, and his warnings to Sarah that something is wrong and they need to flee all fulfill the expected protocols of recent, viral-zombie films, particularly Zach Snyder's *Dawn of the Dead* remake (2004). Players watch Joel lead Sarah outside, where Joel's brother Tommy (Jeffrey Pierce) is waiting with his truck. He reports that "half the people in the city have lost their minds" because of "some sort of parasite or somethin.'" Tommy shares reports of roadblocks, military mobilization, massive deaths, and widespread chaos all across the country. The car passes racing police cars and ambulances, a burning farmhouse, crashed cars, and a desperate family hitchhiking on the side of the road. When Tommy is stopped by a traffic jam, players witness people violently attacking and even killing each other. Tommy tries to navigate a crowd of panicked people, but the car is sideswiped by another vehicle and the screen goes black.

The fusion of cinematic narrative with video game action continues, with very limited player engagement and autonomy, throughout the rest of the exposition sequence. When Joel regains consciousness, gamer control has shifted to him, as the player must command Joel to kick the windshield out of the crashed truck by repeatedly pushing a controller button. Upon escaping the vehicle, a crazed passerby immediately attacks Joel, grabbing him and trying to bite him before Tommy smashes the man in the head with a brick, splattering the "camera" of the game with drops of blood. In fact, if Joel is overwhelmed at any point in this stage of the game, he is bitten violently on the shoulder, and the game immediately reloads, implying death by infection is unavoidable, as in the more recent zombie movies. Because Sarah has broken her leg in the crash, Joel must carry her, requiring players to take a fully defensive posture while following the armed Tommy non-player character (NPC) through the chaos of the city streets. A gas station blows up spectacularly, again evoking the opening sequence of Snyder's zombie film, and players must weave through running NPCs, menacing infected foes, car crashes, and explosions. Players only have one path to take, and if they wait even a moment, Joel is overtaken and killed. If the gamer is quick enough, however, Joel and Sarah will meet an armed soldier, who unfortunately shoots and kills Sarah before Tommy can take him out. Apart from some limited, and perhaps disingenuous, interactivity, the entire prologue section of *The Last of Us* plays out like a film, one drawn almost directly from the existing cinematic zombie cannon.

Similarly, the opening credits for *The Last of Us* firmly tie the video game to the generic and media tradition of similar cinematic narratives. After Sarah's emotional and pathetic death—a hallmark of the game to follow—

the image of a mourning Joel is replaced by the stark words "The Last of Us" in white on a black screen. As with many recent and contemporary films, the opening prologue shifts abruptly into a stylized credits sequence, one that exploits the now ubiquitous montage of a viral outbreak, civil unrest, and social collapse—similar to the opening credits of films such as Marc Forster's *World War Z* (2013) and Matt Reeves' *Dawn of the Planet of the Apes* (2014). Although the clips are audio only, the sound bites could be taken directly from real-world, contemporary news reports and press conferences, adding to the building verisimilitude of the narrative. During this immersive sound-scape, the credits appear on the screen alongside almost abstract visual images of fractal growth, calling to mind the reproductive patterns of molds and fungi. As the credits come to a close, the audio reports shift to a diegetic transmission, one discussing a rebel group called "The Fireflies," an organization dedicated to undermining whatever civil government has implicitly been put into place since the catastrophic—and still unspecified—infectious outbreak and societal collapse. In an efficient, cinematic manner, then, the credits establish the global apocalypse, transport the gamer forward in time, and build the scaffolding of the storyline to follow.

Only at this point in *The Last of Us* does gameplay take priority over the cinematic experience, and the game begins to depart from its filmic antecedents. In 1996—fittingly, the year of *Resident Evil*'s release—Alain Le Diberder famously declared in the prestigious French film journal *Cahiers du Cinéma* that video games represented a "new frontier of cinema,"[25] and as *The Last of Us* moves from its unidirectional storytelling into its interactive gameplay, the potential Le Diberder saw in the medium for crafting complex narratives becomes clear. In the sensorial calm following the opening sequence, the title text "Summer" indicates the beginning of the video game narrative's first act, and the player sees a slightly gray-haired, bearded, and obviously aged Joel waking up "20 Years Later." An unknown woman named Tess (Annie Wersching) bangs loudly on the door to Joel's room, and they begin an exchange that informs the audience much has changed since the game's prologue. The apocalypse has clearly become post-apocalyptic, and gamers control Joel as their avatar to figure out what is going on in this strange and dysfunctional world by exploring the realistic digital environment and playing through the narrative stages of the game. As the player navigates Joel through the city slum, avoiding violent soldiers and eavesdropping on strategically placed NPCs, Joel's abilities expand, including interacting with his environment; jumping, crouching, and climbing; moving key objects such as ladders and planks of wood; and, most importantly for the survival-horror subgenre, loading, aiming, and shooting a gun. In a very gradual way, then, the movie of *The Last of Us* slides into an interactive video game, and the gamer walks through an integrated tutorial phase, which makes that transition manageable. Furthermore, through its expansive storyline, verisimilar characters, vulnerable gameplay, and plausible zombies, *The Last of Us* now begins to forge into new and exciting territory for the subgenre.

The Last of Us: Giving the Zombie Narrative New Life

An increasing number of 21st-century zombie narratives feature story structures based on *movement*, not simply hiding out in one stationary location.[26] In contrast to *Resident Evil* and *Dead Rising*, exploring a fixed location and surviving for a finite period of time are not the primary goals of *The Last of Us*, a narrative that requires players to be constantly on the move from location to location and even across the landscape of a virtual United States. Furthermore, the motivation driving the story of *The Last of Us* is not mere survival but salvation—as Joel, gamers must escort Ellie (Ashley Johnson), a young girl who is somehow immune to the deadly infestation, to a team of doctors so they can find a cure to save the entire human race. The focus on movement belies a new, proactive attitude against societal threats that reflects, among other things, the United States' more aggressive stance against domestic and international threats. As Joel, gamers cannot be satisfied with hiding out and waiting for help from abroad; they must take the initiative and fight various threats—both infected and human alike—head on. Similarly, the optimism manifested by the story's focus on finding a cure reflects a more positive worldview that threats such as the War on Terror, new pandemic infections, or even global climate change *can* be addressed, beaten back, and overcome.

As expected, the world of *The Last of Us* is one in which civilized society has collapsed, with a splintered government, military factions, and gangs of violent vigilantes ruling their own small corners of the fractured and crumbling country. The primary structure of the game, as a result, consists of players navigating Joel through mazelike buildings and richly detailed urban and rural neighborhoods and past increasingly dangerous threats—including both the infected and fast-moving "runners," the mutated and blind "clickers,"[27] and various gangs of heavily armed and depraved humans. With the almost limitless possibilities of digital art design and virtual environmental renderings, *The Last of Us* provides gamers with a rich world, one that they, unfortunately, can only explore within the game's very restrictive and linear pathways. City streets and abandoned houses are rendered with precise detail, and players must search carefully, as established by similar games in the past, to find scarce supplies, weapons, ammunition, and Easter egg bonuses, including a series of comic books and Firefly soldier dog tags. At various points in the game, dark spaces must be cautiously explored with an unreliable flashlight,[28] water-filled spaces navigated both above and beneath the surface, and new pathways created with the aid of salvaged ladders, wooden planks, and movable dumpsters. As the game progresses, players are afforded post-apocalyptic versions of real locations and recognizable landmarks, including downtown Boston, the University of Eastern Colorado, and Salt Lake City, with varying levels of commitment to the actual, real-world locations. The scope of Joel and Ellie's journey resembles that of an ambitious film such as *World War Z*, yet with the interactive, three-dimensional spaces of a video game not possible in a live-action movie.

As an interactive media experience, the real advantage *The Last of Us* has over similar filmic narratives lies in the hosts of enemies the gamer must encounter and overcome through direct, albeit simulated, engagement. The infected zombie creatures, which I will discuss in more detail later, follow the behavioral model of Danny Boyle's infected from *28 Days Later* (2002), living but diseased humans—devoid of their awareness and agency—lurking in the shadows, sprinting with shocking rapidity at their targets, and attacking with brutal violence. While most zombie video games ignore the infectious nature of the zombie plague or virus, resorting to a diminishing health meter that can be recharged with various health items, if Joel is bitten by an infected, *The Last of Us* simply ends with a gory cut scene before reloading at an earlier quick-save point. The human antagonists, on the other hand, inflict more traditional damage on the player's avatar; although, unlike other ultraviolent video games, Joel can only withstand a few blows to the head or shots to the body before he collapses and dies. Similarly, Ellie, while immune to the bite of an infected human, can nonetheless still be killed by them—and by the human foes who regularly target her. If the gamer neglects Joel's role as Ellie's protector and the young girl dies, the game ends just as abruptly as when Joel himself is infected or killed. Unlike most other games—and certainly unlike zombie films—the action ends either when the player avatar dies *or* when efforts to protect others fail.

Beyond the realistic environments and challenging obstacles, what makes *The Last of Us* work so effectively as a captivating narrative are the well developed and emotionally compelling characters, most especially Joel and Ellie. Writing in 2008, Krzywinska claimed that "virtual violence is at the core of the majority of zombie-based games; rarely is the focus on character-based, interpersonal relationships."[29] While this statement was mostly true at the time, *The Last of Us* effectively transcends this kind of limitation, putting human relationships ahead of raw violence. As established in the prologue and gradually developed as the main story progresses, Joel is no superhuman, no seasoned Marine or hardened criminal; instead, he's a middle-aged man who struggles against his physical limitations. While Joel does have some brute strength and a certain physical skill with weapons, he comes across as a relatable everyman, one willing to scavenge comic books for Ellie and put his life on the line to help total strangers, such as brothers Henry (Brandon Scott) and Sam (Nadji Jeter). Ellie represents an even more connective character, due in part to her young age and overt vulnerability. From her introduction, gamers see her as spunky and high-spirited, a girl who thinks she can take care of herself, but who nonetheless needs help from others.[30] Joel must regularly boost her over obstacles or fences, and because Ellie can't swim, gameplay repeatedly requires the player to manipulate floating wooden pallets to transport her across water obstacles. Ellie is also depicted as a caring person who strives to grow closer to Joel, who reads stupid jokes out of a battered paperback, and who thinks to salvage a toy robot for Sam. More than anything, though, these two characters endear themselves to players because of their unexpected and realistic vulnerability—a vulnerability shared by the gamer through the process of *suture*, a process that encourages players to identify with their virtual avatar(s) on numerous levels.

This key feature of gaming makes *The Last of Us* particularly engaging, far beyond the level ever possible by a conventional film. In 2002, the editors of *Cahiers du Cinéma*'s first special issue dedicated entirely to video games declared, "the video game no longer needs to imitate the cinema to exist because it proposes hypotheses that cinema has never been able to formulate, as well as emotions of another nature."[31] Games such as *The Last of Us* explore the possibilities of these hypotheses and other natures by suturing players perceptively and emotionally to their protagonist avatars; rather than simply having strategic camera placement and careful edits determine what viewers see and thus with whom they relate and identify,[32] the video game medium passes character control directly onto its consumer. Furthermore, this control is often hampered and inhibited—and the suture is thus intensified—by the game's verisimilitude. For example, when the player is given control of Sarah in the prologue, she is mostly useless as an avatar—she cannot interact directly with her environment, and she even responds sluggishly to player commands, simulating a young girl struggling to come fully awake. While players gain access to more complex avatar control as the game progresses, moments of verisimilar limitations resurface whenever Joel is burdened or injured and when Ellie is finally made available for player control. In more general terms, the gamer connects empathetically and, to a certain extent, physically because of the rather unusual and unique limitations placed on the avatars throughout the game.

Weise claims that in recent years "there has been a general drift away from the anxiety of disempowerment towards the thrill of empowerment,"[33] but *The Last of Us* restores the helplessness and vulnerability found in the original *Resident Evil* game, drawing players more effectively into the story and bonding them firmly with the characters. Krzywinska rightly claims that "the primary theme of horror is the relationship between power and power-lessness,"[34] and that tension is heightened in *The Last of Us* because, as with the later *Resident Evil* titles and other survival horror video games such as those in Konami's *Silent Hill* franchise (1999–2012), "exploratory play becomes guarded and wary, exacerbated by the scarcity of firepower provided."[35] Thanks to the limits placed upon Joel and Ellie as avatars, *The Last of Us* requires a lot of running away, hiding, and shooting weapons from a safe distance. Unlike other, more contemporary video games, though, Joel doesn't have a limitless supply of ammunition; often times, players must find alternative paths forward than simply relying upon a gun—although many of those options are equally (if not more so) violent: strangling, beating a target to death, or using a shiv. A remarkable narrative feature of *The Last of Us* as yet unseen in any zombie film is the game's insistence that players rely on their auditory senses to facilitate their visual ability. Rather than just seeing obvious threats that they need to shoot, stab, and destroy, gamers experience another layer of verisimilitude because they must regularly stop, hide, and *listen*. While listening carefully, players get a kind of "sonar" version of what Joel hears, allowing them to "see" targets in other rooms and to track the movements of foes, both human and infected alike. With patience, these threats can be efficiently dispatched; in many situations, however, they must simply be avoided.

Gamers must likely learn Joel's limitations and weaknesses the hard way; I certainly had to when I played through *The Last of Us*. Early in the game, during the chapter "The Outskirts," Joel must drop down into a clutch of rooms on the ground floor of a dilapidated office building. A number of runners and clickers populate the space, standing still or wandering the rooms with funereal slowness, and players must advance gradually and cautiously to make the way safe for the waiting Tess and Ellie. If players move Joel too quickly, the runners hear and come running; if they move Joel around a corner without listening carefully first, a clicker grabs him from behind and kills him. Needless to say, the learning curve can be steep; I watched Joel die over and over again before I learned to adopt a more cautious approach. During the "Pittsburgh" chapter, players must get Joel safely across a city square teeming with human renegades. Even though Ellie can protect Joel somewhat with a scoped rifle from a fire escape, players must nonetheless creep warily through the space, crouching behind stalled vehicles, sneaking around corners and up the stairwells of the neighboring buildings, and ducking out of the way of foes at the last possible moment. I navigated this stage of the game by hiding in a room filled with desks and room dividers, waiting for my enemies to patrol the space one at a time so I could jump out and choke them to death. The fear that I might be discovered unprepared or overwhelmed by a mob of villains increased with each kill, and the anxiety I felt was real, not merely simulated. By the time the area was cleared, I was literally sick to my stomach. For those nerve-wracking moments in that digital environment, I *was* Joel, and that subjective identification had been all the more real thanks to the replicated uncertainty and vulnerability.

The Last of Us places gamers in even more perilous and vulnerable situations when they control Ellie, who has limited access to weapons for most of the game and doesn't enjoy the benefits of any of the power-ups players might have assigned to Joel. While she uses a bow and arrow with great efficiency, she cannot kill an enemy with melee weapons as quickly as Joel, although she does have an indestructible switchblade she can use to assassinate targets if she successfully sneaks up on them. While controlling Ellie, then, gamers must be even more cautious and more frugal in their expenditure of health supplies or powerful weapons such as the Molotov cocktail. One of the most challenging sequences in *The Last of Us*, coming at the end of the "Lakeside Resort" chapter, pits the player against the megalomaniacal cannibal leader David (Nolan North), who has locked Ellie in an abandoned restaurant. David stalks Ellie relentlessly around the empty booths and through the kitchen with a machete, and while a single sneak attack with a switchblade has taken out human foes up to this point in the game, David must be successfully stabbed three times before the storyline can progress. The player must keep Ellie crouched low, using her rudimentary listening skill to track David, all the while avoiding shattered plates on the floor that give away her position. While I was playing this sequence of *The Last of Us*, I repeatedly failed at sneaking up on David, and, as a result, I was forced to watch him butcher Ellie over and over with his machete, a murder made all the more upsetting thanks to realistic Foley sound effects and a chilling music cue. The recurring death scenes only heightened my anxiety for my vulnerable avatar, making each attempt to attack David all the more challenging. Hopefully, though, the player will invariably succeed, as I did eventually, kill David, and see gamer control switch back over to the more capable Joel.[36]

While emotional engagement with the protagonist avatars keeps players captivated by the game and its narrative, perhaps the most important question to address when discussing *The Last of Us* as a progressive, inventive, and relevant zombie video game is whether we should even consider it a zombie video game at all. According to Weise, the "contemporary digital zombie" must eat flesh, require the destruction of the brain, move slowly, and infect its victim.[37] The monsters featured in *The Last of Us*, being merely infected humans and not the reanimated dead, fail on at least two of these counts, but does that mean they *aren't* zombies? I have established a kind of notoriety on Twitter for being incredibly myopic when it comes to what constitutes a zombie, but my personal obsession with taxonomy may not be as restrictive as it first appears. For me, the primary quality of a zombie, which goes back to the monster's folkloric origins in Haitian Vodou tradition, is the lack of conscious agency. Since Romero, zombies are often classified as violent and voracious flesh eaters, mindless drones (usually part of a horde or army) that relentlessly attack and feast upon the living, communicating their condition either directly through their bites (as with viral zombies) or indirectly as a result of their victim's death (as in Romero-style zombies). The infected foes of *The Last of Us*—fast-moving runners, aggressive "stalkers," the more dangerous clickers, and the boss-like "bloaters"—demonstrate all of these fundamental characteristics: the infected cannot think or act on their own, they become part of a collective of human-hunting flesh-eaters, and their condition is highly contagious. Yet unlike the inexplicable living dead of Romero's oeuvre or the viral beasts of *28 Days Later* or AMC's *The Walking Dead* television series (2010–), the infected in *The Last of Us* are the result of a kind of plausible fungal infestation.

While Boyle's film presents a credible infection in terms of a mutated "rage" virus and Robert Kirkman's series a kind of viral agent that somehow reanimates the dead, *The Last of Us* proposes a version of the zombie monster founded on an actual, real-life phenomenon. Rather than proposing a pandemic apocalypse originating at the microscopic level, the scenario of *The Last of Us* is mycological, based on the reproductive cycle of a mind-controlling fungus. This unusual focus on the eukaryotic rather than the viral is artfully foreshadowed even before the game beings. The initial setup screen for *The Last of Us* is unexpected for a survival horror title: instead of featuring a violent preview or hi-resolution image of a monstrous foe, this game presents players with an almost static shot of an old, latticed window with peeling paint flanked by torn white curtains that drift lazily in a breeze. Most striking, however, is the intrusive presence of a verdant ivy vine, which has crept its way through one of the open window panels. The image sets up the unique premise of the video game—a post-apocalyptic adventure, yes, as indicated by the decrepit condition of the window, but one focused on biological life different from the more traditional mutants, marauders, or raised dead. After the player has selected a new game and saved the file, the screen goes black, interrupted by a quiet barrage of translucent dots and circles, images that will later be identified as fungal spores—the true monster of the game's narrative. This fungus is inspired by specialized species in the genus *Ophiocordyceps*, types of invasive parasites that effectively turn ants into mindless zombie insects.

In the bizarre tapestry of biological life on this planet, zombies do, in fact, exist. They are humble creatures that have lost control of their minds, and thus their bodies, in the service of ensuring the procreative potential of an invasive, parasitic force. Matt Simon, science writer for *Wired* magazine, explains how this "absurd creature," the zombie ant, works. Many species of the *Ophiocordyceps* fungus exist, and each has evolved to attack only a single species of ant. Once a spore has found its way into a poor ant's brain, the fungus takes over the motor functions of the insect, commanding it to climb a tree until just the right leaf with just the right temperature and in just the right humidity has been located. Its strange and terrifying reproductive process then begins to take place:

> Once the ant has anchored itself by sinking its mandibles into the leaf's vein, it perishes, and from the back of its head erupts a stalk, which, while in a way is quite beautiful, might be considered the world's least desirable hat. This in turn rains spores down onto the ant's fellow workers below, attaching to their exoskeletons and beginning what could euphemistically be called an invasive procedure.[38]

While the zombie ant isn't turned into a rampaging cannibal that directly attacks other ants, it nonetheless does infect its peers in a way that admittedly resembles the zombie plagues depicted in the movies.[39] This highly specialized reproductive cycle, while merely curious when observed in the insect kingdom, would represent a magnificently terrifying threat if *Ophiocordyceps* ever mutated to the point that humans could be infected in the same fashion, and thus the unexpectedly realistic premise of *The Last of Us*.

Rather than being manipulated by the willpower of a nefarious magician or mad scientist, instead of being reanimated by supernatural or cosmic forces, the apocalyptic monsters of *The Last of Us* are victims of an aggressive natural world. A fungus not unlike *Ophiocordyceps* has suddenly and inexplicably begun to infect human beings, sending its spores deep into the brains of its victims to overpower their higher functions while rewiring their basic motor functions. The resultant runners are driven to attack other humans violently, passing on their spores through a bite, feasting on their victim's flesh, or simply killing their targets outright in their madness and rage. As the fungus grows and expands through the ocular cavities, the once-human host loses its vision and must rely upon a primitive kind of echolocation to hunt, facilitated by the robust creature's constant clicking noises. At this point, the fungus may continue to grow and spread, transforming the host into a lumbering behemoth of blind violence, the bloater that rampages from one feckless victim to the next. More likely, however, the fungal influence will encourage its host to locate a dark and damp location, such as the corner of an abandoned building, to lie down and wait. Like zombie ants, the infected in *The Last of Us* find an ideal place to position themselves before the growing pressure of the expanding fungus ruptures through the victim's skull, filling the surrounding area with a dense cloud of parasitic spores, eagerly seeking a new, living target to begin the terrible cycle anew.[40] This kind of zombie, one directly inspired by a real-world phenomenon, presents fans of the subgenre with a plausible version of their beloved monster, one that manifests potential fears and anxieties concerning mortality, infection, and the natural environment itself.

While *The Last of Us* represents an exciting and immersive video game experience, one that pushes the limits of verisimilar computer graphics and interactive gameplay, what makes the game most relevant and important to zombie studies is how it manifests an inversion of the traditional adaptive model of the zombie narrative. As most zombie films and television programs continue to recycle tired story arcs and expected horror tropes, the dynamic and innovative nature of the video game is inspiring—even requiring—original ideas, new storylines, and more realistic zombie monsters. Not unexpectedly, fans of the zombie have grown tired of being passive spectators and now insist on being part of the action. The longer story arcs and more savvy consumers require better story telling, richer environments, more sympathetic and interesting characters, and new levels of anxiety and fear, often the result of greater simulated vulnerability and more plausible monsters. I'm regularly asked if I believe the zombie apocalypse could ever happen, a query I have regularly answered in the negative; however, *The Last of Us* makes me think that perhaps the zombie does indeed represent the *most* likely of the supernatural monsters. If *Ophiocordyceps* could ever mutate and jump to mammalian infestation, it could learn to target human beings. Maybe another natural agent entirely could develop with the potential to attack the human brain, rendering us mindless, voracious monsters. Without the possibility, however remote, of appearing in the real world, monsters can never transcend their status of allegory, and *The Last of Us* reminds us that real monsters are out there, and they are sometimes more strange and terrible than those we invent for speculative storytelling.

Chapter 8

THE NON-ZOMBIE ZOMBIE
The Tragically Misidentified Draugar
of *Dead Snow*

"I reckon you small, spoilt brats couldn't be bothered to read a little
local history about the area before you snow-scootered in here?
Events have occurred here. Events that people prefer to keep quiet
about."

—Turgåer, *Død Snø*

Since September 11, 2001, horror movies in both the U.S. and abroad—
not *just* zombie films—have enjoyed a resurgence in production and popularity that matches, and often directly mirrors, the halcyon days of the 1970s.[1]
Slasher and monster movies have been as popular as ever, and foreign horror
films are building on the popularity of U.S. films while simultaneously taking
advantage of their own culture's folkloric and mythological narratives and
traditions, such as Joon-ho Bong's *Gwoemul* (2006, *The Host*) from South
Korea, J. A. Bayona's *El orfanato* (2007, *The Orphanage*) from Spain, and
Tomas Alfredson's *Låt den rätte komma in* (2008, *Let the Right One In*) from
Sweden. Tommy Wirkola's 2009 Norwegian horror film *Død Snø* (*Dead
Snow*), for example, presents audiences with a refreshingly original and postmodern version of both the stereotypical U.S. slasher movie and the modern
zombie narrative. In the film, a feckless group of medical students hikes into
the frozen backcountry of Norway for an isolated weekend of drinking, par-
tying, and sexual exploits. Much like Drew Goddard's more recent *Cabin the
Woods* (2011), Wirkola's film is not only constantly aware of its own cinematic
antecedents, but the movie's characters are as well. Numerous references to
famous U.S. horror films abound, along with discussions of other aspects of
contemporary popular culture.

This abundant, postmodern self-awareness means the unexpected arrival of a mysterious wanderer at the beginning of the film comes as no real surprise to anyone. As the rugged Turgåer (Bjørn Sundquist) drinks the coffee and beer offered him, he harshly upbraids the med students for being so woefully ignorant of their own Norwegian myths, legends, and history. He weaves a dramatic tale of Nazi soldiers, stolen gold, and vengeful revenants hidden in the frozen wilderness around them. Before storming off into the night, he warns the campers about the dangers awaiting them—and dangers soon abound indeed. In classic horror film fashion, the cabin is soon besieged, not by serial killers or demons but by a relentless army of moldering, reanimated Nazi soldiers. The med students, drawing solely on their knowledge of U.S. horror movies, instantly assume the murderous creatures are zombies—after all, they are animated dead bodies that bite and appear to eat their prey—and they base all their survival plans and efforts on the "rules" that have been established by George A. Romero's films. Everything the students do to combat the relentless Nazi monsters fails, however, and they make rash decisions based on their initial assumptions. In the end, not surprisingly, all but one of the med students is dead and the "zombies" have triumphed.

But here's the rub and the reason I find the film so fascinating: the voracious and unstoppable Nazi creatures are *not*, in fact, zombies, at least not in terms of the U.S. cinematic tradition. If the students had taken Turgåer's cryptic advice, they might have realized they were dealing with *draugar*, a particular kind of supernatural, undead monster native to Norway. These walking dead creatures, unlike either the Vodou or the Romero-style zombies, can think, organize, and use tools and weapons. In addition, they are *not* contagious or even technically cannibalistic—they bite and stab and kill, but all they really want is to protect their treasure from looters. Because the draugar behave more in the manner of vengeful mummies, the med students could have avoided their violent and unnatural deaths if they had only handed over the box of gold and jewels they had found in the remote cabin and made a hasty retreat from the mountain. I read Wirkola's film as a subtle if powerful argument to native Norwegian viewers: don't be so quick to replace the Norse mythology and heritage of Scandinavia with the trivial pop culture of the United States. Instead of memorizing meaningless plots and amassing contemporary trivia, the youth of Norway should learn their *own* folklore and understand their *own* history first.

Dead Snow can be read as a rebuttal of the current Renaissance of zombie films and other such narratives; that is, the zombie isn't the only walking dead creature that has terrifying and moralistic stories to tell. The term *zombie* has specific references and connotations, representing a species of monster unique to modern American culture,[2] and its haphazard application to other creatures, cultures, and narratives belies either a lazy taxonomy or a strategic marketing ploy. *Zombie* has become a popular catchall term for almost any reanimated monster, and one that is likely deployed to take advantage of a broader cultural movement. Because filmgoers are less likely to accept and embrace a new or unfamiliar monster, producers, filmmakers, and distributors use familiar labels—such as *vampire* or *zombie*—to make monster movies more palatable and marketable. However, all countries have their own monsters, and they should be allowed, even encouraged, to tell their stories as well. The imposition of U.S. taxonomies upon the folklore, mythology, and monsters of other nations and cultures is analogous to the established Hollywood practice of remaking successful foreign films, a form of "colonial adaptation" that undermines the value of global storytelling and misses opportunities for cultural education. Zombies, while admittedly pretty great, aren't the only game in town.

Taxonomy of the (Un)Dead

When it comes to fictional beasts, any scientific taxonomy is a tricky proposition, one complicated by the subjective nature of creativity and imagination. When dealing with monstrous creatures, the process is even more difficult, if not futile. Jeffrey Jerome Cohen, author of the "Seven Theses" of monster culture, has tweeted, "The monster is not a category that names a phenomenon but the name for a breakdown of categorization when excluded impurities self assert."[3] Monsters, by their very nature, represent a challenge to traditional, natural, and scientific classification. They are almost always liminal creatures, manifesting either aberrant mutations or unholy fusions. As such, can an inhuman and unnatural monster even be categorized? I propose such an effort has value. Building on Cohen's admonition that "taxonomy is a kind of poetry,"[4] I suggest my argument in terms of a rhetorical poetics. To establish the value of recognizing the monsters of *Dead Snow* as Norwegian draugar instead of American zombies, I will first present a number of "zombie-like" monsters that already appear in horror films and literature—various reanimates and revenants from a variety of cultures and folklores—and build my case that they should be allowed to shine on their own, rather than being nonchalantly misclassified as something more familiar and popular.

Almost every world culture has a tradition of ghosts and the reanimated dead, but not all of those traditions should be casually labeled as "zombies."

Despite similarities present in a variety of folklores and mythologies, the term *zombie* has a specific cultural etymology, one inexorably tied to the Vodou religion of postcolonial Haiti. The original zombie is a human being who has been poisoned by a nefarious *bocor*, rendering him or her a mindless slave, one likely brain damaged or lobotomized, not dead.[5] Not surprisingly, the key characteristic of this post-slave trade terror is loss of autonomy and individuality; the zombie is not a monster to be feared but rather a fate worse than death.[6] Although the postmodern cinematic zombie developed by Romero and his imitators represents a number of major changes to this folkloric antecedent, the core feature of enslavement remains. Romero's zombies, which persist as the most pervasive version in contemporary popular culture, may be animated corpses that attack the living and infect them with their voracious bites, but their condition is fundamentally one of enslavement. Zombies in both cases are creatures without conscious will, enslaved by evil sorcerers, as in *White Zombie* (1932, directed by Victor Halperin); by invading aliens, as with *Invisible Invaders* (1959, directed by Edward L. Cahn); or by a viral infection, as with *28 Days Later* (2002, directed by Danny Boyle).

Four "undead" monsters in particular from a variety of global folklores resemble the American zombie closely enough to warrant closer examination: the Chinese *jiangshi*, the Middle Eastern *ghul*, the Anglo Saxon *revenant*, and the Scandinavian *draugr*. In 2011, the History Channel, eager to add its authoritative voice to the increasingly pervasive discussion concerning the walking dead, broadcast a documentary on the cultural history of the zombie that somewhat sensationally presented these four "zombie-like" monsters as the "real" origins of "true zombies." Rather than providing viewers with a serious academic investigation into the supernatural beliefs of other cultures, however, David V. Nicholson's *Zombies: A Living History* focuses its rhetorical efforts on trying to prove the zombie we all know and love is *not*, in fact, a manifestation of Haitian folk beliefs or even an American cinematic invention. While I obviously disagree strenuously with this reductive and largely unsubstantiated claim, the documentary nevertheless sheds light on a variety of mythologies and folklores that demonstrate the idea of a corpse returning from the dead to menace or even kill the living is a pervasive and universal fear. Furthermore, the special illustrates a host of supernatural creatures just waiting in the wings to be cast as the monstrous stars of their own feature films, books, or video games.

Nicholson claims the modern-day zombie has existed since the second century BCE with China's legend of the jiangshi. According to celebrated zombie novelist Jonathan Maberry, author of *Rot & Ruin* (2010), "the jiangshi is a fascinating and terrible monster from Chinese folklore. It's a hungry ghost that returns to devour the living ... as a retribution for not being properly buried."[7] This account sounds more like a vengeful ghost or poltergeist, but other accounts of the jiangshi speak of the creature as a corporeal manifestation. The online *Mythical Creatures Guide* describes the jiangshi as a reanimated corpse that can appear at various stages of decomposition. An evil necromancer either raises them from the dead, or they appear when the soul is trapped in its body due to a sinful life or suicide.[8] This terrifying creature "cannot speak, has pale skin, long claw-like fingernails, and a long prehensile tongue."[9] Because of rigor mortis, this "stiff corpse" must hop along, and "when it comes across a victim it will suck the life force out of them,"[10] a process that often results in the creation of another jiangshi.[11] The jiangshi has not been traditionally equated with the zombie at all but rather the more familiar vampire, yet the jiangshi isn't technically either—it has its own monstrous identity.

In fact, the jiangshi had already enjoyed a measure of cinematic success in Asia long before our current global fascination with the designation "zombie." One of the earliest appearances of this creature is in Sammo Kam-Bo Hung's 1980 film *Gui da gui* (*Encounter of the Spooky Kind*), a kung-fu action horror film that set a new standard for the subgenre. In the film, the unlikely hero Bold Cheung (Hung) must spend the night in a haunted temple and fight the stiff-armed animated corpse of legend. Ricky Lau's *Geung si sin sang* (*Mr. Vampire*) from 1985 follows in Hung's footsteps, although this later film is more comedic and features jiangshi that bear a closer resemblance to the European vampire. Wei Tung's 1990 film *Qu mo jing cha* (*Magic Cop*), also known as the fifth film in the *Mr. Vampire* series, has more of a horror flavor to it, while remaining nonetheless driven by action and special effects. The "Magic Cop" is Uncle Feng (Ching-Ying Lam), who joins forces with the Hong Kong police department to battle an evil sorceress (Michiko Nishiwaki), who commands both ghosts and jiangshi, although these creatures are admittedly more zombie-like in appearance, despite their skill at martial arts. More recently, versions of the jiangshi have appeared in the television series *Ngo wo geun see yau gor yue wui* (1998, *My Date with a Vampire*) and in the "Chi of the Vampire" episode of the animated *Jackie Chan Adventures* television series (2002, directed by Chap Yaep).

Nicholson's documentary next addresses a legend from ancient Arabian folklore, citing the ghul—more commonly rendered as "ghoul"—as the primary case of an "ur-zombie." Maberry describes this mythological terror as "a female demon ... [or] someone who had fallen from grace with God ... [who had become] a horrific, devouring monster."[12] While this creature might resemble the American zombie in its propensity to consume human flesh,

Maberry clearly refers to the ghoul as a demon, *not* an animated corpse; nevertheless, the monster deserves a closer look. The earliest recorded reference to the ghoul comes from *The Thousand and One Nights*. In Edward Forster's English translation, Shehrazade tells the sultan, "Your majesty knows that Ghouls of either sex are demons, which wander about the fields. They ... surprise passengers, whom they kill and devour. If they fail in meeting with travelers, they go by night into burying places to dig up dead bodies and feed upon them."[13] According to Robert Lamb, an inaccurate (perhaps even fabricated) French translation of the tale by Antoine Galland resulted in this version of the story; nevertheless, that account is likely responsible for the type of ghoul that appears in William Beckford's 1786 novel *Vathek* and other Gothic narratives.[14] Monsters similar to the ghoul appear in other cultures as well, including the Indian *pey*, which fed on the blood of dying soldiers, and the Tibetan *Pishachi*, which are physical manifestations of denied emotions that torment their victims psychologically.[15]

As indicated, the ghoul has enjoyed a rich literary tradition, appearing in stories and poems for centuries. Lord Byron briefly references the creatures in his 1813 poem "The Giaour," and Hans Christian Andersen describes their feasting on human corpses rather vividly in his fairy tale "The Wild Swans" (1838). Edgar Allan Poe refers to ghouls in his poems "Ulalume" (1847) and "The Bells" (1848), albeit with little description or detail, and H. P. Lovecraft arguably draws upon the legend of the ghoul for both his "Pickman's Model" (1926) and the novella *The Dream-Quest of Unknown Kadath* (1926). Types of ghouls have appeared in a number of recent novel series, including Larry Niven's *Ringworld* books (1970–2004), Chelsea Quinn Yarboro's ongoing *Saint-Germain* saga (1978–), Laurell K. Hamilton's popular *Anita Blake* series (1993–), and Jim Butcher's *The Dresden Files* novels (2000–). Ghouls feature prominently in Neil Gaiman's *The Graveyard Book* (2008), and rather harmless versions of the creatures can be found in J. K. Rowling's *Harry Potter* series (1997–2007). The ghoul has been less successful in cinema—apart from Freddie Francis's *The Ghoul* (1975), which actually uses the term to describe a human cannibal, and perhaps Luca Bercovici's *Ghoulies* (1984) and its many sequels—although Romero did, of course, chose that designation to describe the monsters he created for *Night of the Living Dead* (1968).

A more likely kin to the modern-day zombie comes in the form of the revenant as recorded by the 12th century English historian William of Newburgh. Maberry presents Newburgh's records as undisputed fact, claiming, "His writings became very important to the church at the time, because they were a doorway into trying to understand, identify, and eventually exterminate these monsters that were returning to plague the living."[16] Despite this sensational presentation of William of Newburgh as the world's first zombie hunter, the revenants described in the actual record are far more benign.[17] The stories recounted in *Historia rerum Anglicarum* tell of ghostlike creatures that represent a "serious nuisance," but not monsters that attack and kill the living.[18] Nevertheless, he does record a frightening phenomenon that apparently occurred with some frequency:

> It would not be easy to believe that the corpses of the dead should sally (I know not by what agency) from their graves, and should wander about to the terror or destruction of the living, and again return to the tomb, which of its own accord spontaneously opened to receive them, did not frequent examples, occurring in our own times, suffice to establish this fact, to the truth of which there is abundant testimony.[19]

In French historian Claude Lecouteux's study on ghosts in pagan traditions, he describes anything that returns from the grave to influence the living—even during the daytime—as a revenant.[20] However, he also emphasizes that revenants are *not* evanescent but "flesh and blood individuals"[21]; that is, these kinds of menacing "ghosts" are always corporeal, but as such, the term is often applied to any reanimated or resurrected being, including both vampires and zombies. With this definition, hundreds of books and movies could be classified as "revenant" narratives, with the most overt being Robin Campillo's 2004 film *Les revenants* (*The Returned*) and the 2012 television adaptation of the same name from creator Fabrice Gobert.

Lastly, Nicholson addresses the draugar from Scandinavian mythology, powerful and vengeful creatures that relentlessly guard their burial sites and treasure. A draugr—also known as an *aptrgangr*, or "after-goer"[22]—is a reanimated corpse that "comes forth from its grave-mound, or shows restlessness on the road to burial."[23] These Scandinavian revenants are "large, alarming, and sometimes black in color, and often harmful. They inhabit the mounds and tumuli, and, unable to find peace there, return. They are also spirits of a kind that guards treasures."[24] Nicholson's documentary boldly describes the Norwegian revenant as "history's most savage zombie," and *Fangoria* writer Rebekah McKendry describes the draugar as "people who had come back from the dead ... as unstoppable machines."[25] In addition to supernatural strength, Maberry claims the Norwegian draugr also retains "some degree of its own intelligence, which makes it a little more frightening because it knows what it is and delights in what it is."[26] Despite the claims made by the documentary, these featured experts systematically describe a monster that sounds more like a mummy—a conscious, unstoppable monster returned from the grave to seek vengeance upon the trespassing living.

Each of these folkloric creatures pay more than a passing resemblance to the monsters currently called "zombies"; however, even the most superficial of investigations reveals these creatures possess unique attributes and abilities that unequivocally separate them from both voodoo-style zombies and Romero's apocalyptic, viral zombies. As I have shown, the jiangshi, far from being a "missing link" in the evolution of the Western zombie, is actually a somewhat successful cinematic monster in Asian culture already, and the ghoul, while not featured as often on the screen, appears in a number of Gothic texts and strongly influenced Romero's creative process. The monster that hasn't enjoyed as much success on its own merit is the draugr, a wonderfully terrifying creatures that has, until quite recently, been languishing in the obscurity of ancient Scandinavian heroic sagas. But things are changing for the aptrgangr, which does feature in the 1980 novel *The Sword and the Satchel* by Elizabeth H. Boyer, the first in her *World of the Alfar* series, and they appear as "draugs" in Rachel Caine's *The Morganville Vampires* series (2006–2014). Additionally, the draugar are particularly prominent foes in the video game *The Elder Scrolls V: Skyrim* (2011, directed by Todd Howard), in which the mummy-like creatures guard various tombs and crypts. Wirkola has certainly brought these monsters into the mainstream with *Dead Snow*, in which he has repurposed the draugar for a modern audience while taking on the global popularity of the zombie at the same time.

The Nazi Draugar of *Dead Snow*

Wirkola's film begins like so many well-known horror movies, with a panicked woman running aimlessly through a dark forest as shadowy, nondescript shapes pursue her. Paying no mind to whipping branches or deep snowdrifts, she rushes on, pausing only once to look behind her. Her flight is accompanied somewhat unexpectedly by a classical score, but the significance of Norwegian Edvard Grieg's "In the Hall of the Mountain King" (1867), which tells the tale of barbaric trolls ruling a mountain kingdom, becomes increasing clear as the film unfolds. Indeed, when the woman stops to scan the dark woods behind her carefully, a monstrous figure, a gray and moldering soldier, suddenly springs out of nowhere, as if rising from the very ground before her. She runs on, trips, falls, and crashes down a hillside. Crumpled and helpless at the bottom, she is set upon by three superhuman soldiers, creatures that move with lightning speed, growl like wild animals, and rend and tear her soft flesh with their teeth and claws. At first glance, the undead warriors of *Dead Snow* do bear some resemblance to the modern zombie—

especially the viral, fast-moving creatures of films such as *28 Days Later* (2002, directed by Danny Boyle)—but more details remain to be revealed. Viewers familiar with "cabin in the woods"-style slasher films and zombie apocalypse narratives may think they know what they are getting into, but Wirkola has many secrets and surprises in store.

After the blood-red title "Dead Snow" appears starkly against the dark sky next to the full moon, the film cuts to the next day and continues to establish itself as a stereotypical slasher movie, one deliberately operating in the tradition of *Friday the 13th* (1980, directed by Sean S. Cunningham), *The Evil Dead* (1981, directed by Sam Raimi), *April Fool's Day* (1986, directed by Fred Walton), and *Evil Dead II* (1987, also directed by Raimi). Wirkola's intentionality is clear here, as the characters of the film will come to compare their situation to all four of these films by name. These eight friends and acquaintances—an even number of men and women, to maximize the sexual potential—are heading into the woods for a long weekend of recreation, play, and fraternization. The four men, all riding together in one car, innocuously discuss the dangers of venturing into the backwoods, specifically the risks associated with avalanches. Roy (Stig Frode Henriksen) tells the chilling story of a man who died buried in the snow because he had become disoriented and had dug his way down instead of up. Vegard (Lasse Valdal), the driver of the car and most familiar with the area, sneers at the stupidity of the feckless victim. He had been taught in the military to spit when buried in snow to determine which way to dig—since the spit would fall down, one should always dig in the opposite direction. This conversation, while resembling the kind of mindless blather typical of low-budget slasher films, might appear insignificant at first, but it foreshadows how the young med students would be wise to take the simplest, most logical course of action to survive the terror awaiting them, a course of action they will all subsequently fail to follow.

Two more conversations take place that establish Wirkola's movie is both aware it's a stereotypical horror film and defiant against the established Hollywood entertainment industry. As six of the students hike along the snowmobile track Vegard has left behind him to guide their way, Erlend (Jeppe Beck Laursen), the group's pop-culture expert and "world's biggest movie nerd,"[27] asks how many horror movies begin with a group of people going to a remote mountain cabin with no cell phone service for the weekend.[28] The group laughs him off and chides him for his obsession with U.S. cinema, but, then again, the group *is* about to find themselves in a stereotypical horror film. Regardless, they arrive without incident at the cabin, an isolated and dusty old shack clearly coded as an antiquated Gothic location, and after a cheerful montage of inner tubing, eating hotdogs, and playing in the snow, some of the group take part in a spirited game of Twister. With an air of disgust, Roy asks, "Why do we play this game?" From his position entangled with two women on the game mat, Erlend replies, "Because Hollywood told us it's so much fun." The line is played for laughs, but I think it's the key to understanding the entire film. From this point on, the characters act and react *not* based on the scientific logic espoused by Vegard but rather in an attempt to do what Hollywood, through horror movies in general and zombie films in particular, *tells* them to.

Just after dark, the cabin is visited by a harbinger of doom, an older man whose voice will cry unheeded in the wilderness like so many of his kind in other horror movies. Turgåer reproaches the med students for their frivolity and lack of respect for the countryside around them. As he rolls a cigarette, he spits, "I reckon you small, spoilt brats couldn't be bothered to read a little local history about the area before you snow-scootered in here? Events have occurred here. Events that people prefer to keep quiet about." In a decidedly unsettling monologue, Turgåer educates them in "local history," a tale of Nazi occupation, wholesale theft, and village uprising. According to Turgåer, the brutally evil Colonel Herzog, who had tortured and tormented the villagers for three years, led his soldiers in the pillaging of Øksford when he realized the war was about to end. The outraged citizens organized and, bearing any weapons they could muster, attacked the German force at night. Many of the soldiers were killed, but the devil Herzog and his remaining troops fled into the mountains with all the community's gold, silver, and jewels. While the Germans likely froze to death, Turgåer cautions his attentive young audience that one must still tread cautiously. "There is an evil presence," he concludes. "An evil one does not want to awake." As would be expected, the students scoff at the story, especially the ever-skeptical Roy, who thinks their schooling will save them, and Turgåer suddenly lashes out, grabbing Roy tightly by the throat and asking him, "If you stand with your own intestines in your hands, then what do you do? Or get your limbs torn off? What will you do then? Did they teach you that?" The stunned students have no answers, and Turgåer storms back out into the dark night.

Unbeknownst to the young, lighthearted med students, Turgåer is talking about a troop of Nazi draugar, living dead monsters that haunt the surrounding woods to protect both their burial place and their ill-gotten treasure. As mentioned above, these creatures can be understood as Scandinavia's version of the Egyptian mummy. According to Rudolf Simek's *Dictionary of Northern Mythology*, draugar are powerful and violent revenants found in burial mounds across northern Europe that "might involve grave robbers in fights and who became a threat to both men and animals especially at midwinter."[29]

In addition to these defining features, Lecouteux ascribes four chief characteristics to the draugar: (1) corporeality, (2) retention of any wounds suffered in life, (3) the ability to disappear into the ground, and (4) immense resilience, as their bodies must be completely destroyed for them to be defeated.[30] Antiquarian Hilda Roderick Ellis-Davidson identifies even more supernatural attributes associated with some versions of the draugar from Nordic sagas, including the ability to change their shape and size, control the weather, or even see into the future.[31] While Wirkola's monsters fail to exhibit any of these latter paranormal traits, they do adhere to the other definitive qualities, particularly the four enumerated by Lecouteux, in their unflagging efforts to guard their icy tombs and stolen treasure.

The students might have enjoyed their long weekend unmolested if they had only avoided disturbing the draugar and threatened their spoils of war. This violation implicitly occurred before the events depicted in *Dead Snow*, for Sara (Ane Dahl Torp), the owner of the cabin, was the poor woman murdered by the draugar in the film's pre-title sequence. When Erlend takes a six-pack of Pilsner beer from the cold-storage compartment sunk into the cabin's floor, a subtle puff of white smoke or mist is sucked into the glowing keyhole of a small wooden chest hidden there. That night, Vegard has a nightmare in which he sees the long-overdue Sara closing the trapdoor to the compartment, a space now full of glowing mist. She goes outside, and he follows to find her standing in the dark with blood oozing from her mouth. The portent of the vision is clear: at some recent point, Sarah found a chest of the Nazi's stolen treasure and hid it in her family's cabin, and she has now paid the ultimate price for her apparent transgression. The next morning, Erlend (wearing a *Braindead* T-shirt,[32] no less) finds the hidden chest and opens it with the others gathered closely around. Their faces are illuminated by a warm glow coming from the gold coins, jewelry, and other trinkets lying inside.[33] In their excitement, they each touch, fondle, and even don some of the treasure, thus implicating them all as Sara's criminal accomplices. Martin (Vegar Hoel) puts a stop to their play, reasoning the gold isn't theirs to take, but Hanna (Charlotte Frogner) slips a single coin into Martin's pants pocket. From that moment, the gold marks the students for death, in much the same was as the cursed treasure plundered from a pharaoh's Egyptian tomb.

Giving the monsters of *Dead Snow* such a pointed, purposeful, and *personal* reason for their murderous rampage certainly challenges the generic conventions of most zombie narratives. These fiends are not operating at the behest of some evil sorcerer or alien race, nor are they merely driven by blind instinct and ravenous desire. As stated, the Norse draugar behave more like the classic mummy, returning from the dead to protect their burial sites and treasure. Ellis-Davidson says that in most of the folkloric tales, "[t]he majority of these battles [between the living and the dead] take place in the burial mound itself, when the living man has broken his way in to take possession of the treasures in the guardianship of the dead,"[34] and Wirkola, working with co-screenwriter Stig Frode Henriksen, scripts a chilling scene drawn directly from this legend. While those back at the cabin carelessly play with the plundered gold, Vegard, in his search for Sara, falls through the ice and into a system of caves. As he explores them, he finds some open graves, a clutch of World War II-era weapons, a Swastika flag, a row of helmets ... and Sara's decapitated head. He has apparently stumbled into a kind of burial mound, a lair filled with the draugar's possessions and trophies. As a trespasser, Vegard is soon attacked by the animated corpse of a German soldier, a growling beast that punches him repeatedly in the face, tries unsuccessfully to stab him with a bayonet, and only then attempts to bite him.[35] Vegard must bite back to enable his escape, and even then, just temporarily.

Needless to say, both the motivations behind the draugar attacks and the manner of their violent assaults differ significantly from the actions of most rampaging zombies. Ellis-Davidson writes how the draugr "is possessed of superhuman strength and unlimited malice."[36] Turgåer, camping by himself, is set upon by a swift figure that cuts his throat before jumping on him and hitting him over and over in the face with very powerful blows.[37] Back at the cabin, a draugr pulls Chris (Jenny Skavlan) backwards into the pit of the outhouse, slashes her viciously across her stomach, and then decapitates her and holds her head up to one of the windows to scare the other students,[38] a final malicious act that shows conscious thought, calculation, and wicked, sinister intent. Yet despite these differences from traditional zombie behavior, the isolated cabin is soon surrounded by reanimated Nazis, making *Dead Snow* a siege narrative reminiscent of so many post–Romero zombie movies, and as the monsters begin their assault, the students try to block and fortify all the doors and windows.[39] However, Erlend, despite all the wisdom he has allegedly gleaned from watching horror films, panics and allows himself to be grabbed by a monster reaching through a broken window; the draugr pulls his skull in half with its bare hands, causing Erlend's brain to fall wetly on the floor. These brutal attacks resemble not only those foreshadowed by Turgåer, but also those described from the folklore by Lecoutreux, who writes that when a draugr assaults a human, "he tears him to pieces, breaking all his bones."[40] Clearly, these beasts are more than mere mindless animals or reanimated corpses.

Despite Erlend's earlier declaration that they are dealing with zombies and should avoid being bitten at all costs, the monsters repeatedly demonstrate non-zombie-like attributes and behaviors. When the Nazi monsters of *Dead Snow* bleed, for example, their blood comes out in pulsing bursts, implying a beating heart, and they are repeatedly shown breathing, even gasping for breath. They rise up out of the ground (or out of the snow, at least); they punch and fight with their fists; and they can climb trees. Furthermore, and perhaps most tellingly, although Vegard is bitten by one of the fiends, he doesn't die from the wound nor come back as one of them.[41] In fact, none of the murdered protagonists rise from the dead or return as monsters themselves, key generic features of almost every zombie narrative. Finally, these creatures don't die, even when stabbed in the brain, shot with a machine gun, or dismembered—none of the solutions offered by Romero's films seem to work. And why would they? Because the beasts of *Dead Snow* are draugar, the Nazi monsters can only be destroyed by decapitation followed by cremation,[42] something the doomed med students, acting on Hollywood's lead alone, instead of an awareness of Norwegian folklore, simply don't know.

Once again following the expected protocols of the slasher subgenre, the protagonists of *Dead Snow* foolishly separate, and the thrilling violence accelerates to the film's conclusion. Martin and Roy accidentally light the cabin on fire in their inept efforts to defend it, and, at this point, the film devolves slightly in tragicomic farce, once again evoking Raimi's *Evil Dead* films, especially when the two survivors arm themselves with tools from the shed, including the obligatory chainsaw. Then, with less than a third of the movie left, the audience finally gets to see the reanimated Colonel Herzog (Ørjan Gamst), a monster that continues to take pride in his uniform and rank. He also retains the power to order the other fiends about like the loyal soldiers they still are, and he organizes his troops for a climatic assault against the ignorant interlopers. Accompanied by Norwegian pop music, Martin and Roy make their last stand, facing down a rushing platoon of Nazi draugar, slicing, dicing, and smashing their way to perceived freedom.[43] In the meantime, Vegard has somewhat recovered from his wounds and mounted a relic machine gun to the steering column of his snow scooter, and he arrives just in time to save his friends, like some kind of Western cavalry officer. In a glut of abject excess, he mows the Nazis down with his acquired weapon, runs them over with his snow scooter, and even uses its engine to grind one of their numbers into a soupy pulp.

The surviving women, on the other hand, have been desperately trying to flee the mountain to get help, but they are of course unsuccessful in their efforts. Draugar soldiers chase after Liv (Evy Kasseth Røsten) and Hanna, separating them from each other, and the only way Liv manages to best her pursuers is by activating one of the soldier's antique grenades. Before she does, however, she watches as the monsters methodically disembowel her—they don't appear to *eat* any of her flesh, and neither do those that later pull Vegard limb from limb. Unlike Romero-style zombies, these foes have no interest in recruiting others to their ranks; in fact, as I have stated, they *can't*, despite Erelend's hasty assessment of the situation. Once again, the tragicomic play of *Dead Snow* comes to bear, for when one of the monsters bites Martin on the arm, all he can think about is Erlend's pop culture advice: "Remember what Erlend said? Remember? Do not get bitten. Not matter what you do, don't get bitten.... You'll be infected if.... You'll become like them." Despite Roy's desperate plea that the creatures had slaughtered Vegard instead of turning him into a monster, Martin impulsively amputates his own limb with the chainsaw and efficiently cauterizes the stump. The punch line of the entire film, perhaps, comes when another draugr rises up from the snow and bites Martin firmly in the genitals, resulting in a wounded body part Martin is *not* willing to amputate.

By the end of the movie, violence has been proven to be the province of the monsters, not the tragic humans, but another solution to their plight might still be obtainable. Herzog, who appears to be the last draugr standing, confronts the two surviving men and growls, "Arise!" Dozens of fresh, new Nazis answer his call, and Martin and Roy have no choice but to make a mad dash back to the smoldering cabin. Roy never makes it, though—fulfilling Turgåer's dark prophecy, he dies with his intestines ripped from his body. Herzog approaches the corpse and gently removes a gold watch from Roy's pocket, providing concrete evidence that what primarily drives the creatures is the reacquisition of their stolen treasure. Martin sees, and he finally figures out the secret of the mountain. Amidst the crumbling wreckage of the cabin, he scavenges the treasure chest and hands it over to one of the Nazi soldiers. Herzog takes the box and holds it close, and the soldiers appear to be satisfied—a shift in the film's score to more serene, triumphant music certainly supports this interpretation. Martin, exhausted, wounded, and bleeding, staggers out of the woods and back to the waiting automobiles. He climbs into the driver's seat of Vegard's car, but as he reaches to insert the key into the ignition, one gold coin falls from his pocket, the coin Hanna had playfully hidden there earlier. Before Martin can do anything, Herzog suddenly smashes his fist through the window and the screen cuts to the closing credits. Like the draugar of legend, these monsters fulfill their unholy task and reclaim their stolen treasure.

While *Dead Snow* could merely be viewed as one of the latest in a series of twenty-first century zombie variants—a new take on an established narrative, a revisionist approach to a formula that might be growing stale—the film lends itself to a richer reading when viewed through the lens of Scandinavian folklore. Simply put, it's not a zombie movie. After all, Herzog only murders Roy to retrieve the gold watch he had stolen from the wooden chest, and Martin fails in his triumphant escape because of the coin left in his pocket. Rather than being pursued by a mindless horde of ravenous zombies, the tragic protagonists of *Dead Snow* are systematically punished for transgressing the supernatural laws of Norway, laws governing the respect required for the dead and their possessions, despite their being Nazis guarding stolen treasure. If authors and filmmakers were given the encouragement to pursue less popular, less familiar folkloric, mythological, and international legends, tales, and monsters, the world of horror storytelling would be fuller, more diverse, and less predictable. Frankly, I almost hope the next "big thing" in zombie cinema won't be zombies at all.

Chapter 9

THE ROMANTIC ZOMBIE
Warm Bodies
and the Monstrous Boyfriend

"I guess you can't be all that bad, Mr. Zombie."
—Julie, *Warm Bodies*

Over the past few decades, the popular conception of the vampire has shifted from a dangerous, bloodthirsty *monster* that threatens the safety of young women to a dangerous, bloodthirsty *hero* who represents the acme of romantic love for young women. This transformation of the original supernatural monster began, arguably, with Anne Rice's *Interview with the Vampire* (1976) and has reached worldwide profusion with Stephenie Meyer's popular *Twilight* series (2005–2008) and its many imitators. Even a cursory look at paranormal romance titles proves Karen Backstein's claim that "today's vampire—at least, that particular type of vampire who serves as the narrative's male lead and the heroine's love interest—has transformed into an alluring combination of danger and sensitivity, a handsome romantic hero haunted by his lust for blood and his guilt for the humans he killed in the past."[1] With the recent rise in popularity of the zombie monster, no one should be surprised many fans of the "walking dead" have longed for a similar version of their beloved creature, one they could also root for as a sympathetic protagonist. Yet as Peter Dendle rightly asserts, no creature should be "less conducive" to touching romance narratives than the zombie; nonetheless, the monster has certainly "held its own" in recent years.[2] Indeed, Fred Botting, writing about the modern zombie, claims, "no longer objects of hate or fear, monstrous others becomes sites of identification, sympathy, desire, and self-recognition."[3] As if on cue, then, the past few years have seen the birth of what Craig Derksen and Darren Hudson Hick have called the "agent zombie,"[4] or the thinking, feeling, evolved version of George A. Romero's famous flesh-eating foe.[5] Following in the footsteps of Rice and Meyer, narratives such as the web video *Zombie-American* (2005, directed by Nick Poppy), the film *Wasting Away* (2007, directed by Matthew Kohnen), and S.G. Browne's romance novel *Breathers: A Zombie's Lament* (2009) have given contemporary audiences zombies that are much more sympathetic, if not even lovable.

While the fully formed zombie romantic hero has been developing for years in the pages of paranormal romance and young adult titles, Jonathan Levine's zom-rom-com *Warm Bodies* (2013), based on the 2010 novel by Isaac Marion, marks the first mainstream feature film that offers audiences a zombie they can really fall for, the sweet and innocent "R" (Nicholas Hoult), anemically attractive, who knows how to treat a girl right—when he's not killing and eating her boyfriend, of course.[6] Although zombies, by their very nature, "reveal the ugliest human truth" that "we are piles of matter that consume and excrete other piles of matter,"[7] *Warm Bodies* asks audiences to rethink the definition of "monster," proposing zombies may simply be misunderstood victims who suffer at the brutal hands of uncaring humans. For Botting, this redirection of the traditional zombie narrative works by recoding difference as something desirable: "Otherness is rendered attractive in that it delivers a curious specialness: pain and trauma mark out the individual's irreducible uniqueness, and authorize its rights to speak against normative social pressures."[8] The zombies of *Warm Bodies* are indeed unique and have literal voices of their own, but the film remains unavoidably problematic. Like Edward Cullen before him, Levine's R is a monster in a more troubling way than simply his unfortunate existence as a walking corpse: he's a "bad-boy" who represents the kind of narcissistic and abusive partner to whom far too many women find themselves irresistibly attracted. Because of the way R manipulates the hybristophilic Julie (Teresa Palmer)—who begins the narrative as an essentially strong and confident woman—audiences are told to see romance where only selfish control and psychological abuse exist. More disturbing, however, is the prevailing theme *Warm Bodies* and similar paranormal romances propose, that what I call the "monstrous boyfriend" *can* change if a woman is only willing to love him deeply and truly enough.

Romeo, Edward and R the Zombie

Perhaps one of the most influential and archetypical romantic monstrous boyfriend narratives—or at least one that establishes the trope of love complicated by the male partner being an unacceptable Other—is William Shakespeare's *Romeo and Juliet* (1597), based on an ancient Italian tale of a doomed young couple. Famously the story of "star-cross'd lovers" who cannot openly express their feelings because of the "ancient grudge" that exists between their warring families,[9] *Romeo and Juliet* romanticizes forbidden emotions and attractions and presents the only viable outcome to be the death of both parties. In her astute analysis of the *Twilight* saga, Glennis Byron argues, "*Romeo and Juliet* has always had a particular appeal for adolescents, partly because it epitomizes *young* love in Western society, partly because it is so widely taught in schools, and perhaps also because of the frequent sentimentalization and modernization of the play by those who teach it."[10] The familiarity of the play enables a kind of romantic "short hand" most young adults will readily recognize, and its sentimentality and rather grim morbidity understandably resonate with angst-ridden adolescents. The appropriation of *Romeo and Juliet* by the modern paranormal romance world is a clear no-brainer, resulting in a wide array of books, graphic novels, movies, and television programs about lovelorn vampires, ghosts, werewolves, and, now somewhat ubiquitously, zombies.

By recasting the rather egotistical and fickle Romeo as a supernatural monster, a monster othered from his beloved Juliet because of his inhumanity, Shakespeare's tale can be marketed to an entirely new generation. Arguable the most successful of these retellings is Meyer's *Twilight* series, in which Romeo has become the lustful vampire Edward and Juliet the wide-eyed, innocent teenage girl Bella. In Shakespeare's masterwork, Romeo is portrayed as brash, spirited, and violently passionate, an immature young man who shifts his hormonal obsession from the lovely Rosaline to the verboten Juliet with hardly a second thought. Friar Laurence is quick to note the flaw in young Romeo's character, declaring,

> Holy Saint Francis, what a change is here!
> Is Rosaline, that thou didst love so dear,
> So soon forsaken? Young men's love then lies
> Not truly in their hearts, but in their eyes.[11]

Romeo desires whatever appeals to his senses, and Juliet inflames his lust (and extinguishes his judgment) because of the way she looks. In *Twilight*, Meyer's ancient vampire Edward reacts to his first encounter with Bella in much the same way. Despite his many years and supposed great experience and wisdom, the vampire quickly abandons both tradition and reason because Bella overwhelms his senses, specifically his olfactory ones. When Bella first walks past Edward, he "suddenly [goes] rigid in his seat,"[12] a sexually coded reaction to her physiological presence, later established to be her biological odor.

Romeo and Edward are thus presented as atavistic lovers, drawn to their respective objects of affection because of biological desire and—in the vampire's case—palpable hunger. However, with *Twilight* and similar supernatural romances, "the quintessential Gothic monster and the iconic 'star-crossed lovers' have been simplified and commodified, emptied of threat and tragedy, welcomed into the collective iconography of popular culture, and now, merged together."[13] This lessening of threat and tragedy for modern readers is problematic; yet, not surprisingly, this kind of merger has made its way into the world of the zombie apocalypse narrative as well. In fact, the ties among *Romeo and Juliet, Twilight*, and *Warm Bodies* are anything but subtle. For example, the first thing audiences see when they play the *Warm Bodies* DVD is the trailer for *Breaking Dawn: Part II* (2012, directed by Bill Condon), the fifth film in the *Twilight* franchise. On the one hand, this association is simply a matter of smart marketing: the *Twilight* books and films have been hugely successful among teens and adults alike, and the producers and distributors of *Warm Bodies* are understandably hoping for the same level of commercial success. On the other, though, the film is pre-coded as a similar kind of retelling of *Romeo and Juliet*, the story of a romanticized, somewhat monstrous young man and his insatiable desire for a beautiful young woman. However, whereas *Twilight*'s association with Shakespeare's classic is largely implicit, especially in its first installment, *Warm Bodies* presents itself as an intentional adaptation: the hero's name starts with an "R," his love interest is named "Julie," her best friend is training to be a nurse, he courts her at the base of a balcony, etc. *Warm Bodies* has the benefit of presenting itself in the same tonality as two iconic romantic narratives, and those associations insure a built-in, pre-established audience.

As with Romeo, R's attraction to Julie is initially coded in terms of how she delights his eye with her romanticized physical beauty; however, she is presented in terms of scent as well, as her human biology must be masked to prevent other zombies from attacking and devouring her. Because the zombies of *Warm Bodies* are robbed of speech, at least initially, their only form of contact with others, aside from the occasionally random physical collision, is staring awkwardly at each other. In other words, as with *Romeo and Juliet*, the "romance" of *Warm Bodies* is couched almost immediately in terms of a man's look, or what Laura Mulvey has famously called the "male gaze."[14] Mulvey's analysis of cinematic pleasure, while a bit dated and often challenged, rightly claims how scopophilia takes "other people as objects, subjecting them to a controlling and curious gaze,"[15] and R's behavior is no exception. In fact, his ocular aggression towards Julie, coupled with the narrative being presented from his cognitive perspective as well, leads the viewing audience to be complicit in the objectification of Julie. From the outset, she is presented as a "thing" to be possessed and controlled—admittedly with varying levels of success. Furthermore, R uses scent to brand Julie as his own. To bond her to him, and to keep the other zombies at bay, he smears blood and ichor on Julie's face, ostensibly masking the sensory output of her living biology while making her an object for his future "consumption." At a very visceral level, then, Julie becomes R's possession in both her visual appearance and her physical odor in ways that emulate the film's inspirational antecedents.

Furthermore, all three narratives share the same plot device to make the otherwise joyous union of two young lovers a dramatic complication: the ancient grudge or feud between their "families." For Shakespeare, this grudge amounts to little more than a multi-generational standoff between two aristocratic dynasties; in the paranormal romance world, however, the presented feud is about the divisions between humans and monsters, between prey and hunters. Byron points out how "[t]he conflict provided by the feud [of *Romeo and Juliet*] provides a perfect template for the problems encountered in romances between vampire and werewolf or vampire and human"[16]—or, in the case of *Warm Bodies*, between zombie and human. The first scene of Shakespeare's play foregrounds the longstanding familial dispute with the Capulets Sampson and Gregory exchanging first words and later drawn swords with the Montagues Abraham and Balthasar. A similar scene occurs in the first chapter of *Twilight*; while the initial interaction between the vampires and the humans lacks harsh words or an exchange of violence, Edward and his clan are nonetheless presented as aloof and alienated high school students who consciously separate themselves from everyone else in the cafeteria. *Warm Bodies'* first climatic scene more closely resembles Shakespeare's; through the use of cross-cut editing, the factions of zombies and humans appear almost as rival gangs, the hungry zombies shuffling ever closer to a group of human teenagers scavenging the apocalyptic wasteland for medical supplies. All three narratives firmly establish the othering of the male hero from the group associated with his future female obsession, thus setting up the romantic conflict that follows.

Despite such similarities, *Twilight* and *Warm Bodies* demonstrate diametrically opposite attempts to redeem the plot of *Romeo and Juliet* for the paranormal romance genre. While both stories retell the archetypal story of the impassioned star-crossed lovers with decidedly happy endings, they do so through contrasted resolutions to the protagonists' initial dissimilarities. In tragic climax of Shakespeare's play, the insurmountable differences between the Capulets and Montagues become as irreconcilable as those between life and death. Romeo, having killed himself when confronted with the illusion of Juliet's death, forever separates himself from his love by consuming a poisoned draught. The only way for Juliet to join him is in death, and she does so expediently with his dagger. Unfortunately, as Shakespeare largely relates a realistic romance, their shared death does little to provide either the young lovers or their families any kind of positive resolution. Over the course of the *Twilight* saga, however, audiences enjoy a fantasy that resolves the tragedy of *Romeo and Juliet* with a joyous outcome. Meyer's Romeo is *already* dead, and remains so throughout his love affair with Bella. When she ultimately joins her lover in death, the tragedy of *Romeo and Juliet* is cheated because of the characters' *un*death. In other words, Meyer holds true to Shakespeare's original tale, but she uses the loophole of vampirism to offer her fans a happy ending that resolves her Romeo and Juliet's differences by making them members of the same paranormal clan.

Warm Bodies, in contrast, proposes an even more supernatural resolution: the healthy transformation and even resurrection from R's monstrous condition of walking death. For R's story of angst and love to be even possible, the story must take many liberties with established zombie characteristics. On the one hand, R begins his tale with the expected limitation of grunting instead of speaking; shuffling about with a slow, plodding gait; and lacking the ability for higher-order thinking. On the other, though, he proves to be surprisingly dexterous—able to use a record player, for example—and, if the film's voice-over narration is to be accepted as literal, he actually *does* possess an extremely cogent thought process. Whereas the zombies of the 20th century were primarily devoid of human consciousness, independent thought, and agency, characteristics representing some of the only ties remaining between cinematic zombies and those depicted in Vodou folklore, modern zombies such as R understandably need a developed sense of self and personal identity to tell their own stories, especially romantic ones. And in the case of *Warm Bodies*, the story is essentially one of loneliness and love, requiring zombies such as R to have a heart as well as a mind. As his love for Julie develops and deepens, that heart begins to beat—literally—once more. R slowly remembers how to speak, learns to master his cannibalistic urges, and even finds a way back from his fate as a zombie. Whereas Edward's bite makes Bella undead like himself, Julie's love resurrects R and turns him back into a real, live boy who can safely love her in return.

Another key point of differentiation that contrasts *Twilight* and *Warm Bodies* from each other, not to mention their shared source material, lies in their oppositional target audiences and their perspectival foci. While *Romeo and Juliet* is largely a neutral presentation of the young lovers, *Twilight* is overtly written to fulfill a female reader's fantasy and to tell its story from

Bella's subjective point of view. Meyer's entire series is written in first person, giving readers exclusive insight into Bella's perspective, desires, and insights; as such, the series addresses female desire and sets the stage for the classic "bad boy" romantic scenario. Unlike *Twilight*, however, *Warm Bodies* is presented, for the most part, as R's story, told from his point of view and perspective through both anachronistic voiceover narration and subjective camera shots and editing. Rather than romanticizing the story of an "everywoman" girl seeking true love from a potentially dangerous source, then, *Warm Bodies* is the story of that potential danger personified, the monstrous boyfriend's quest to find love and not the other way around. At best, *Warm Bodies* seeks to fulfill male fantasies about obtaining the unobtainable woman; at worst, it advocates indulgence in narcissistic, selfish, and even sociopathic behavior to treat women as objects of both desire and possession. Perhaps even more troubling, *Warm Bodies* uses the sympathetic perspective of the manipulative, dangerous boyfriend to champion the misguided myth that a woman can transform her abusive lover into a caring, sensitive individual.

R, the Dark Triad and the Monstrous Boyfriend

The audience doesn't know much about R from the beginning of *Warm Bodies*, despite his insightful voiceover narration, because the zombie doesn't really know much about himself. What viewers come to learn, however, demonstrates R, like Edward before him, has something of a "dark" personality, belonging to what psychologists Delroy L. Paulhus and Kevin M. Williams have called the "Dark Triad." This collusion of three related traits of "offensive yet non-pathological personalities" includes narcissism, psychopathy, and Machiavellianism.[17] While acceptance and use of this personality model remains somewhat contested in clinical psychology,[18] it nevertheless affords cultural studies a fascinating framework with which to study the antihero or, in the case of the paranormal romance, the monstrous boyfriend, especially since males score much higher on the Dark Triad scale than women.[19] In their analysis of the antihero in popular culture, Peter K. Jonason et al. explore the specific personality qualities associated with the Dark Triad in an effort to understand the appeal in both fiction and real life of "bad boy" figures. The application of these traits reveals why a narrative such as *Warm Bodies* appeals to both men and women; as Jonason et al. argue, "men will be drawn to these shows as exemplars of how to live" and "women will be drawn to these shows because of the sexual appeal these 'bad boys' have."[20] However, as a monstrous "bad boy" figure, R evinces decidedly antisocial, dangerous, and disturbing behavior towards Julie, who allows herself to be manipulated and endangered in response. The appeal of a Dark Triadic anti-hero is therefore problematic at best.

While R presents himself through his endearing voiceover as something of a reluctant monster, the lonely young victim of some unspecified zombie apocalypse, his comments and behavior at the outset of the film establish him to be decidedly narcissistic. According to Jonason et al., narcissistic people demonstrate "grandiosity, need for admiration, lack of empathy, a sense of entitlement, and self-admiration."[21] Somewhat by definition, zombies are self-centered monsters, creatures driven by little more than their irrepressible desire to glut their carnal need to consume flesh and blood. That aspect of R's personality aside, he reveals himself to be narcissistic in other ways as well. Like the young, rich, and attractive heroes of other generic romances, R thinks only of himself, his needs, and his creature comforts. Like a vain Romantic hero, R's opening lines belie his desire for admiration, sharing how he wants to be respected by others despite his pale appearance and poor posture. As he wanders around an abandoned airport teeming with zombies similar to him-self, he wallows in self-pity because of his lack of memory, his loneliness, and his wish for contact with others, at the same time mocking the other zombies for how awful they look. More importantly, and very much unlike the other walking dead around him, R has appropriated a passenger airplane and turned it into a grandiose private residence that is part bachelor pad and part shrine. He's a zombie who feels entitled to his own space and privacy, surrounding himself with toys, trinkets, and phonographic music. When he does interact with his one zombie friend M (Rob Corddry), it's to satisfy his wish to go hunting, to fulfill the narcissistic desire that consumes all such ghouls. And, of course, R is no follower; when he shuffles towards the city, his gang of loyal zombie toadies follows on his heels.

As a zombie who hungers for human flesh, R expectedly behaves psy-chopathically as well. Hervey M. Cleckly and Robert D. Hare variously describe psychopathic behavior and emotions to include "low remorse, low fear, low empathy, egocentrism, exploitativeness, manipulativeness, impulsiv-ity, aggression, and criminality,"[22] and these traits surface in R repeatedly. When his gang finally makes it to the pharmacy where Julie's salvage team is working, he's the first through the door; and although he has commented repeatedly on the slow speed of himself and the other zombies, he suddenly exhibits superhuman physical abilities. R's aggression forces him into the fray with no fear and with no thought of his prey; in fact, when he attacks Julie's boyfriend Perry (Dave Franco), his only consideration is the quality of Perry's watch, not his identity as a human victim. He bashes Perry's head repeatedly against the floor, attempting to excuse his behavior to the audience by telling them he's not proud of his actions and asking them to look away. Despite his professed shame and vocalized apology, R nonetheless devours part of Perry's brain, for, in doing so, R can experience and enjoy Perry's memories, thoughts, and feelings—including intimate ones about Julie. R tells viewers, "I don't want to hurt you; I just want to feel what you felt," but stealing another's mind through violence is narcissistic, egocentric, and immoral. While the film asks the audience to tolerate R's behavior as an unavoidable consequence of his "new hunger," it's hard to see him as anything more than a voracious, terrifying monster.

When it comes to Julie, R's psychopathy extends beyond mere violence to impulsivity, manipulativeness, and exploitativeness. Stuffing his pockets full of Perry's brains for later voyeuristic consumption, R makes the rather rash and impulsive decision to act on his newly acquired memories and emotions by kidnapping Julie, with whom he has suddenly and inexorably fallen in love. In one of the film's most disturbing scenes, R creeps up on Julie while managing to whisper her name. Although she had been destroying zombies left and right with great success, Julie is suddenly rendered passive and inert, sliding onto the floor in a paralyzed heap. R exhales her name once more, strokes Julie's face, and sniffs deeply of her hair. He smears her with Perry's blood and gray matter, marking her as his own, and brings her into his herd of zombie followers with the ironic promise she is now "safe." The now lovesick R takes advantage of Julie's trauma at having just witnessed her boyfriend's murder and manipulates her fear of death, forcing her to follow him back to the airport. As R ruminates on his impulsive exploitation of Julie, he tells the audience, "I don't know what I'm doing. What's wrong with me? These other guys would never bring a living person home. You know why? Because that's crazy." R's inability to understand his own actions reveals more of his narcissistic and psychotic behavior, and he presents viewers with a romantic hero they should hardly see in desirable terms. After all, as a ravenous zombie, R is a viscerally frightening monster; as an obsessed stalker, his actions are perhaps even more terrifying.

After R has taken Julie back to his abandoned airplane lair, he reveals his Machiavellian side through his concerted efforts to seduce her. Anna Gunnthorsdottir, Kevin McCabe, and Vernon Smith identify the three main components of Machiavellian social strategy to be "cynicism, manipulativeness, and a view that the ends justify the means,"[23] and while R is understandably cynical about his chances with Julie, he does just about anything he can to change the way she feels about him. As mentioned, R manipulates her through her fear, placing her in the center of a large community of zombies so she must look to him for safety and sustenance—a blanket, some soothing music, and a can of fruit cocktail. To win Julie over further, R elects to take the admittedly "unorthodox method" of eating her dead boyfriend's brains so he can get to know her better. Since he can't really have a conversation with her over coffee, R sees no other way forward with his courtship, embracing a horrific course of action he can justify if she ends up falling in love with him in return. Indeed, once the incarcerated Julie has some food in her stomach and a beer in her hand, she looks at R with bright eyes and smiles, her recent trauma and loss apparently forgotten. R learns quickly all Julie needs is safety and basic creature comforts to begin to change the way she thinks about him.

After Julie recovers from her initial shock, she recognizes R doesn't represent a threat to her at all, a change in attitude that necessitates R upping his manipulative game. When Julie expresses her appreciation to R for his saving her life, R must think as quickly as his presumably dead brain can, and he once again threatens her with the danger the *other* zombies pose to her. Seeing her captivity as a necessary evil that will only inconvenience her for a few days, Julie relaxes and agrees to her captor's terms. A classic romance montage follows, with R seducing the vulnerable Julie with a red convertible sports car, more cans of fruit, and his hipster-enviable collection of vintage vinyl records. They listen to music, dance, look at stereographic photos of couples in love, try on sunglasses, and play games. And all the while, R is sweet and even cute, with his sideways smile and his tendency to shrug awkwardly at everything Julie asks. The entire sequence would fit perfectly in a normal romantic narrative—would even be delightful and lovely—but in *Warm Bodies*, the film conveniently asks viewers to forget how R murdered Perry and has been holding Julie prisoner. His efforts to entertain her, even seduce her, constitute an intentional enactment of Stockholm Syndrome designed to make her forget the reality of her situation in favor of the alternative reality R has chosen. Through these efforts, both intentional and coincidental, R manifests the characteristics of the Dark Triad, but he does so in such a romantic manner that Julie—and, by extension, the audience—forgets the monster he truly is.

As a zombie, R is literally a monstrous boyfriend, but, as demonstrated, his behavior parallels real psychological tendencies and social problems abusive men manifest in their treatment of women. For example, R's reliance on Perry's brains to give him access to the dead boyfriend's memories—what R calls the closest thing zombies get to dreaming—resembles the invasive efforts of online stalkers who use social media to uncover personal and private things about the objects of their obsession. Perhaps more overtly, the emotional "trips" R enjoys from his cerebral snacks mirror the secretive drug abuse and addiction that plagues so many human relationships. R indulges on Perry's brains repeatedly, always without Julie's knowledge, and when he ends up reliving the memories of Perry's death, R experiences the zombie equivalent of a "bad trip." Through the memories, the zombie must see himself as others see him, as a mindless, voracious monster, and, ostensibly, he experiences something of Perry's fear as well.[24] A horrified R spits out the masticated gray matter, implicitly resolving to give up the habit, much in the same way remorseful drug addicts attempt to commit to going on the wagon. R, inspired to change for the woman he now loves, tracks down his suddenly missing captive and defends her against a circle of hungry zombies led by M. Once again, R saves Julie's life, this time channeling his preternatural strength and violence against his own kind. While R continues to refrain from psychopathic behavior towards Julie directly, he does act against others; and he continues to be secretive, manipulative, and deceptive. As they escape the airport together, R does let Julie drive, though.

As the film comes to a climax, R changes substantially from his initial Dark Triad tendencies as a result of his prolonged contact with Julie, her love and acceptance of him, and the memories and emotions he has commandeered from Perry's brain matter. As a result of this miraculous and fanciful transformation, R is able to step more directly into the shoes of the heroic Romeo. In addition, *Warm Bodies* allows R and his group of zombies to be sympathetic by introducing a new foe, a creature unseen in other zombie films: the Boneys. These creatures are zombies who have decomposed too much, have given up all of their human remnants and become skeletal monsters. As R begins to change, and as other zombies are inspired to hope for a similar transformation, the Boneys declare war on zombies and humans alike, and the film enjoys a *deus ex machina* that shifts R from the camp of the monsters into the camp of the humans. At first, he simply fights alongside them; later, he literally becomes one of them. R's great moment of redemptive selflessness comes when he saves Julie's life one last time, jumping with her from a great height to escape the Boneys and breaking her fall in a shallow fountain with his body. As a "corpse," however, R knows he can survive the fall, so perhaps it's not such a sacrificial move after all, but it *does* save Julie's life. Furthermore, the moment is apparently the last step to R's becoming truly human again, and he emerges from the water, as if from baptism, renewed and ready to accept Julie's grateful kisses. R's dark psychological traits forgotten, he lays aside his monstrous outside as well, becoming human as a direct result of Julie's love, a problematic chain of causal events that reveal more about Julie's—and, by extension, the film's—delusion than R's monstrous character.

Julie, Self-Verification
and the Myth of Monstrous Reformation

Even though *Warm Bodies* primarily relates R's story from his cognitive and visual perspective, Julie's role in the "good girl/bad boy" dyad contributes to the overall problems of the text as a laudable romance. Whereas R, like so many of his antecedental predecessors, manifests the destructive qualities of the Dark Triad, Julie, like a battered wife or abused girlfriend, falls victim to her own desire for damning self-verification. William B. Swann and Stephen J. Read proposed the idea of "self-verification" theory in 1980, which claims people "may actively seek, elicit, and recall social feedback that confirms their self-conceptions, thereby promoting the stability of these conceptions."[25] Because people take so much comfort and put so much stock in the way they see themselves, they are drawn to partners who confirm their self-images, whether positive or negative. In fact, "people who perceive themselves as dislikable may be more attentive to interaction partners who they think view them unfavorably."[26] Furthermore, "familiar stimuli should be more perceptually fluent and more easily processed than unfamiliar stimuli,"[27] so Julie is understandably drawn to men—and zombies—who resemble her father Grigio (John Malkovich). Their relationship is a weak one, to say the least, for Grigio "goes weeks without checking in," despite the fact that his wife is deceased, leaving Julie largely on her own. Late in the film, when Julie suggests going to her father for help because "he was a reasonable guy once," Nora (Analeigh Tipton) reminds her, "It was your mom that was the reasonable one. It was your dad that grounded you for a year for stealing peach schnapps." Grigio isn't a loving, compassionate man; instead, he's a cold, pragmatic leader who treats Julie in a similar fashion, and, like so many young women before her, Julie finds herself attracted to just that kind of man.

R's subjective, first-person perspective and personalized commentary only accompanies part of *Warm Bodies*; the audience is also provided with the objective story of Julie and her camp of surviving humans. At first, Julie appears as an independent girl with a gun of her own who is part of a team of teenagers who have volunteered to risk a scavenging run outside the community's fortified walls. As she and her group watch the pre-departure "pep-talk" video from Grigio, her rebellious streak manifests as well, one directed against her father not only as a civic authority figure but also on a personal level. "Corpses look human. They are not," Grigio cautions. "They do not think. They do not bleed.... They are uncaring, unfeeling, incapable of remorse." "Sound like anyone you know, Dad?" Julie replies to the digital image. Despite this urge to defy her overbearing and uncaring father, Julie is coded as subservient to another male figure, her boyfriend. As the orientation video winds down, Julie tries to hold Perry's hand for support, but he shrugs her off, indicating the need for them both to pay attention to her father's words—and authority. Perry's behavior mirrors the attitude of Julie's father, and her desire for him belies a complicated paternal relationship. When the group reaches a pharmacy to look for medical supplies, Julie's somewhat antagonistic relationship with Perry draws into clearer focus: he insists on doing exactly what Julie's father says, on following orders, by the book. When Julie tells him he sounds just like her dad, Perry replies with a curt "Thank you," followed by Julie pointing out it wasn't meant as a compliment. Yet her thirst for rebellion and independence collapses as she allows Perry to make all the decisions for the group, including staying on the scene even when Julie thinks they should leave. She may wish to be independent, but her actions show a willing subservience to both her father and his proxy, her boyfriend.

After her abduction, when Julie arrives at R's airplane bachelor pad—devoid of a male authority figure to follow—she crawls into a corner and weeps, showing no sign of the plucky, rebellious, and competent woman viewers had met at the beginning of the film. Instead, Julie is a cowed and meek kidnapping victim, a victim who is not only incapacitate by her powerlessness but also one who will soon succumb to Stockholm Syndrome. Thanks to R's efforts to hide Julie from the other zombies, Julie apparently forgets R is the bloodthirsty monster that killed her boyfriend and asks what, instead, R might be. Julie finds herself fascinated with the creature's unexpected behavior and apparent emotional depth. When R leaves the plane to find her some food, Julie does make a half-hearted attempt to escape, but she is quickly surrounded by zombies, sniffing the air like expectant hound dogs. R intercedes once again, and this time when he smears the remains of Perry's brain on her face, she responds with an impassioned "thank you." Even more incredulously, after R gives Julie the first beer she's had in ages, she tells him, "I guess you can't be all that bad, Mr. Zombie." R's character thus parallels that of most "bad boys"; he may be monstrous and violent and dangerous, but not *all* of the time, and those moments of kindness are all someone like Julie needs to see him in a favorable light.

Julie's passivity grows more alarming as she seeks new leadership and guidance from a man in her life, and as R is the closest thing she has, she attaches her subservient self to him. Perhaps in a direct homage to *Romeo and Juliet*, part of R's charm lies in the way he woos Julie with words. A few stumbling, stuttered words and short phrases are hardly sophisticated iambic pentameter, but R's verbal efforts and progressive abilities cause Julie to stare and marvel at him in disbelief: "Are there others like you?" she asks. "I mean, I've never, ever heard a corpse talk before." As she grows closer to R, she distances herself from Perry as well, revealing things weren't great between the two, and she awkwardly comes to terms with his death: "My boyfriend—he died back there.... It's just—in my world—people die all the time. So, you know, it's not like I'm not sad that he's gone, 'cause I am, but I think I've been preparing for it for a really long time." Perhaps Julie is simply being pragmatic about Perry, having lost her mother to the zombies already, and she just sees the practical advantages of R's protection. Yet Julie seems almost happy to be charmed by a mildly loquacious zombie and to bypass any kind of mourning for the dead Perry.

Before long, Julie is officially attached to her new "bad boy" boyfriend. When R finally allows Julie to leave the airport, he must escort her through a throng of hungry zombies. Julie, for the first time displaying her growing affection for her zombie captor, takes R's hand. In a telling doubling with the beginning of the film, R welcomes Julie's touch in contrast to how Perry had rejected it. That night, the two fugitives hole up in an abandoned house, and when Grigio leads an armored search party through the neighborhood, Julie illogically tells R to stay away from the windows. She actively hides from her father, from the chance at rescue, to protect her own kidnapper. Like Patty Hurst, Julie is now actively colluding with the enemy, choosing the "bad boy" over her father. An "operation of evolutionary logic" may be the key reason why women such as Julie would remain in relationships with controlling or abusive partners. According to evolutionary psychologist Satoshi Kanazawa, "In our ancestral environment, violent men probably did very well in their intrasexual competition for status, and thus for mating opportunities.... Aggressive, violent, and ruthless men often made the best warriors and political leaders throughout human evolutionary history."[28] Like Julie's father, R has proven himself as a violent and capable "warrior" leader, and he can potentially give her everything she needs, albeit his ability to serve as a mating partner is greatly suspect.

Julie's complete surrender to R despite Perry's death at his hands reaches a climax later that night. While lying in bed, Julie ponders R's unique place in the world, and, in the process, reveals the depths of her fascination with him as her developing object of obsession. "It must be hard, being stuck in there," she says, to R, lying chastely on the floor, referencing his mind or soul trapped inside his clumsy and decomposing body. "You know, I can see you trying—that's what people do. You know, we try to be better. Sometimes we kind of suck at it, but when I look at you and you try so much harder than any human in my city. You're a good person, R." In this impassioned bout of sympathy, Julie calls R a "person" twice, but the zombie potentially spoils the mood when he breathes, "It was me." When Julie asks what he means, R places Perry's watch on the bedside table. Julie picks it up slowly and contemplates it, but instead of running screaming from the house, she simply utters, "Oh. I mean—I guess I kind of knew that." When R gasps, "You did?," Julie simply replies, "Yeah—I ... I guess I hoped you didn't. I'm sorry." At this moment, Julie must recognize how she has allowed herself to be seduced by the voracious murder in the room, but the realization has apparently come too late. Her negative self-image and passivity vis-à-vis a powerful male authority figure—first her father, then Perry, and now R—are starkly reconfirmed in this scene, particularly in her choice to apologize to R instead of demanding one of him. Julie does sneak away from R in the morning, but her facial expressions and repeated backward glances imply she isn't leaving him because she is repulsed by him or afraid of him but rather that she knows she must go home and he cannot go with her.

With Julie's apparent forgiveness of R and her ambiguous apology, *Warm Bodies* shifts from a story about a kidnapping victim who comes to love her captor to a battered-woman's fantasy in which Dark Triadic traits can be overcome through attention, perseverance, and love. While contact with Julie did indeed cause R's atrophied heart to beat again, at least once, her acceptance of his murderous acts—and thus of him—begin to transform R from an unacceptable monster into the kind of boy she can take home to her father. For starters, R sleeps and has a dream, two things impossible for the zombies of *Warm Bodies*. In his first dream, he watches Julie, Nora, and Perry talking about their hopes for the future. When Perry sees R, he is understandably hostile, but Julie says R can dream if he wants to. She accepts him as he is and supports his choices. More changes manifest when he wakes up and notices Julie has left him. R, no longer particularly impulsive, rash, or needy, decides he should quit pretending to be something he's not and go back to the airport. On his way, he not only grows cold when it starts raining, but he also runs into a group of like-minded zombies lead by M. He and M shake hands and even hug. Julie's acceptance of and love for R has not only begun to change R, her "bad boy" lover, but also all the zombies she has come into contact with (except the "Boneys," of course). Suddenly, R has transformed into a kind of "zombie messiah," leading his new, kinder-and-gentler zombie followers to the human city and Julie.[29]

Julie makes it back to the walled city alive, and her father is relieved, if not overjoyed, to see her again. For Julie, though, the reunion is more bitter than sweet, and she immediately begins second-guessing her decision to leave R behind. While talking with Nora on her bed, Julie says, "No, I'm serious,

Nora. I mean, 'corpse' is just a ... a stupid name for a state of being we don't understand.... I gotta tell you something.... I actually miss him." A shocked Nora teases Julie about having feelings for her "zombie boyfriend," and the lovesick girl doesn't deny those claims or labels are accurate. Julie then goes out alone onto her balcony to complete the narrative's careful references to Shakespeare's source material. Granted, all R can muster is a weak, "Julie. Julie!"—hardly seductive poetry—but it's enough to convince Julie to let him into her bedroom, especially when he awkwardly declares, "Came to see you." Julie responds, "I actually missed you," before embracing him. R's fantastic transformation has apparently been continuing in Julie's absence, for she notes, "It's funny—You feel warmer than I remember," and Nora points out R doesn't smell rotten either. When Julie asks why he has come, R says, "Show everyone ... that we can change." This transformation of R from a bad boy to a good boy, from a zombie to a human, is symbolized by a comical makeover sequence through which Julie and Nora use makeup to help R pass through the city unnoticed. Their efforts are more than effective; Nora declares the disguised R to be outright "hot," and Julie makes a point to tell him he looks "nice." In this romantic fantasy, the woman is *literally* changing her "bad boyfriend" into something more beautiful and acceptable.

As mentioned, R's final sacrifice for Julie's wellbeing symbolizes a redemptive baptism, but, perhaps more importantly, it is coded in terms of death and resurrection. R fulfills the romantic ideal by sacrificing himself for the woman he loves, the ultimate gesture signifying the end of the "bad boy." The monster, formerly only disguised by a surface reformation represented by makeup, goes into the water to "die"; he rises again, washed clean and sporting the natural flushed skin tone of a living human. As alluded to in R's mystic dream of Julie, she has accomplished R's "exhumation," drawing him from the water as if from the grave. Finally, Julie can kiss R, for he is no longer a zombie acting like a human but a real human being. She has saved her "bad boy" and reformed him into the romantic hero of her dreams, and his eyes magically transform, indicating his completed resurrection. Unfortunately, Julie's father doesn't see what she does, and he shoots R in the shoulder. However, this act only serves to prove R is alive because he starts bleeding (and one of Grigio's unwavering rules is "corpses don't bleed"), and it softens Grigio's heart when he sees that perhaps, indeed, the human race *can* get a second chance. As a triumphant Julie rushes out of the fountain to embrace her father, the audience realizes that her love, devotion, and hope have not only saved the "bad boy" that was her boyfriend but also her father. A fantastic happy ending for everyone, indeed.

The romantic mythology of *Warm Bodies* literalizes the delusion battered and abused women cling to when they insist on staying with their "bad boy" partners. The plot of *Warm Bodies* centers on the idea that love can change a man into something else, that all it takes is the love and devotion of a dedicated woman to turn a monster into an angel. However, if self-verification theory is to be believed, Julie would never accept the reformed version of R; she would come to need a new partner who would treat her badly as before. By resolving the emotional conflicts of the film with a Hollywood-style "happy ending," *Warm Bodies* defies the problems that plague real dysfunctional relationships by presenting a romanticized view of the world. R becomes human again, despite the decay and rot his body has presumably been undergoing for months (if not years), not to mention his various gunshot and knife wounds. While it may seem foolish to try to apply logic and reasoning to something as fantastic as a zombie narrative, the inexplicable impossibility of R's redemptive transformation back into a warm, living, and breathing human simply *makes no sense*. However, this lack of reason underscores the fantasy of not only the romance genre in fiction but also the fantasy held to by so many who love monstrous partners. The film ends with the hopeful and poignant image of the city's wall being demolished, allowing humans and zombies to coexist peacefully, but it's all just a nice dream.

Some will undoubtedly argue I'm taking this family-friendly, lighthearted, and perhaps even satirical film far too seriously in my close analysis and criticism. After all, it's quite well made, clever, and makes the zombie apocalypse genre more accessible to a broader demographic. However, while I openly acknowledge that *Warm Bodies* is a comedy—and as such, it likely isn't supposed to be taken too seriously—it's also a *romantic* comedy, and any text that portrays itself as an exploration into matters of love and human interaction should carry with it some kind of obligation to treat such relationships responsibly. The problem with paranormal romantic fantasy such as *Twilight* and *Warm Bodies*—to name just two of dozens of successful narratives featuring the monstrous boyfriend trope—lies in the messages such texts convey to young readers and viewers, both male and female. These stories advocate that stalking a woman is an acceptable form of courtship, that dominant male behavior backed by the threat of violence and bodily harm is a normal expression of love and devotion, and that a woman can find common ground with a potentially dangerous partner by simply loving him enough or by becoming monstrous herself. Such messages are not only essentially misogynistic but are also potentially dangerous, as they could serve to put impressionable women into destructive relationships with skewed and invalid expectations. Not exactly the standards the zombie narrative should be shooting for.

CONCLUSION—
THE TELEVISION ZOMBIE
The Future(s) of the Walking Dead

> One of the most remarkable features in our domesticated races is
> that we see in them adaptation, not indeed to the animal's or plant's
> own good, but to man's use or fancy.
> —Charles Darwin, *On the Origin of Species*

Despite their visceral appeal as amassed hordes of ferocious, flesh-eating, contagious, rotting, uncanny beasts, modern-day zombies actually represent one of the most unsophisticated of monsters. As George A. Romero conceived them, zombies are, quite simply, reanimated corpses with an existential desire to kill and eat their former kin. Their bite is usually poisonous or infectious, and anyone bitten by a zombie invariably becomes one. While some variations on this ghoulish creation have existed long enough to be included in the narrative canon—fast-moving zombies, living zombies, talking zombies, and zombies that only consume brains—the basic characteristics of these foes remain relatively unchanged. Now, however, with the walking dead appearing ubiquitously on the big screen, on television, in video games, in books and comics, in phone apps, on T-shirts, and even down toy aisles, "zombie fatigue" is perhaps beginning to set in. For creatures—even fictitious creatures—to survive, they must evolve and adapt. Luckily, creative minds are practicing a kind of "unnatural selection" on the zombie foe, determining which variations work best, which are most effective, and which are most popular. As the zombie becomes an increasingly desirable property for media producers—in the television industry in particular—the creators of these stories must consciously discern the most bankable course of zombie evolution.

A number of these potential trajectories already exist most accessibly on television. The first is the more classical depiction, zombies following the protocols established by Romero, as in serials such as *The Walking Dead* (2010–), its still-in-development spinoff *Fear the Walking Dead* (2015),[1] and relative newcomer *Z Nation* (2014–), although the latter does feature fast zombies and explores the ideas of a possible cure and zombie hybrids. But sympathetic zombie portrayals are gaining traction as well, including former zombies struggling through rehabilitation, as in the British series *In the Flesh* (2013–), or zombies clinging desperately to their humanity, as in the recent procedural drama mash-up *iZombie* (2015). Then again, while contagious zombies are all the rage—pun intended—perhaps it's time to look back to the beginning, to the source, and pilot a television series grounded in folklore, mythology, and the Vodou religion; a series featuring the authentic zombie could be very fresh and original indeed—as has already been attempted to some extent by *American Horror Story: Coven* (2013–2014). Of course, perhaps the best future for "Zombie TV" won't be one that engages with zombies at all; other kinds of revenants already *do* exist, after all, including mummies, *draugar, jiangshi*, golems, reanimates, or the otherwise resurrected, as seen in the French series *Les revenants* (2012– , *The Returned*).[2] Regardless, the cure for zombie fatigue must be found through insightful adaptation, variations that look to the future as much as they do the past. I believe television affords the zombie its best shot at sustainable longevity, and the right productions will see the multifarious creature well into a new generation of fans and scholars alike.

Because the best zombie narratives engage with the human characters and explore what happens to them as they change and adapt to their increasingly unfamiliar and challenging environment, long-arc storylines with sufficient time for substantial character development must be an essential part of zombie evolution and development. When I concluded my first book, *American Zombie Gothic*, at the end of 2009, I made just such a prediction concerning the then-only-proposed television series *The Walking Dead*:

> Ultimately, however, the future of the zombie narrative lies not in variation and transplantation but in a careful adaptation of the traditions of the past—taking the established zombie invasion narrative and playing it out on a large scale and over a longer view, thereby tracking the development of the human protagonists over many years as they attempt to rebuild the post-apocalyptic world they now inhabit.[3]

While I will take up the problematic first portion of this claim later, the rest of what I had observed has come to prove somewhat prescient. Granted, I had already seen this kind of long-arc story developed successfully in Robert

Kirkman's comic series *The Walking Dead* (2003–), and I was cautiously optimistic about the planned television adaptation. Little did I fully comprehend that the show would explode in popularity, becoming not only one of the most successful basic-cable television shows of all time,[4] but also a text that has garnered substantial critical attention from the academic community.[5] Over five seasons, and multiple years of narration time, the characters of *The Walking Dead* have faced increasingly demanding challenges, and many of those who were present at the beginning of the series have not survived. Seeing how these characters grow and adapt—and, frankly, finding out which beloved character will die a gruesome death in each midseason and season finale— keeps bringing viewers back for more.

Six years ago, I had hoped a television production such as *The Walking Dead* "would finally give the zombie narrative the time it need[ed] to map out the complicated relationships that would result from a zombie infestation that ends normal society."[6] After sixty-seven progressive episodes (so far), the television version of Kirkman's apocalyptic vision has certainly provided its human characters the time required to experience a myriad of relationships and to both progress and digress in their human development. Gary Farnell explains why much of the draw to the series stems from the journeys undertaken by the human protagonists, not the zombie creatures: "The subject of the show is the 'inner lives' of the main protagonists, delineated through the various moral dilemmas they face."[7] These "inner lives" can only be fully explored in a long-arc narrative, as shown particularly in the characters of Carol (Melissa McBride) and Daryl (Norman Reedus).[8] Thanks in a large part to the zombie apocalypse, which brings her into the company of strong and independent women, Carol finally finds the strength in the first season to stand up to her abusive husband Ed (Adam Minarovich).[9] She has developed gradually over five seasons from a passive and downtrodden woman to a fierce, independent survivalist and treasured asset to the group of survivors, especially when she rescues them all from the cannibalistic Hunters at the beginning of the fifth season.[10] Similarly, Daryl begins the series as little more than a submissive man living in the shadow of his oppressive older brother Merle (Michael Rooker).[11] When the two brothers eventually reunite after a prolonged separation, Daryl has changed for the better, calling Merle "a simple-minded piece of shit" to his face and abandoning him for the kinship of Rick (Andrew Lincoln) and his group.[12] By Season 4, Daryl has become something of a celebrity among the community of survivors at the prison, providing food with his crossbow and leadership through his unexpected position on the ruling council,[13] and he has continued to be a vital member of the group throughout Season 5.

Of course, not all the character development in *The Walking Dead* has been positive or represents desirable evolutionary progress, but the series affords those types of developmental explorations nonetheless. Throughout the first two seasons of *The Walking Dead*, Dale (Jeffrey DeMunn) acts as the "moral center" of the group; therefore, when a rogue walker kills him,[14] viewers likely begin to worry about what will become of the survivors.[15] As in Kirkman's comic series, which I explore in Chapter 4, the progression of *The Walking Dead*'s protagonists has become progressively violent and atavistic, and viewers may be increasingly shocked to learn to what lengths Rick and his team will go to keep themselves and their loved ones safe. Shane (Jon Bernthal) has no qualms about making tough decisions if it means protecting Lori (Sarah Wayne Callies), the object of his unwanted affection. Shane shoots Otis (Pruitt Taylor Vince) in the leg, sacrificing him to the zombies to facilitate his own survival,[16] and he murders the defenseless prisoner Randall (Michael Zegen) to draw Rick out into the woods where he hopes to kill him.[17] Rick isn't making it through the zombie apocalypse unscathed either; as in the comic series, he brutally kills a band of thugs with his bare hands and teeth,[18] and he leads his group in the wholesale slaughter of the remaining Hunter cannibals—before the altar of a church, no less.[19] This kind of sophisticated character development, both evolutionary and de-evolutionary, could less effectively be explored in a narrative shorter than 120 minutes, as with a film, or one driven primarily by combat and puzzle solving, as in a video game.

The Walking Dead certainly delivers on its dynamic cast of human characters, but what many have longed to see are fully realized and sympathetic zombie characters, even protagonists, who appear in serious, not comedic narratives. The British mini-series *In the Flesh*, created by Dominic Mitchell and produced by BBC Drama Productions,[20] has realized this careful balancing act, presenting viewers with fascinating zombie characters that are more than just shallow stereotypes or visual sight gags. This innovative series recounts the unusual story of Kieren Walker (Luke Newberry), a quiet teenager-turned-zombie who had certainly never wanted to come back from the dead; in fact, he hadn't wanted to be alive at all. He had killed himself years earlier because he had felt responsible for his best friend's death in Afghanistan. When an unexplained event known as "The Rising" occurred, Kieren had awoken unexpectedly in his casket as a zombie—or, in more politically correct terms, as a sufferer of "Partially Deceased Syndrome" (PDS)— and he had been forced to claw his way out of his own grave to search out human flesh to eat. But Kieren is fundamentally different from the flesh-eating foes that have come before him. While almost all zombies share a loss of personal autonomy, the creatures at the heart of *In the Flesh* tell their own stories to the viewing audience through both traumatic flashbacks and subjective dialogue, thanks to a governmental treatment program that allows them to regain their former brain functions.

At the time of the series, the conflict with the "rotters" has largely come to a peaceful resolution, and the work to reintegrate the surviving zombies back into society has begun—but not everyone is happy about it. Thanks to Neurotriptyline, an experimental drug that must be injected daily directly into the spines of PDS suffers, the former rotters regain their human memories and reestablish control over their own minds. Nevertheless, they remain partially dead: they can't eat; they can still only be killed by a traumatic brain injury; and they must wear contacts and skin-tone makeup to "pass" among living humans. The narrative focuses on the small community of Roarton, a village that had survived the Rising thanks in large part to the valiant efforts of their militia, the Human Volunteer Force (HVF), lead by the hypermasculine Bill Macy (Steve Evets). Kieren has completed his "reconditioning," a process presented overtly in terms of a drug-rehabilitation program, and is ready to come home to his anxious but loving parents. Kieren's sister, however, is far less excited to see her revived brother; Jem (Harriet Cains) had been an ardent member of the HVF—in fact, she continues to wear the armband and go on patrols despite the new, politically correct laws concerning the partially deceased. Jem initially rejects Kieren for two painful reasons: on the one hand, Jem has been conditioned to hate all rotters, having seen them kill many of her friends, but on the other, she still harbors strong feelings of resentment towards Kieren for his suicide, an act that had scarred her deeply.

Running for just three episodes, the first season of the series presents viewers with an allegory of intolerance, one read best through a queer lens. In fact, while *In the Flesh* does have its share of violence and gore—especially when members of the HVF take it upon themselves to be judge, jury, and executioner for any rabid rotters they find—the show is really "a domestic drama that sensitively explore[s] a range of issues[, including] prejudice, suicide, [and] loss."[21] The living humans of Roarton fear what they don't understand, but most of the PDS sufferers fear what they have become just as much, if not more. Kieren had already struggled to fit in *before* the Rising, when he had been a quiet, shy teenager harboring strong feelings towards his best friend Rick Macy (David Walmsley). He had already been "othered" and ostracized by the community, teased by the other boys about being too effeminate, and downright hated by Rick's myopically intolerant father, Bill. Now that he has returned, things are even worse, mostly because he really *is* an Other now, a liminal character far beyond his implied homosexuality. As *The Guardian* reviewer David Renshaw observes, Kieren "hangs nervously between life and death as he attempts to build bridges with alienated loved ones and a local community whose pitchforks are twitching to impale this Peter Pan lookalike they see as 'a rotter.'"[22] His efforts are primarily hindered by the oppressive ideological institution of the church, represented by Vicar Oddie (Kenneth Cranham), who vehemently demonizes the PDS Domicile Care Initiative, part of the new Protection Act: "They are vicious killers," he preaches. "End. Of. Story. And now the government is putting these 'dangerous fiends' back into our community. Passing laws to protect the beast?" Oddie stokes the fire of bigoted hatred in Bill and his HVF troops, so much so that Kieren must be smuggled back into Roarton by his parents and hidden day and night in the house.

As with many cases of discriminatory and bigoted behavior, some of the most intolerant people in *In the Flesh* are the ones suffering from denial, either intentionally or unintentionally. Ken Burton (Ricky Tomlinson), for example, is initially one of the most vocal opponents to the reintegration process and the new laws, shouting loudest and longest at the town meetings, but viewers—along with the Vicar—learn he is actually hiding his wife Maggie (Sue Wallace), a recovering PDS victim, in his home. Apprised of the news, Bill puts together a lynch mob of loyal HVF members, and he executes the harmless and pathetic woman coldly in the middle of the street. However, Bill must soon confront his own prejudicial demons head on when he receives conflicting news: his son Rick has been found in Afghanistan and will soon be coming home, but not alive; Rick is now a recovering rotter, the very thing Bill hates more than anything else in the world. Nevertheless, Bill welcomes his son home as a war hero, and he insists the rest of the town does as well. Yet Bill refuses to recognize his son as a zombie, much in the same way he has long refused to acknowledge even the possibility of his son's homosexuality. To enforce what he thinks is "normal," Bill takes Rick target shooting, makes him wear his military medal (despite his being out of uniform), lets him drink with the HVF troops in the otherwise segregated local pub, and even drags him out on a hunt for rabid rotters. Bill invasively overcompensates with his son, trying to make him into something he simply is not.

The night of the rotter hunt, Rick and Kieren finally have some time alone together, and they revisit the end of their human relationship. Rick asks how Kieren had died, and Kieren tells him, "When you died, everything turned to shit. Life didn't mean anything anymore." The thought of his friend killing himself when he had had so much to live for sends Rick into a rage. He thought they had said goodbye and that Kieren had simply moved on with his life; however, Kieren denies this interpretation of events, exclaiming, "We drank a bottle of White Lightening, smoked a few fags, messed around, and then you said, 'all right, see you tomorrow.' Next thing I know, you'd gone to Preston for basic training. I didn't hear nothing from you after that. Nothing.... I wrote thousands of letters; why didn't you reply to me?" Kieren had assumed Rick had regretted their relationship and pushed Kieren out of his life, but Rick had never received any of the letters. Because Bill had banned Kieren from his house years ago simply for giving Rick a mix CD, it's entirely likely the homophobic father had intercepted the letters. Now that both Kieren and Rick are back, Bill once again sees Kieren as a threat to his son, a threat because of both their potential and obvious similarities. Bill insists Rick kill his dear friend: "He's not a person, Rick, he's an animal. Worse than an animal. He might walk and talk, but rotters are evil. This has to be done.... Do you want to be in the good books or the bad books?" Rick is understandably distraught—he wants to be a good son, but obeying his father would ultimately mean denying who he truly is.

The hatred many in Roarton feel towards PDS suffers results largely from a powerful religious rhetoric of hate and intolerance, a rhetoric that hauntingly mirrors that often used against the LGBTQ community today. At Bill's request, Vicar Oddie gives an impassioned fire-and-brimstone sermon on the evils of this perceived threat to the Christian community: "Do not be fooled. Those things are not what they appear to be. They are not your neighbors, not your friends; they are imposters, changlings of the highest order. The undead are the pale horseman personified, intent on destruction and evil, and they must be judged." The Vicar sees the liminal PDS sufferers in apocalyptic terms, and he convinces many of his flock to demonize their former friends and family because of their perceived differences. Bill certainly believes God sanctions his hatred for Kieren, and he shows Rick how to kill a rotter with a knife so he can murder his best friend. Rick goes into the bathroom, though, clearly distraught, and looks at himself in the mirror, covering up the wounded half of his face so he can remember what he used to look like, who he *used* to be. Then Rick takes off his makeup and removes his contacts to confront his father as he is *now*, essentially "coming out." He tells his father, "I don't want to hurt Ren. He's me best mate. If Ren's evil, Dad, then so am I." Bill hugs his disfigured son, telling him it's going to be all right, before stabbing Rick through the back of his head and dumping the body at Kieren's house. Bill has convinced himself Rick isn't really his son—he's just an imposter, and the real Rick will return to him in the glory of God's resurrection.

In addition to using the zombies of *In the Flesh* as metaphors for homosexuality, the series also explores the complex and troubling issue of teenage suicide. As Renshaw declares, "Writer Dominic Mitchell deserves huge credit for exploring sexuality, suicide and teenage angst with insight and heart,"[23]and the series is, at its core, about a family trying to recover from the trauma of their son's death. Kieren's suicide, a result of his struggles with his sexuality and his overwhelming depression, had almost destroyed his surviving family, making Jem blindly angry and causing his father Steve (Steve Cooper) to withdraw and shut down. Now that Kieren has returned, his mother Sue (Marie Critchley) finds herself conflicted between being happy her son is back but also furious with him because of what he had put her through. After Rick dies the second time, Kieren goes back to the cave where he had killed himself, a powerfully symbolic location, as it was the place where he and Rick had secretly met to be together. Kieren feels trapped, perceiving the same things are happening all over again, but this time, his mother intervenes. Sue pleads with him that this time things need to be different—he needs to live. She tells him how she had once loved an RAF pilot, but the man had left her for her friend, a young woman who had been more "socially acceptable." She reveals to Kieren that she had wanted to kill herself too, but the local pharmacist had refused to give her any drugs. Instead, he had listened to her, and that was how she had met Steve, Kieren's father. They return home, and the family finally gets a second chance to be together and work things out.

In the Flesh demonstrates how zombie narratives can be more than just violent, apocalyptic gore-fests with simple characters and shallow plotting; instead, the zombie creature can be employed in tales spanning a variety of genres to tell captivating stories, stories that challenge the established conventions of the tradition. Thanks to the serialized format of television programs, and perhaps also their general aesthetic focus on character and dialogue, zombies and zombie stories have tremendous potential to develop gradually over time. The long-arc narrative structure will continue to be explored by *The Walking Dead*, hopefully for years to come, and I am optimistic its spinoff series will hold much promise, especially if it explores some variation in the zombie creature, as does *Z Nation*. The zombie protagonist will also continue to have a potentially bright future ahead of it on television. Even though BBC3 has already canceled *In the Flesh* (after just two seasons),[24] Rob Thomas has developed an adaptation of Chris Roberson and Michael Allred's comic series *iZombie* (2010–2012) for the CW Television Network. While the pilot episode demonstrates a dramatic departure from the source material—the protagonist sports the groan-inducing name "Liv Moore" (Rose McIver), and she works in a coroner's office instead of as a grave digger—the show *does* emphasize the lead zombie's unusual status as a special kind of revenant who can maintain her humanity while eating a brain now and then.[25] Unfortunately, the comic's diverse cast of ghosts, vampires, werebeasts, and mummies is sadly missing,[26] and the series runs the risk of devolving into a romantic soap opera and not a supernatural horror narrative.

Yet what *iZombie* proves is that maybe we all should simply redefine and broaden our definition of "zombie," exploring more radical versions and variations of the walking dead.[27] I quoted myself earlier as once writing "the future of the zombie narrative lies not in variation and transplantation," a sentiment from 2009 that I no longer fully support. As Tommy Wirkola's *Død snø* (2009, *Dead Snow*) demonstrates, exciting and innovative tales *can* be woven around other forms of revenants, a host of creatures, monsters, and sympathetic protagonists that have returned from the grave for various reasons. While these types of explorations and evolutions have been developing for years in a variety of media, the non-zombie revenants of the French series *Les revenants*, created by Fabrice Gobert, represent a particularly interesting and successful example of such possibilities. Conceptually inspired by Robin Campillo's 2004 film of the same name (also known as *They Came Back*), *Les revenants* begins by introducing its viewers to Camille (Yara Pilartz), a teenager who dies tragically when her school bus careens off a winding mountain road. Four years later, for no discernible reason, Camille suddenly returns, and she climbs up the embankment and walks back home. For her, no time has passed, and she soon finds her new surroundings disorienting and frightening.[28] She knows she is different, of course, telling her childhood crush Frédéric (Matila Malliarakis), "I'm not like other girls. I come from another world, a world of dead souls who hide from the sun—and drink blood!"[29] And Camille is not the only one who has returned so abruptly; a host of the dead have returned, and not all of them are happy about their return or the community that in various ways betrayed them. Reminiscent of David Lynch's *Twin Peaks* (1990–91), *Les revenants* weaves a complex story of death, resurrection, and retribution, all the while engaging with common anxieties associated with these very issues.[30]

Based on recent developments across a variety of media, I am confident we have many years of great zombie storytelling ahead of us, especially as extended television narratives. However, the Zombie Renaissance can only endure, and continue to be exciting and rewarding, if artists find new ways to tell new stories. In the conclusion to *American Zombie Gothic*, I quote from Fred Botting's 2008 study *Gothic Romanced*, and his insights into narrative development are as relevant to today's discussion of zombie tales as they ever were. Botting sagely reminds us, "[O]nce formulas become too repetitious and familiar, they are perceived as mechanical and boring. Without difference and variation, generic codes become obvious and predictable. Excitement, interest, and affect wanes. Desire moves on, in search of innovation, stimulation, and reinvigoration."[31] As the past few years of the Zombie Renaissance have shown us, while the tried-and-true formula of the zombie as infectious, apocalyptic scourge can remain popular and engaging, new variations, new versions, new stories, and new formats are essential for keeping this wonderful monster relevant and captivating. Every apocalypse has its own story to tell, and those stories shouldn't always be told from the point of view of survivalists in the United States. Every zombie has its own story to tell as well, and sometimes the zombie itself can best tell that story. And, of course, not all zombies have to be the hungry, reanimated dead. As a society, we need monsters to help us make sense of the world around us, and because our world is constantly changing, our monsters must change as well. I look forward to the next "big thing" in zombies, whatever that may be.

FILMOGRAPHY

"A," *The Walking Dead* (Michelle Mac-Laren, 2014)

Aaah! Zombies!! (see *Wasting Away*)

Airplane! (Jim Abrahams, David Zucker, and Jerry Zucker, 1980)

Aliens (James Cameron, 1986)

Alone in the Dark (Infogrames, 1992)

April Fool's Day (Fred Walton, 1986)

"Beside the Dying Fire," *The Walking Dead* (Ernest R. Dickerson, 2012)

"Better Angels," *The Walking Dead* (Guy Ferland, 2012)

Bio Hazard (see *Resident Evil*)

The Birds (Alfred Hitchcock, 1963)

Black Swan (Darren Aronofsky, 2010)

Blazing Saddles (Mel Brooks, 1974)

Braindead (Peter Jackson, 1992), also known as *Dead Alive*

Breaking Dawn: Part II (Bill Condon, 2012)

Cabin the Woods (Drew Goddard, 2011)

"Camille," *Les revenants* (Fabrice Gobert, 2012)

"Chi of the Vampire," *Jackie Chan Adventures* (Chap Yaep, 2002)

"Coda," *The Walking Dead* (Ernest R. Dickerson, 2014)

Colin (Marc Price, 2008)

Dawn of the Dead (George A. Romero, 1978)

Dawn of the Dead (Zack Snyder, 2004)

Dawn of the Planet of the Apes (Matt Reeves, 2014)

Day of the Dead (George A. Romero, 1985)

Dead Alive (see *Braindead*)

Dead Heat (Mark Goldblatt, 1988)

Dead Island (Techland, 2011)

Dead Rising (Yoshinori Kawano, 2008)

Dead Set (Yann Demange, 2008)

Dead Snow (see *Død snø*)

Diary of the Dead (George A. Romero, 2007)

Doc of the Dead (Alexandre O. Philippe, 2014)

Død snø (Tommy Wirkola, 2009), also known as *Dead Snow*

Doom (id Software, 1993)

Dracula (Tod Browning, 1931)

The Earth Dies Screaming (Terence Fisher, 1964)

The Elder Scrolls V: Skyrim (Todd Howard, 2011)

Encounter of the Spooky Kind (see *Gui da gui*)

The Evil Dead (Sam Raimi, 1981)

Evil Dead II (Sam Raimi, 1987)

The Exorcist (William Friedkin, 1973)

Fido (Andrew Currie, 2006)

"Four Walls and a Roof," *The Walking Dead* (Jeffrey F. January, 2014)

Friday the 13th (Sean S. Cunningham, 1980)

Friday the 13th (Marcus Nispel, 2009)

Geung si sin sang (Ricky Lau, 1985), also known as *Mr. Vampire*

The Ghost Breakers (George Marshall, 1940)

The Ghoul (Freddie Francis, 1975)

Ghoulies (Luca Bercovici, 1984)

Gui da gui (Sammo Kam-Bo Hung, 1980), also known as *Encounter of the Spooky Kind*

Gwoemul (Joon-ho Bong, 2006), also know as *The Host*

Halloween (John Carpenter, 1978)

Halloween (Rob Zombie, 2007)

"Home," *The Walking Dead* (Seith Mann, 2013)

The Host (see *Gwoemul*)

House of the Dead (Uwe Boll, 2003)

I Walked with a Zombie (Jacques Tourneur, 1943)

I Was a Teenage Zombie (John Elias Michalakis, 1987)

In the Flesh (Jonny Campbell, 2013)

Independence Day (Roland Emmerich, 1996)

Indiana Jones and the Temple of Doom (Steven Spielberg, 1984)

Invasion of the Body Snatchers (Don Siegel, 1956)

Invisible Invaders (Edward L. Cahn, 1959)

Juan de los Muertos (Alejandro Brugués, 2011), also known as *Juan of the Dead*

Juan of the Dead (see *Juan de los Muertos*)

"Judge, Jury, Executioner," *The Walking Dead* (Greg Nicotero, 2012)

King of the Zombies (Jean Yarbrough, 1941)

Land of the Dead (George A. Romero, 2005)

The Last House on the Left (Wes Craven, 1972)

The Last House on the Left (Dennis Iliadis, 2009)

The Last Man on Earth (Ubaldo Ragona and Sidney Salkow, 1964)

The Last of Us (Neil Druckmann and Bruce Straley, 2013)

Låt den rätte komma in (Tomas Alfredson, 2008), also known as *Let the Right One In*

Left 4 Dead (Mike Booth, 2008)

Let Sleeping Corpses Lie (see *Non si deve profanare il sonno dei morti*)

Let the Right One In (see *Låt den rätte komma in*)

Lethal Weapon (Richard Donner, 1987)

Magic Cop (see *Qu mo jing cha*)

Das Millionenspiel (Tom Toelle, 1970), also known as *The Millions Game*

The Millions Game (see *Das Millionenspiel*)

Minecraft (Markus "Notch" Persson, 2009)

Mr. Vampire (see *Geung si sin sang*)

Mr. Vampire 5 (see *Qu mo jing cha*)

My Date with a Vampire (see *Ngo wo geun see yau gor yue wui*)

Ngo wo geun see yau gor yue wui (Sap Sam Chan, 1998), also known as *My Date with a Vampire*

Night of the Living Dead (George A. Romero, 1968)

A Nightmare on Elm Street (Wes Craven, 1984)

A Nightmare on Elm Street (Samuel Bayer, 2010)

"No Sanctuary," *The Walking Dead* (Greg Nicotero, 2014)

Non si deve profanare il sonno dei morti (Jorge Grau, 1979), also known as *Let Sleeping Corpses Lie*

The Odd Couple (Gene Saks, 1968)

"Once Bitten," *SpongeBob SquarePants* (Stephen Hillenburg, 2006)

El orfanato (J.A. Bayona, 2007), also known as *The Orphanage*

The Orphanage (see *El orfanato*)

The Plague of the Zombies (John Gilling, 1966)

Plants vs. Zombies (George Fan, 2009)

Le prix du danger (Yves Boisset, 1983), also known as *The Prize of Peril*

The Prize of Peril (see *Le prix du danger*)

Qu mo jing cha (Wei Tung, 1990) also known as *Magic Cop* and *Mr. Vampire 5*

Resident Evil (Paul W. S. Anderson, 2002)

Resident Evil: Apocalypse (Alexander Witt, 2004)

Resident Evil Director's Cut (Shinji Mikami and Mitsuhisa Hosoki, 1996), also known as *Bio Hazard*

The Return of the Living Dead (Dan O'Bannon, 1985)

The Returned (see *Les revenants*)

Les revenants (Robin Campillo, 2004), also known as *The Returned* and *They Came Back*

"Save the Last One," *The Walking Dead* (Phil Abraham, 2011)

Scooby-Doo on Zombie Island (Hiroshi Aoyama, Kazumi Fukushima, and Jim Stenstrum, 1998)

Scream (Wes Craven, 1996)

"Serge et Toni," *Les revenants* (Frédéric Mermoud, 2012)

Shaun of the Dead (Edgar Wright, 2004)

The Silence of the Lambs (Jonathan Demme, 1991)

The Sixth Sense (M. Night Shyamalan, 1999)

"The Suicide King," *The Walking Dead* (Lesli Linka Glatter, 2013)

Survival of the Dead (George A. Romero, 2009)

The Texas Chainsaw Massacre (Tobe Hooper, 1974)

The Texas Chainsaw Massacre (Marcus Nispel, 2003)

"30 Days Without an Accident," *The Walking Dead* (Greg Nicotero, 2013)

They Came Back (see *Les revenants*)

Thriller (John Landis, 1983)

28 Days Later (Danny Boyle, 2002)

Uninvited (ICOM Simulations, 1986)

Vacation (Harold Ramis, 1983)

"Vatos," *The Walking Dead* (Johan Renck, 2010)

The Walking Dead: Season One (Sean Vanaman, Jake Rodkin, Dennis Lenart, Eric Parsons, Nick Herman, and Sean Ainsworth, 2012)

War of the Worlds (Steven Spielberg, 2005)

Warm Bodies (Jonathan Levine, 2013)

Wasting Away (Matthew Kohnen, 2007), also known as *Aaah! Zombies!!*

White Zombie (Victor Halperin, 1932)

World War Z (Marc Forster, 2013)

Zombi (Yannick Cadin and S. L. Coemelck, 1986)

Zombi 2 (Lucio Fulci, 1979), also known as *Zombie*

Zombie (see *Zombi 2*)

Zombie-American (Nick Poppy, 2005)

Zombieland (Ruben Fleischer, 2009)

Zombies: A Living History (David V. Nicholson, 2011)

Zombies of Mora Tau (Edward L. Cahn, 1957)

CHAPTER NOTES

Preface

1. Bishop, "Raising the Dead."
2. Bishop, *American Zombie Gothic*.
3. See Phillips, "Zombie Studies Gain Ground on College Campuses."
4. "New Course Explores Use of Zombies in Pop Culture."
5. "Michigan College Offers Course in Zombies, Apocalypse."
6. Accomando, "SDSU Offers Its First Zombies Class to Reanimate Students."
7. "SW290."
8. Phillips, "Feed Your Brain with Brains."

Introduction

1. Lauro and Embry, "A Zombie Manifesto," 85–86.
2. Poole, *Monsters in America*, 21.
3. Lauro and Embry, "A Zombie Manifesto," 87.
4. Cohen, "Monster Culture (Seven Theses)," 4; Poole, *Monsters in America*, 5.
5. Ackermann and Gauthier, "The Ways and Nature of the Zombi," 468.
6. Davis, *Serpent and the Rainbow*, 83.
7. Seabrook, *The Magic Island*, 101.
8. Hurston, *Tell My Horse*, 195.
9. Gary D. Rhodes has written the definitive work on Halperin's film, *White Zombie: Anatomy of a Horror Film* (2001).
10. Russell, *Book of the Dead*, 23.
11. The modern-day conception of zombies as infectious, overpowering hordes of mindless monsters might actually have its origins in a narrative as unlikely as Peyo's Belgian comic series *Les Schtroumpfs* (*The Smurfs*). In 1959, he and Yvan Delporte created *Les Schtroumpfs noirs* (*The Black Smurfs*, repub-

lished in English as the less-racially offensive *The Purple Smurfs*), the tale of a blue Smurf that is stung by a "Bzz" fly and turned into a raving, black-skinned Smurf that can only say "Gnap!" and is driven to bite and subsequently infect other Smurfs. These "black Smurfs" evince some intelligence, and the condition can luckily be cured, which Papa Smurf manages (albeit accidentally) (Peyo, *The Purple Smurfs*). In my research, I have found no evidence Romero was inspired by the comic—or even aware of it—but it is certainly worth noting.
12. See Bishop, "Assemblage Filmmaking," for a lengthier discussion of Romero's adaptation process.
13. Poole, *Monsters in America*, 194.
14. Lauro and Embry argue this also makes the zombies not just metaphors for slaves but also for slave rebellion ("A Zombie Manifesto," 90).
15. See Poole, *Monsters in America*, 197–200.
16. Cohen, "Undead (A Zombie Oriented Ontology)," 405.
17. "Box Office/Business for Day of the Dead (1985)" and "Box Office/Business for The Return of the Living Dead." *Day of the Dead* actually made three times as much money per screen as *The Return of the Living Dead*, but the fact that Romero's film had such a limited release underscores a clear shift in studio interest to comedic zombie films.
18. "Box Office/Business for Resident Evil."
19. For some reason, I am most often asked whether I think slow or fast zombies are "better," and the Internet is rife with animated and passionate debates on the subject. For the record, I prefer slow zombies; I find their relentless, unstoppable plodding (not unlike the persistent Pepé Le Pew) more uncanny and thus more

terrifying than the animistic ferocity of preternaturally strong and fast zombies.

20. Derksen and Hick, "Your Zombie and You," 15.

21. Released on DVD in the U.S. as *Aaah! Zombies!!*

22. Pokornowski, "Burying the Living with the Dead," 53.

23. See "What Is Humans vs Zombies."

24. See *Zed Events* and *Zombie Survival Course.*

25. See "A Zombie Infested 5K Obstacle Course Race."

26. See Hill, "Undead Ahead."

27. See Ma, *The Zombie Combat Manual*, and Kielpinski, *Surviving the Zombie Outbreak.*

28. See Shandrow, "As 'The Walking Dead' Thrives, So Do Zombie Survival Camps," and "Survive the Apocalypse."

29. See Richards, *The Zombie Cookbook*, and Wilson and Bauthus, *The Art of Eating through the Zombie Apocalypse.*

30. I explore and attempt to explain the allure of these "zombie lifestyle desires" in my recent contribution to *Zombie Renaissance in Popular Culture.* See my "The Contemporary Zombie as Seductive Proselyte," 26–38.

31. See *Zombie Research Society.*

32. See *Zombie Science: Zombie Institute for Theoretical Studies.*

33. See De Vise, "Exploring the Undead."

34. See Ryan, "'Walking Dead' Comes Alive in the Online Classroom."

35. Magistrale, *Abject Terrors*, xiii.

36. See Leverette, "The Funk of Forty Thousand Years," 203; Hubner, Leaning, and Manning, "Introduction," 7; and Manning, "Zombies, Zomedies, Digital Fan Cultures and the Politics of Taste," 164.

37. Dendle, "The Zombie as a Barometer of Cultural Anxiety," 54.

38. See CNN, "New Species of 'Zombifying' Fungi Discovered in Brazil's Atlantic Rain Forest."

39. See Koerth-Baker, "Attack of the Zombie Maples."

40. See Welsh, "Zombie Caterpillars Rain Death from Treetops."

41. See Macintosh, "Sun Eruption May Have Spawned Zombie Satellite."

42. See "'Zombie' Stars Cast Light on Dark Energy."

43. See Boyle, "Only Mostly Dead."

44. See Zimmer, "Could an Inner Zombie Be Controlling Your Brain?"

45. See Landau, "Inside Zombie Brains."

46. See Verstynen and Voytek, *Do Zombies Dream of Undead Sheep?*

47. See Fetherston, "Addicts Depicted as 'Zombies' in Drug Treatment Clinic Row."

48. See Strickland, "How Zombie Computers Work."

49. See Wagenseil, "New OS × Trojan Lays Groundwork for Mac Zombie Army."

50. See Randall, "Bankers See $1 Trillion of Zombie Investments Stranded in the Oil Fields."

51. See Clarke, "Zombie Stormont."

52. See Charbonneau, "Professor Uses Mathematics to Defend against the Zombie Apocalypse."

53. See Singel, "Zombie Computers Decried as Imminent National Threat."

54. See "Europe's Zombie Banks: Blight of the Living Dead."

55. See Alonso-Zaldivar, "'Zombie' in the Budget."

56. See Centers for Disease Control and Prevention, "Zombie Preparedness."

57. Bishop, *American Zombie Gothic*, 36.

58. Cohen, "Undead (A Zombie Oriented Ontology)," 401.

59. See Lauro and Embry, "A Zombie Manifesto."

Chapter 1

1. This narrative structure manifests repeatedly in Robert Kirkman's comic series *The Walking Dead* (2003–), as well as the television adaptation from the American Movie Classics network (2010–), arguably the most popular and widely consumed apocalyptic zombie narrative to date. While much of my argument about the "new" zombie Gothic applies to both versions of this text, this chapter focuses exclusively on zombie cinema (I examine Kirkman's comic series in Chapter 4 and look briefly at the television series in my Conclusion).

2. This idealized conception of the New World as the utopian community to which all other human societies look for inspiration and guidance was appropriated from the New Testament (Matt 5:14) by John Winthrop in his 1630 sermon "A Modell of Christian Charity," and it continues to enjoy a strong presence in current U.S. political rhetoric.

3. Hogle, "Introduction," 2.

4. Savoy, "The Face of the Tenant," 9.

5. Byron, "Introduction," 3.

6. Hogle, "Introduction," 2.

7. Ibid, 4.

8. Freud, "The Uncanny," 124.

9. For sake of space, I will be focusing on Romero's six zombie films, as most of the other successful zombie narratives have followed, imitated, revisited, and embraced these movies and their generic features as canonical.

10. Botting, *Gothic*, 4.

11. Bruhm, "The Contemporary Gothic," 264.

12. Botting, "Aftergothic," 284.

13. Ibid, 282.

14. Savoy, "The Rise of American Gothic," 168.

15. Ibid, 172.

16. Ibid, 175.

17. Savoy, "The Face of the Tenant," 10.

18. Byron, "Introduction," 9.

19. Edwards and Monnet, "Introduction," 2.

20. Hogle, "The Ghost of the Counterfeit in the Genesis of the Gothic," 25.

21. Botting, *Gothic*, 3.

22. Botting, "Aftergothic," 279.

23. Edwards and Monnet, "Introduction," 12.

24. Botting, "Aftergothic," 277.

25. I explore the relationship between zombie cinema and zombie video games in more detail in Chapter 7.

26. Bruhm, "The Contemporary Gothic," 268.

27. Botting, "Aftergothic," 293.

28. Ibid, 279.

29. Botting, *Gothic*, 15.

30. Bruhm, "The Contemporary Gothic," 273.

31. For an insightful analysis of Brooks' novel in terms of the globalgothic, see Botting, "Globalzombie" 197–200.

32. "Zombie," *Box Office Mojo*.

33. Edwards and Monnet, "Introduction," 3.

34. Byron, "Introduction," 1.

35. I discuss (and critique) *Warm Bodies* in detail in Chapter 9.

36. Byron, "Introduction," 3.

37. The races and nationalities of the various characters are not always overtly stated or established in the film itself, so I am relying on demographic information about the actors who portray them as well.

38. Botting, *Gothic*, 199.

Chapter 2

1. Dirks, "The 'Best Picture' Academy Awards." In fact, only two supernatural horror films have ever even been *nominated* for the Best Picture Oscar: *The Exorcist* (1973, directed by William Friedkin) and *The Sixth Sense* (1999, directed by M. Night Shyamalan), although I suppose a case could be made for Darren Aronofsky's *Black Swan* (2010).

2. Cohen, "Undead (A Zombie Oriented Ontology)," 401.

3. Dargis, Review of *Zombieland*, C10.

4. See in particular Linda Badley's "Zombie Splatter Comedy from *Dawn* to *Shaun*" on zombie splatter comedy and the fifth chapter of my *American Zombie Gothic*.

5. In my earlier academic work, I labeled the "zombie comedy" subgenre the *zombedy*, but I am now using the more concise and widely used term *zomedy*.

6. Cohen, "Undead (A Zombie Oriented Ontology)," 401.

7. "Box Office/Business for *Zombieland*."

8. "*Zombieland* (2009)."

9. Collis and Nashawaty, "Zombies A–Z."

10. See Chapter 1 for my discussion of the new American zombie Gothic and its embracing of mobility rather than stability.

11. Frye, *Anatomy of Criticism*, 163. In fact, the *Entertainment Weekly* box office report for October 23, 2009, declares, "Horror films usually drop off more than 50 percent in their second weekends. But with only a 40 percent drop from its $24.7 million debut, the gory-but-hilarious monster flick is performing more like a comedy" ("The Chart," 46).

12. Frye, *Anatomy of Criticism*, 33–34.

13. Ibid, 35.

14. Ibid, 207.

15. See Frye, *Anatomy of Criticism*, 37.

16. Frye, *Anatomy of Criticism*, 38.

17. Ibid, 219.

18. Although the couple is initially presented as the "Adam and Eve" of the post-apocalyptic society of the shopping mall, Francine ends up refusing Stephen's gift of a wedding ring, and she appears increasingly in shots that frame her apart from her male companions.

19. Frye, *Anatomy of Criticism*, 208–209.

20. Ibid, 210.

21. Ibid, 209.

22. Released in English as *Let Sleeping Corpses Lie*.

23. Also known as simply *Zombie*.

24. Released in the United States as *Dead Alive*.

25. Campbell, *The Hero with a Thousand Faces*, 51.

26. This pair of films illustrate how the claims I present in Chapter 1 about the Gothic zombie film also pertain to the zomedy: *Braindead*, produced in the latter century, represents a static narrative founded on the defense of a single location; *Shaun of the Dead*, on the other hand, is structured as a quest narrative and road trip in which the protagonists are constantly on the move as they seek increasingly safer places of refuge.

27. For an in-depth analysis of Wright's film, see Lynn Pifer's "Slacker Bites Back."

28. Frye, *Anatomy of Criticism*, 186.

29. Russell, *Book of the Dead*, 157.

30. Frye, *Anatomy of Criticism*, 34.

31. In *Anatomy of Criticism*, Frye argues the catharsis that occurs during the dramatic comedy is not one of pity and fear, as in the tragedy (37), but rather sympathy and ridicule (43).

32. See Frye, *Anatomy of Criticism*, 44.

33. Frye, *Anatomy of Criticism*, 44.

34. Ibid, 187.

35. See Frye, *Anatomy of Criticism*, 35.

36. Frye, *Anatomy of Criticism*, 203.

37. Ibid, 203.

38. Ibid, 189.

39. Ibid, 44.

40. Frye emphasizes how "the appearance of this new society is frequently signalized by some kind of party of festive ritual" (*Anatomy of Criticism*, 163), and Pacific Playground can be seen as a place of the *carnivalesque*, in Mikhail Bakhtin's sense of the word.

Chapter 3

1. Cohen, "Undead (A Zombie Oriented Ontology)," 401.

2. For a concise discussion of the history and development of "survivalism" as a literary subgenre, see my "Survivalism" article in Grossman, *Sense of Wonder*, 928–930.

3. For a quick overview of apocalyptic fiction and literature, see Irene Sywenky's article "After the End: Post-Apocalyptic Science Fiction" in Grossman, *Sense of Wonder*, 438–440.

4. Ryan's novel has many of its themes and much of its plot and structure in common with Justin Cronin's epic post-apocalyptic horror novel *The Passage* (2010) as well, yet as the latter work was published just shortly after *The Forest of Hands and Teeth*, the two works appear to merely manifest a shared zeitgeist rather than the one directly influencing the other.

5. Tellingly, when the episode was adapted as a children's book, the title was changed from "Once Bitten" to *Attack of the Zombies!* (2011, written by Alex Harvey).

6. Lubar, *My Rotten Life*, 13–14.

7. Ibid, 36.

8. Ibid, 64.

9. Ibid, 64.

10. McGillis, "The Night Side of Nature," 231.

11. Jackson, Coats, and McGillis, "Introduction," 8.

12. Carroll, *The Philosophy of Horror*, 158.

13. Smith, "The Scary Tale Looks for a Family," 131.

14. In fact, Stine references *Night of the Living Dead*, along with Romero's other zombie films, in his introduction to *Zombie Town*, establishing his intentionality vis-à-vis this source material.

15. Jackson, Coats, McGillis, "Introduction," 1 & 9.

16. Stine, *Zombie Town*, Chapter 4.

17. Ibid, Chapter 11.

18. Smith, "The Scary Tale Looks for a Family," 133.

19. Stine, *Zombie Town*, Chapter 12.

20. McGillis, "The Night Side of Nature," 227.

21. I originally presented my theory of "assemblage" texts in Bishop, "Assemblage Filmmaking"; see particularly 269–270.

22. Jackson, Coats, and McGillis, "Introduction," 9.

23. Most notably in Campbell's landmark work, *The Hero with a Thousand Faces* (1949).

24. Nilsen and Donelson, *Literature for Today's Young Adults*, 20–38.

25. Rosen, *Apocalyptic Transformation*, xi.

26. Bishop, *American Zombie Gothic*, 94.

27. Ibid, 19.

28. Consider the opening credit sequence of Edgar Wright's romantic zombie-comedy film *Shaun of the Dead* (2004), which deftly blurs the lines between teenagers on cellphones and listening en masse to iPods and the invading army of the walking dead.

29. Nilsen and Donelson, *Literature for Today's Young Adults*, 20.

30. Ryan, *The Forest of Hands and Teeth*, 1.

31. Ibid, 3.

32. Nilsen and Donelson, *Literature for Today's Young Adults*, 29–30.

33. Ryan, *The Forest of Hands and Teeth*, 10.

34. Ibid, 2.

35. Ibid, 12–13.

36. Jackson, Coats, and McGillis, "Introduction," 11.

37. Ryan, *The Forest of Hands and Teeth*, 11.

38. Ibid, 2.

39. As Romero shows in *Night of the Living Dead*, when the dead wear the faces of former friends and loved ones, they become much more dangerous; they inject grief and remorse into the otherwise protective reactions of fear and self-preservation.

40. Rosen, *Apocalyptic Transformation*, xiii–xiv.

41. Ryan, *The Forest of Hands and Teeth*, 13.

42. Ibid, 42.

43. Campbell, *The Hero with a Thousand Faces*, 49–58.

44. Ryan, *The Forest of Hands and Teeth*, 12–13.

45. Nilsen and Donelson, *Literature for Today's Young Adults*, 28.

46. Ryan, *The Forest of Hands and Teeth*, 15.

47. Cummins, "Hermione in the Bathroom," 178.

48. Ryan, *The Forest of Hands and Teeth*, 22.

49. Ibid, 24.

50. Ibid, 26.

51. Ibid, 35.

52. Jackson, Coats, and McGillis, "Introduction," 4.

53. Ryan, *The Forest of Hands and Teeth*, 45.

54. Smith, "The Scary Tale Looks for a Family," 139.

55. Ryan, *The Forest of Hands and Teeth*, 52.

56. Ibid, 52.

57. Ibid, 67.

58. Ibid, 68.

59. Ibid, 72.

60. Ibid, 83.

61. Ibid, 99.

62. McGillis, "The Night Side of Nature," 229.

63. Rosen, *Apocalyptic Transformation*, xii.

64. Ibid, xx.

65. See Cohen, "Monster Culture (Seven Theses), 4.

66. See Dendle, "The Zombie as a Barometer of Cultural Anxiety."

67. McGillis, "The Night Side of Nature," 229–230.

Chapter 4

1. Dendle, *The Zombie Movie Encyclopedia*, 12.

2. In addition to the "serious" zombie narratives that present the human protagonists as monstrous—which is the focus of this chapter—many zombie comedies, such as Andrew Currie's *Fido* (2006) and Matthew Kohnen's *Wasting Away* (2007), offer a similar inversion. These "zomedies" ask audiences to consider the zombies in sympathetic terms, pitted against cruel and menacing human antagonists, but such texts are beyond the scope of this discussion. But I do consider the romantic zombie protagonist in Chapter 9.

3. Although the AMC television series *The Walking Dead* (2010–) has already proven it will head in the same dark direction as its antecedent source material, I have limited this chapter to an investigation of Kirkman's comic series alone. For in-depth discussions of the television series, See *"We're All Infected": Essays on AMC's* The Walking Dead *and the Fate of the Human* (2014), edited by Dawn Keetley.

4. Nietzsche, *Beyond Good and Evil*, 85.

5. Boon, "Ontological Anxiety Made Flesh," 33.

6. Ibid, 34.

7. Cohen, "Monster Culture (Seven Theses)," 6.

8. Ibid, 4.

9. Banes, "A Word of Warning about Zombies," 7.

10. See Feldstein, "The Thing from the Grave."

11. Such as Dick Beck's "Horror of the Mixed Torsos" (1953) and Wally Wood's "The Thing from the Sea" (1954).

12. Streeter, "I Am a Zombie," 17.

13. Kenemore, "Rick Grimes: A Zombie Among Men," 189.

14. At the 33rd International Conference on the Fantastic in the Arts, China Miéville argued that humans, by definition, cannot be "monsters" but only described as "monstrous" ("Special Panel: The Monstrous"), thus my attempts to delineate the difference between a liminal Other acting according to its inherent violent nature and a human being making horrifying and destructive—yet fully conscious—choices.

15. Pokornowski, "Burying the Living with the Dead," 41.

16. Kirkman and Moore, *Days Gone Bye*.

17. Ibid.

18. Ibid.

19. Riley, "Zombie People," 92.

20. Pokornowski, "Burying the Living with the Dead," 44.

21. Kirkman and Moore, *Days Gone Bye.*

22. Kirkman, Adlard, and Rathburn, *Miles Behind Us.*

23. Kenemore, "Rick Grimes: A Zombie Among Men," 193.

24. Kirkman, Adlard, and Rathburn, *Safety Behind Bars.*

25. Kirkman. Adlard, and Rathburn, *The Heart's Desire.*

26. Kirkman, Adlard, and Rathburn, *Safety Behind Bars.*

27. On 30 September 2011, U.S.-born Anwar al-Awlaki was killed in a drone strike in Yemen on the direct orders of President Obama ("Islamist Cleric Anwar al-Awlaki Killed in Yemen"). Critics of the military action claim that since al-Awlaki was still a U.S. citizen, he should have been tried in a court rather than being killed without due process and outside of an active war zone (see Jacob, "Anwar Al-Awlaki").

28. Pokornowski, "Burying the Living with the Dead," 48.

29. Kirkman, Adlard, and Rathburn, *The Heart's Desire.*

30. Ibid.

31. Ibid.

32. This totalitarian approach to safety and order is made more explicit in the AMC television adaptation of *The Walking Dead*, when Rick's rule is cynically designated a "Ricktatorship" ("Beside the Dying Fire" [2012, directed by Ernest R. Dickerson]).

33. Kirkman, Adlard, and Rathburn, *This Sorrowful Life.*

34. Kirkman, Adlard, and Rathburn, *The Heart's Desire.*

35. Ibid.

36. Kenemore, "Rick Grimes: A Zombie Among Men," 187.

37. Kirkman, Adlard, and Rathburn, *Fear the Hunters.* This sequence represents one of the few times the AMC television series exceeds the graphic violence of its source material. Having successfully ambushed the remaining hunters in Father Gabriel's (Seth Gilliam) church, Rick (Andrew Lincoln) and his team brutally slaughter them before the altar, using rifle butts, knives, and a machete simply because Rick "didn't want to waste the bullets" ("Four Walls and a Roof" 2014, directed by Jeffrey F. January).

38. Ibid.

39. Kirkman, Adlard, and Rathburn, *This Sorrowful Life.*

40. Riley, "Zombie People," 96.

41. Kirkman, Adlard, and Rathburn, *Too Far Gone.*

42. Ibid. Italics added.

43. Ibid.

44. Department of Justice, "Highlights of the U.S. Patriot Act."

45. Kirkman, Adlard, and Rathburn, *Too Far Gone.*

46. Kirkman, Adlard, and Rathburn, *No Way Out.*

47. Kirkman, Adlard, and Rathburn, *We Find Ourselves.*

48. Ibid.

49. Ibid.

50. Kirkman, Adlard, Gaudiano, and Rathburn, *A New Beginning.*

51. Kirkman, Adlard, and Rathburn, *Too Far Gone.*

52. Ibid.

53. Kirkman, Adlard, and Rathburn, *Life Among Them.*

54. Kirkman, Adlard, and Rathburn, *What We Become.*

Chapter 5

1. Bishop, "Raising the Dead," 197–201, and Bishop, *American Zombie Gothic*, 12–13, 38–42, and 59–63.

2. Although zombie narratives were largely absent from more traditional forms of literature until the twenty-first century, versions of the zombie and variations on the vengeful dead returned from the grave were prevalent in a number of horror comics, especially those produced by *EC Comics*, during the 1950s. See Diehl, *Tales from the Crypt*, and Yoe and Banes, *Zombies.*

3. Pagano, "The Space of Apocalypse in Zombie Cinema," 75.

4. Harvey, "The City as a Body Politic," 27.

5. DeRosa, "September 11 and Cold War Nostalgia," 59.

6. In *Zone One*, readers never learn the protagonist's real name, but he picked up the nickname "Mark Spitz" after telling his road-clearing crew he didn't know how to swim: "they laughed. It was perfect: from now on he was Mark Spitz" (Whitehead, 147). This joke only becomes ironically clever when readers realize the protagonist is African-American (which doesn't become overt until page 231 of the 259-page novel).

7. Hoberek, "Living with PASD," 406.

8. Ibid, 407–08.

9. Anders, "Colson Whitehead's *Zone One* Shatters Your Post-Apocalyptic Fantasies."

10. DeRosa, "September 11 and Cold War Nostalgia," 64.

11. In Schulman, "My Horrible '70s Apocalypse."

12. Whitehead, *Zone One*, 212.

13. Ibid, 187.

14. Ibid, 34.

15. Ibid, 168.

16. Harvey, "The City as a Body Politic," 37.

17. Ibid, 34.

18. Ibid, 33.

19. Ibid, 25.

20. Ibid, 25.

21. Harvey points to the beneficial reconstruction efforts undertaken by both Germany and Japan after World War II, unexpected opportunities for "creative destruction" that helped lead both nations into beneficial economic renaissances ("The City as a Body Politic," 26).

22. Harvey, "The City as a Body Politic," 26.

23. Ibid, 37.

24. Ibid, 28.

25. Whitehead, *Zone One*, 88.

26. Ibid, 35.

27. Ibid, 61.

28. Ibid, 79.

29. Ibid, 88.

30. Ibid, 97.

31. See Walsh, "George W. Bush's 'Bullhorn' Moment."

32. Whitehead, *Zone One*, 4.

33. Ibid, 5.

34. Ibid, 6.

35. Ibid, 6.

36. Ibid, 61.

37. Ibid, 64.

38. Ibid, 62.

39. Ibid, 63.

40. Ibid, 89.

41. National Cancer Institute, "Understanding Cancer Series."

42. Whitehead, *Zone One*, 48.

43. Ibid, 14.

44. Ibid, 48.

45. Ibid, 75.

46. Ibid, 76–77.

47. National Cancer Institute, "Understanding Cancer Series."

48. Whitehead, *Zone One*, 48–49.

49. Ibid, 50.

50. Ibid, 86.

51. Whitehead consciously references Romero's *Night of the Living Dead* here, quoting Sheriff McClelland (George Kosana).

52. Whitehead, *Zone One*, 96.

53. Ibid, 82.

54. Ibid, 52.

55. Ibid, 31.

56. Ibid, 12.

57. Ibid, 61.

58. Ibid, 38.

59. Ibid, 242.

60. Ibid, 243.

61. Ibid, 248.

62. Ibid, 65.

63. Ibid, 65.

64. Nora, "Between Memory and History," 7.

65. Whitehead, *Zone One*, 5.

66. Nora, "Between Memory and History," 12.

67. Ibid, 12.

68. Whitehead, *Zone One*, 23.

69. Ibid, 38.

70. Ibid, 46.

71. Ibid, 48.

72. Ibid, 4.

73. Ibid, 5.

74. Ibid, 6.

75. Ibid, 86.

76. Ibid, 70.

77. Ibid, 70–71.

78. See Freud, "The Uncanny."

79. Whitehead, *Zone One*, 54.

80. Hoberek, "Living with PASD," 412.

81. Whitehead, *Zone One*, 55.

82. Ibid, 54.

83. Ibid, 53.

84. Harvey, "The City as a Body Politic," 41.

85. Ibid, 41.

86. Ibid, 43.

87. Anders, "Colson Whitehead's *Zone One* Shatters Your Post-Apocalyptic Fantasies."

88. Whitehead, *Zone One*, 14.

89. Ibid, 15.

90. Ibid, 16.

91. Ibid, 24.

92. Ibid, 26.

93. Ibid, 59.

94. See Pagano, "The Space of Apocalypse in Zombie Cinema," 84.

95. Whitehead, *Zone One*, 223.

96. Ibid, 224.

97. Ibid, 225.

98. Ibid, 228.

99. Ibid, 244.

100. Ibid, 257–58.

Chapter 6

1. For a discussion of zombie affectation through simulated performance, see my "The Contemporary Zombie as Seductive Proselyte" (26–38).

2. Recent stage adaptations include Keith Tadrowski's 1994 production of *Night of the Living Dead: The Play*, Lori Allen Ohm's 2003 stage version, and *Night of the Living Dead Live*, created and produced in Toronto by Christopher Harrison and Phil Pattison in 2013.

3. Wessendorf, Email interview.

4. The story was adapted in 1970 for German television as *Das Millionenspiel* (*The Millions Game*, directed by Tom Toelle) and again in 1983 as the French film *Le prix du danger* (*The Prize of Peril*, directed by Yves Boisset).

5. Andrejevic, *Reality TV*, 102.

6. Johnson, "Televising the Panopticon," 2.

7. Andrejevic, *Reality TV*, 102.

8. Johnson, "Televising the Panopticon," 3.

9. Baudrillard, *Simulacra and Simulation*, 1.

10. Ibid, 12.

11. Ibid, 12.

12. Ibid, 13.

13. Trottier, "Watching Yourself, Watching Others," 260.

14. Johnson, "Televising the Panopticon," 2.

15. Foucault, *Discipline and Punish*, 200.

16. Andrejevic, *Reality TV*, 103.

17. Johnson, "Televising the Panopticon," 3.

18. Foucault, *Discipline and Punish*, 217.

19. Baudrillard, *Simulacra and Simulation*, 29.

20. Mathiesen, "The Viewer Society," 219.

21. Ibid, 219.

22. Ibid, 220–21.

23. Hill, *Reality TV*, 118.

24. Andrejevic, *Reality TV*, 128.

25. Trottier, "Watching Yourself, Watching Others," 260.

26. Egginton, "The Best of Worst of Our Nature," 179.

27. Andrejevic, *Reality TV*, 176.

28. Egginton, "The Best of Worst of Our Nature," 191.

29. In "Storm Hits Fox's New 'Temptation Island.'"

30. In Carter, "Some Sponsors Can't Accept Racy Reality."

31. Andrejevic, *Reality TV*, 189.

32. Foucault, *Discipline and Punish*, 217.

33. Baudrillard, *Simulacra and Simulation*, 30.

34. Hand and Wilson, *Grand-Guignol*, ix.

35. Ibid, 4–5.

36. Ibid, 9.

37. Ibid, x.

38. Carroll, *The Philosophy of Horror*, 15.

39. See Hand and Wilson, *Grand-Guignol*, 53–66, for a detailed discussion of the technical aspects of the Grand-Guignol, including its use of practice effects.

40. Foucault, *Discipline and Punish*, 58.

41. In Fournier, "Zombie Reality Show."

42. Wessendorf, Email interview.

43. In Fournier, "Zombie Reality Show."

44. Ibid.

45. Hall and Wilson, *Grand-Guignol*, 27.

46. Hand and Wilson recount how "Maurey added a *médecin de service*, or house-doctor, to the permanent staff of the theatre to attend personally to members of the audience who were taken ill during the performance" (*Grand-Guignol*, 12).

47. *Uncle Vanya and Zombies*, Playbill.

48. Ibid.

49. Hall and Wilson, *Grand-Guignol*, 32.

50. Mathiesen, "The Viewer Society," 222.

51. As mentioned, the characters in the play go by the real names of the actors portraying them, resulting in a hyperreality that blurs the lines between play and reality.

52. Hall and Wilson, *Grand-Guignol*, 11.

53. Pierron, *Le Grand Guignol*, xiii.

54. Hall and Wilson, *Grand-Guignol*, 50.

55. Andrejevic, *Reality TV*, 190.

56. Hall and Wilson, *Grand-Guignol*, 35–36.

57. Ibid, 36.

58. Ibid, 44.

59. I tip my hat to Wessendorf's creativity here; with all the zombie narratives I have consumed over the years, I have *never* seen a zombie on a treadmill.

60. Walt's inappropriate behavior is reminiscent of tactless news reporters who insist on interviewing people who have just survived or witnessed a debilitating tragedy.

61. Andrejevic, *Reality TV*, 187.

Chapter 7

1. Bishop, *American Zombie Gothic*, 16.

2. Krzywinska, "Zombies in Gamespace," 159.

3. Originally released in Japan as *Bio Hazard*.

4. Weise, "How the Zombie Changed Videogames," 153.

5. Russell, *Book of the Dead*, 172.

6. Weise, "How the Zombie Changed Videogames," 153.

7. Krzywinska, "Zombies in Gamespace," 153.

8. Even if the zombie foes are living creatures, humans merely infected by a virus or other kind of pathogen, players may consider them "dead already," as the games almost never include a method by which the monstrosity can be cured.

9. Russell, *Book of the Dead*, 171.

10. Ibid, 171.

11. Weise provides an excellent and concise "pre-history of digital zombies" that explains these early zombie video games in more detail ("How the Zombie Changed Videogames," 154–155).

12. Krzywinska, "Zombies in Gamespace," 157.

13. Weise, "How the Zombie Changed Videogames," 156.

14. In Feature Creature, "Creating Evil Incarnate," 33.

15. Schott, "Digital Dead," 143.

16. Ibid, 144.

17. Weise, "How the Zombie Changed Videogames," 158.

18. In Feature Creature, "Creating Evil Incarnate," 32.

19. Russell, *Book of the Dead*, 171.

20. Weise, "How the Zombie Changed Videogames," 157.

21. Ibid, 154.

22. Schott, "Digital Dead," 147. For further analysis, see Schott's thorough close reading and discussion of *Dead Rising* ("Digital Dead," 146–150).

23. Weise, "How the Zombie Changed Videogames," 152.

24. Krzywinska, "Zombies in Gamespace," 156.

25. Le Diberder, "L'interactivité, une nouvelle frontier du cinema," 122.

26. I discuss this point at some length in Chapter 1.

27. While not unique to *The Last of Us*, another innovation of the game are zombies that pass through different phases of development: the infected change into different kinds of monsters as the fungus invades more and more of the human body before finally killing the host.

28. When the flashlight sputters out, players must shake their controller to get it working again, a nice piece of verisimilitude that further engages the gamer directly with the action.

29. Krzywinska, "Zombies in Gamespace," 155.

30. A post-apocalyptic scenario in which an adult must care for a relatively defenseless child has a rich tradition, from films such as James Cameron's *Aliens* (1986) to novels such as Cormac McCarthy's *The Road* (2006). This trope has becoming increasingly common in video games; in fact, much of what makes *The Last of Us* such an engaging, personal story of human survival could be found first in Tell-Tale Game's critically acclaimed *The Walking Dead: Season One* (2012), a strikingly similar game in which players control Lee Everett (Dave Fennoy) as he tries to survive a zombie apocalypse while protecting his young surrogate daughter Clementine (Melissa Hutchison).

31. Quoted in and translated by Wolf and Perron, "Introduction," 8.

32. See Kaja Silverman's *The Subject of Semiotics* for a thorough explanation of how cinema confers subjectivity upon its viewing audience (194–215).

33. Weise, "How the Zombie Changed Videogames," 165.

34. Krzywinska, "Zombies in Gamespace," 164.

35. Ibid, 161.

36. I don't interpret Ellie's weaknesses as any kind of insidious sexism; she is weaker than Joel because she is only fourteen years old, and the storyline relies too heavily on her needing Joel's protection for her to become suddenly equally capable as an avatar.

37. Weise, "How the Zombie Changed Videogames," 159.

38. Simon, "Absurd Creature of the Week."

39. Simon explains how other "hyperparasitic fungi" have developed that attack the *Ophiocordyceps* spores in return, a system of checks and balances that prevents an infected zombie ant from wiping out its entire species, thus robbing the fungus of the hosts needed to maintain its system of reproduction ("Absurd Creature of the Week").

40. Whenever players encounter rooms full of these spores, Joel automatically dons his gasmask and gameplays continues as usual. *The Last of Us* could have made better use of this aspect of the infestation, though, by giving gamers control over the gasmask—failure to do so at the right moments could result in death or, better yet, infection—or by having the equipment hamper their ability to see clearly or fight effectively.

Chapter 8

1. These remake pairs include films such as *The Last House on the Left* (Wes Craven's in 1972 and Dennis Iliadis's in 2009), *The Texas Chainsaw Massacre* (Tobe Hooper's in 1974 and Marcus Nispel's in 2003), *Dawn of the Dead* (George A. Romero's in 1978 and Zack Snyder's in 2004), *Halloween* (John Carpenter's in 1978 and Rob Zombie's in 2007), *Friday the 13th* (Sean S. Cunningham's in 1980 and Marcus Nispel's in 2009), and *A Nightmare on Elm Street* (Craven's in 1984 and Samuel Bayer's in 2010).

2. Bishop, *American Zombie Gothic*, 12.

3. Cohen, "The monster is not a category."

4. Cohen, "[T]axonomy is a kind of poetry."

5. Hurston, *Tell My Horse*, 182–183. For additional first-hand accounts concerning the Haitian zombie, see Seabrook, *The Magic Island*, and Davis, *The Serpent and the Rainbow*.

6. According to Wade Davis, "In Haiti, the fear is not of being harmed by zombis; it is fear of becoming one" (*The Serpent and the Rainbow*, 187).

7. In Nicholson, *Zombies: A Living History*.

8. "Jiang Shi."

9. "Chinese Vampire."

10. "Jiang Shi."

11. "Chinese Vampire."

12. In Nicholson, *Zombies: A Living History*.

13. Bussey, *The Thousand and One Nights*, 196.

14. Lamb, "How Ghouls Work."

15. Ibid.

16. In Nicholson, *Zombies: A Living History*.

17. In William of Newburgh's *Historia rerum Anglicarum*, Book Five, Chapter 22, he records instances of the dead coming back to life, such as the following:

A certain man died, and, according to custom, by the honorable exertion of his wife and kindred, was laid in the tomb on the eve of the Lord's Ascension. On the following night, however, having entered the bed where his wife was reposing, he not only terrified her on awaking, but nearly crushed her by the insupportable weight of his body. The next night, also, he afflicted the astonished woman in the same manner, who, frightened at the danger, as the struggle of the third night drew near, took care to remain awake herself, and surround herself with watchful companions. Still he came; but being repulsed by the shouts of the watchers, and seeing that he was prevented from doing mischief, he departed.

18. William of Newburgh, *Historia rerum Anglicarum*.

19. Ibid.

20. Lecouteux, *The Return of the Dead*, 84.

21. Ibid, 130–131.

22. "The Walking Dead."

23. Ellis-Davidson, *The Road to Hel*.

24. Lecouteux, *The Return of the Dead*, 132.

25. In Nicholson, *Zombies: A Living History*.

26. Ibid.

27. Erlend represents a key character trope found increasingly in postmodern horror films; like Randy (Jamie Kennedy) from Wes Craven's *Scream* (1996) and Marty (Fran Kranz) from *The Cabin in the Woods*, Erlend recalls the Fool from Shakespeare's *King Lear* (1606), the one character who knows what's going on but to whom no one will listen. Of course, as with so many of the topes and themes appearing in the film, Wirkola will come to undermine Erlend's role, revealing him to be a fool in fact, not merely in archetype.

28. Martin later makes an emergency phone call from the cabin, a comedic scene used to lighten the mood rather than keep with the continuity of the plot.

29. Simek, *Dictionary of Northern Mythology*.

30. Lecouteux, *The Return of the Dead*, 179.

31. Ellis-Davidson, *The Road to Hel*.

32. The shirt is a clever nod to Peter Jackson's zombie film from 1992, and continues to enforce *Dead Snow*'s postmodern self-referentiality.

33. In another subtle reference to U.S. popular culture, Erlend says, "Fortune and glory, kid," in English, glibly quoting *Indiana Jones and the Temple of Doom* (1984, directed by Steven Spielberg).

34. Ellis-Davidson, *The Road to Hel*.

35. Online folklorist The Viking Answer Lady writes, "The presence of great wealth within the burial mound attracted the attention of grave-robbers.... However, the would-be grave-robber had to be wary, for the haugbui [mound dweller] was a jealous guardian of its treasures, and would viciously attack those who disturbed him in his house" ("The Walking Dead"). Yet the draugar don't simply stay within the confines of their burial mounds: "While the haugbui was often content to re-

main within its grave, harming only those who trespassed upon its domain, the draugr was known to venture outside the mound, causing great harm to the living" (ibid), a loophole in the folk legend that Wirkola exploits with increasingly gory exuberance.

36. Ellis-Davidson, *The Road to Hel*.

37. While Turgåer has no direct connection to the draugar's treasure, the monsters might target him regardless because of his efforts to warn the med students; then again, once the creatures have been awakened, they might just kill any hapless human victim without needing a logical reason.

38. Chris dies shortly after having sex with Erlend, the typical and thus expected result of promiscuity in these kinds of slasher films.

39. Lecouteux describes the attack pattern of the draugar: "revenants were always trying to lure outside—far from the light that gleamed fitfully in the common room—those they wished to hurt" (*The Return of the Dead*, 138).

40. Lecouteux, *The Return of the Dead*, 177.

41. A fact that makes Martin's self-amputation of his arm near the end of the film all the more tragic.

42. See Ellis-Davidson, *The Road to Hel*, and Simek, *Dictionary of Northern Mythology*.

43. At one point, Roy destroys one of the Nazi revenants with a hammer and sickle, which he first crosses in front of him in a clever evocation of the symbol on the flag of the former Soviet Union, the country that drove the Nazis out of Norway at the end of the war.

Chapter 9

1. Backstein, "(Un)safe Sex: Romancing the Vampire," 38.

2. Dendle, *The Zombie Movie Encyclopedia: 2000–2010*, 1.

3. Botting, "Aftergothic," 286.

4. Derksen and Hick, "Your Zombie and You," 15.

5. See Dendle, *The Zombie Movie Encyclopedia: 2000–2010*, 5.

6. Because of the film's wide dissemination and commercial success, this chapter will focus exclusively on Levine's version of *Warm Bodies* instead of the source novel.

7. Tenga and Zimmerman, "Vampire Gentlemen and Zombie Beasts," 80.

8. Botting, "Love Your Zombie," 29.

9. Shakespeare, *Romeo and Juliet*, Prologue 6 & 3.

10. Byron, "Romeo and Juliet in the 'Twilight' Zone," 176.

11. Shakespeare, *Romeo and Juliet*, 2.3.65–68.

12. Meyer, *Twilight*, 23.

13. Byron, "Romeo and Juliet in the 'Twilight' Zone," 169.

14. Mulvey, "Visual Pleasure and Narrative Cinema," 203.

15. Ibid, 200.

16. Byron, "Romeo and Juliet in the 'Twilight' Zone," 173.

17. Paulhus and Williams, "The Dark Triad of Personality," 556.

18. See Jonason, et al., "The Antihero in Popular Culture," 193 & 197.

19. Paulhus and Williams, "The Dark Triad of Personality," 559.

20. Jonason, et al., "The Antihero in Popular Culture," 197.

21. Ibid, 194.

22. In Jonason et al., "The Antihero in Popular Culture," 194.

23. Ibid, 195.

24. Despite the film taking care to often use the camera to replicate R's point of view, when the zombie experiences Perry's memories, he does *not* see things from a subjective POV; instead, he views the so-called memories from an omniscient, third-person perspective. In addition to being an inaccurate representation of memory, the oversight prevents viewers from identifying with Perry at all.

25. Swann and Read, "Self Verification Processes," 352.

26. Ibid, 354.

27. Swann, Chang-Schneider, and Angulo, "Self-Verification in Relationships as an Adaptive Process," 56.

28. Kanazawa, "Why Do Some Battered Women Stay?"

29. R's journey to the human city, a host of zombies in tow, resembles in many ways the climax of Romero's *Land of the Dead* (2005). As many credit that film, along with the earlier *Day of the Dead* (1984), with the birth of the agent zombie, this sequence may indeed by a conscious homage to Romero's influence.

Conclusion

1. The creator of *The Walking Dead* comic series, Robert Kirkman, is helming the creation of this spinoff series, which is currently in the development stage. A pilot will allegedly be di-

rected by Adam Davidson and will likely premier on the AMC network in fall of 2015 (Jeffery, "Everything We Know So Far").

2. I survey and consider these "zombielike" foes in some detail in Chapter 8.

3. Bishop, *American Zombie Gothic*, 204.

4. For example, the most recent episode of *The Walking Dead*, the mid-season finale for Season 5, "Coda" (2014, directed by Ernest R. Dickerson) was watched by 14.8 million viewers, which outperformed Sunday Night Football for the fifth time that season (Patten, "'Walking Dead' Shatters Winter Finales Ratings Record").

5. Consider, for example, the dedicated collections of critical essays *Triumph of The Walking Dead* (Lowder, 2011) and *"We're All Infected"* (Keetley, 2014). Specific chapters also explore *The Walking Dead* in the scholarly anthologies *Undead in the West* (Miller and Van Riper, 2012), *Thinking Dead* (Balaji, 2013), and *Zombie Renaissance in Popular Culture* (Hubner, Leaning, and Manning, 2015).

6. Bishop, *American Zombie Gothic*, 207.

7. Farnell, "'Talking Bodies' in a Zombie Apocalypse," 177.

8. I have analyzed the emotional progression of these two characters and what the zombie apocalypse has afford their personal identities in a soon-to-be-published essay titled "Apocalyptic Psychotherapy: Emotion and Identity in AMC's *The Walking Dead*," which I initially presented in 2013 at the Identity and Emotions in Contemporary TV-Series workshop at the University of Navarra in Pamplona, Spain.

9. Beginning in the Season 1 episode "Vatos" (2010, directed by Johan Renck).

10. See "No Sanctuary" (2014, directed by Greg Nicotero).

11. Carol reveals to Beth (Emily Kinney) in the Season 3 episode "The Suicide King" (2013, directed by Lesli Linka Glatter) the unfortunate kinship she shares with Daryl: "Men

like Merle get into your head. Make you feel like you deserve the abuse."

12. "Home" (2013, directed by Seith Mann).

13. See "30 Days Without an Accident" (2013, directed by Greg Nicotero).

14. "Judge, Jury, Executioner" (2012, directed by Greg Nicotero).

15. Farnell, "'Talking Bodies' in a Zombie Apocalypse," 182.

16. "Save the Last One" (2011, directed by Phil Abraham).

17. "Better Angels" (2012, directed by Guy Ferland).

18. "A" (2014, directed by Michelle MacLaren).

19. "Four Walls and a Roof" (2014, directed by Jeffrey F. January)

20. The first season of *In the Flesh*, which is the focus my discussion, was directed by Jonny Campbell and presented as a miniseries in the spring of 2013.

21. "*In the Flesh* BBC Three, 10 p.m."

22. Renshaw, "Your Next Box Set: *In the Flesh*."

23. Ibid.

24. Emma Daly suggests Amazon Prime might pick up *In the Flesh* so the series could continue ("Could *In the Flesh* Be Saved by Amazon?").

25. "Pilot" (2015, directed by Rob Thomas)

26. See Robertson and Allred, *iZombie*.

27. Although, as I explain in Chapter 8, I personally would rather we all use the proper cultural terms to describe each of the zombie variants.

28. "Camille" (2012, directed by Fabrice Gobert)

29. "Serge et Toni" (2012, directed by Frédéric Mermoud)

30. A similar television series is currently enjoying a successful run in the U.S. as well: ABC's *Resurrection* (2014–).

31. Botting, *Gothic Romanced*, 22.

BIBLIOGRAPHY

Accomando, Beth. "SDSU Offers Its First Zombies Class to Reanimate Students." *News.* KPBS Public Broadcasting, 28 March 2014. http://www.kpbs.org/news/2014/mar/28/sdsu-offers-zombies-101.

Ackermann, Hans W., and Jeanine Gauthier. "The Ways and Nature of the Zombi." *Journal of American Folklore* 104.414 (1991): 466–494.

Alonso-Zaldivar, Ricardo. "'Zombie' in the Budget: Long-term Health Care Plan." *Politics on NBC News.* MSN, 8 October 2011. http://www.nbcnews.com/id/448 31153/#.UmUofBaxNFI.

Anders, Charlie Jane. "Colson Whitehead's *Zone One* Shatters Your Post-Apocalyptic Fantasies." *io9*, 29 December 2011. http://io9.com/5871998/colson-whiteheads-zone-one-shatters-your-post-apocalyptic-fantasies.

Andersen, Hans Christian. "The Wild Swans." 1838. Translated by Jean Hersholt. *The Hans Christian Andersen Center.* University of Southern Denmark, 8 October 2013. http://www.andersen.sdu.dk/vaerk/hersholt/TheWildSwans_e.html.

Andrejevic, Mark. *Reality TV: The Work of Being Watched.* Lanham, MD: Rowman & Littlefield, 2004.

Backstein, Karen. "(Un)safe Sex: Romancing the Vampire." *Cineaste* Winter (2009): 38–41.

Badley, Linda. "Zombie Splatter Comedy from *Dawn* to *Shaun*: Cannibal Carnivalesque." In McIntosh and Leverette, *Zombie Culture*, 35–53.

Balaji, Murali. *Thinking Dead: What the Zom-bie Apocalypse Means.* Lanham, MD: Lexington, 2013.

Banes, Stephen "Karswell." "A Word of Warning about Zombies." In Yoe and Banes, *Zombies*, 7–9.

Baudrillard, Jean. *Simulacra and Simulation.* 1981. Translated by Sheila Faria Glaser. Ann Arbor: University of Michigan Press, 1994.

Beck, Dick. "Horror of Mixed Torsos." *Dark Mysteries* #13. August 1953. In Yoe and Banes, *Zombies*, 50–55.

Beckford, William. *Vathek.* 1786. Oxford: Oxford University Press, 2013.

Bishop, Kyle William. *American Zombie Gothic: The Rise and Fall (and Rise) of the Walking Dead in Popular Culture.* Jefferson, NC: McFarland, 2010.

_____. "Assemblage Filmmaking: Approaching the Multi-Source Adaptation and Reexamining George Romero's *Night of the Living Dead*." In *Adaptation Studies: New Beginnings*, edited by Christa Albrecht-Crane and Dennis Cutchins, 263–277. Teaneck, NJ: Fairleigh Dickinson University Press, 2010.

_____. "Battling Monsters and Becoming Monstrous: Human Devolution in *The Walking Dead*." In *Monster Culture in the 21st Century: A Reader*, edited by Marina Levina and Diem-My Bui, 73–85. London: Bloomsbury, 2013.

_____. "L'émergence des *Zombie studies.* Comment les morts-vivants ont envahi l'Académie et pourquoi nous devrions nous en soucier." In *Z pour Zombies*, edited by Antonio Dominguez Leiva, Samuel Archibald, and Bernard Perron,

31–44. Montréal, QC: Presses de l'Université de Montréal, 2015.

———. "'I always wanted to see how the other half lives': The Contemporary Zombie as Seductive Proselyte." In Hubner, Leaning, and Manning, *Zombie Renaissance in Popular Culture*, 26–38.

———. "The New American Zombie Gothic: Road Trips, Globalization, and the War on Terror," *Gothic Studies*, first published online 8 June 2015, DOI: http://dx.doi.org/10.7227/GS.0003.

———. "Raising the Dead: Unearthing the Non-Literary Origins of Zombie Cinema." *Journal of Popular Film and Television* 33.4 (2006): 196–205.

———. "Survivalism." In Grossman, *Sense of Wonder*, 928–930.

———. "Vacationing in *Zombieland*: The Classical Functions of the Modern Zombie Comedy." *Journal of the Fantastic in the Arts* 22.1 (2011): 24–38.

Blumberg, Arnold T., and Andrew Hershberger. *Zombiemania: 80 Movies to Die For*. London: Telos, 2006.

Boluk, Stephanie, and Wylie Lenz. *Generation Zombie: Essays on the Living Dead in Modern Culture*. Jefferson, NC: McFarland, 2011.

Boon, Kevin Alexander. "Ontological Anxiety Made Flesh: The Zombie in Literature, Film and Culture." In Niall, *Monsters and the Monstrous*, 33–43.

Botting, Fred. "Aftergothic: Consumption, Machines, and Black Holes." In Hogle, *Cambridge Companion to Gothic Fiction*, 277–300.

———. "Gobalzombie: From *White Zombie* to *World War Z*." In Byron, *Globalgothic*, 188–201.

———. *Gothic*. 2nd ed. The New Critical Idiom, edited by John Drakakis. London: Routledge, 2014.

———. *Gothic Romanced: Consumption, Gender and Technology in Contemporary Fictions*. New York: Routledge, 2008.

———. "Love Your Zombie: Horror, Ethics, Excess." In *The Gothic in Contemporary Literature and Popular Culture: Pop Goth*, edited by Justin Edwards and Agnieszka Soltysik Monnet, 20–36. Routledge Interdisciplinary Perspectives on Literature. London: Routledge, 2014.

"Box Office/Business for Day of the Dead (1985)." *The Internet Movie Database*. Amazon, 1990–2015. http://www.imdb.com/title/tt0088993/business.

"Box Office/Business for Resident Evil." *The Internet Movie Database*. Amazon, 1990–2015. http://www.imdb.com/title/tt0120804/business.

"Box Office/Business for The Return of the Living Dead." *The Internet Movie Database*. Amazon, 1990–2015. http://www.imdb.com/title/tt0089907/business.

"Box Office/Business for Zombieland." *The Internet Movie Database*. Amazon, 1990–2015. http://www.imdb.com/title/tt1156398/business.

Boyer, Elizabeth H. *The Sword and the Satchel*. 1980. New York: Del Rey, 1983.

Boyle, Alan. "Only Mostly Dead: Astronomers Puzzle over Zombie Comet ISON." *NBC News Science*. NBC News, 29 November 2013. http://www.nbcnews.com/science/only-mostly-dead-astronomers-puzzle-over-zombie-comet-ison-2D11674274.

Brooks, Max. *World War Z: An Oral History of the Zombie War*. New York: Crown Publishers, 2006.

———. *The Zombie Survival Guide: Complete Protection from the Living Dead*. New York: Three Rivers Press, 2003.

Browne, S. G. *Breathers: A Zombie's Lament*. Portland: Broadway Books, 2009.

Bruhm, Steven. "The Contemporary Gothic: Why We Need It." In Hogle, *Cambridge Companion to Gothic Fiction*, 259–276.

Bussey, George Moir, ed. *The Thousand and One Nights*. Translated by Edward Forster. New York: Carleton, 1872.

Byron, G.G. Lord. "The Giaour: A Fragment of a Turkish Tale." 1813. *Ready to Go Books*. J. G. Hawaii Publishing, n.d. http://readytogoebooks.com/LB-Giaour.htm.

Byron, Glennis. "'As one dead': Romeo and Juliet in the 'Twilight' Zone." In *Gothic Shakespeares*, edited by John Drakakis and Dale Townshend, 167–185. Accents on Shakespeare Series, edited by Terence Hawkes. New York: Routledge, 2008.

———, ed. *Globalgothic*. Manchester: Manchester University Press, 2013.

———. "Introduction." In Byron, *Globalgothic*, 1–10.

Campbell, Joseph. *The Hero with a Thousand*

Faces. 1949. Princeton: Princeton University Press, 1973.

Carroll, Leslie. *You Can't Hang the Dead*. New York: Mitre Press, 1944.

Carroll, Noël. *The Philosophy of Horror: or Paradoxes of the Heart*. New York: Routledge, 1990. Print.

Carter, Bill. "Some Sponsors Can't Accept Racy Reality." *New York Times*, Late Edition, 29 January 2001. *ProQuest Newsstand*.

Centers for Disease Control and Prevention. "Zombie Preparedness." *Office of Public Health Preparedness and Response*. Centers for Disease Control and Prevention, 18 August 2014. http://www.cdc.gov/phpr/zombies.htm.

Charbonneau, Léo. "Professor Uses Mathematics to Defend against the Zombie Apocalypse." *University Affairs*. AUCC, 20 August 2014. http://www.university affairs.ca/news/news-article/prof-uses-math-to-defend-against-the-zombies.

"The Chart: Box Office." *Entertainment Weekly*, 23 October 2009: 46.

Chekhov, Anton. *Uncle Vanya*. 1898. Mineola, NY: Dover Thrift, 1998.

"Chinese Vampires." *TV Tropes*. TV Tropes Foundation, n.d. http://tvtropes.org/pmwiki/pmwiki.php/Main/ChineseVampire.

Christie, Deborah, and Sarah Juliet Lauro, eds. *Better Off Dead: The Evolution of the Zombie as Post-Human*. New York: Fordham University Press, 2011.

Clarke, Liam. "Zombie Stormont: Prospect Looms or a Dead-Man Walking Assembly, Limping to the May Elections." *Politics*. Belfast Telegraph, 18 December 2014. http://www.belfasttelegraph.co.uk/news/politics/zombie-stormont-prospect-looms-of-a-deadmanwalking-assembly-limping-to-the-may-elections-30845902.html.

CNN. "New Species of 'Zombifying' Fungi Discovered in Brazil's Atlantic Rain Forest." *This Just In*. Turner Broadcasting System, 3 March 2011. http://news.blogs.cnn.com/2011/03/03/new-species-of-zombifying-fungi-discovered-in-brazils-atlantic-rain-forest.

Cohen, Jeffrey Jerome. "Monster Culture (Seven Theses)." In *Monster Theory: Reading Culture*, edited by Jeffrey Jerome Cohen, 3–25. Minneapolis: University of Minnesota Press, 1996.

_____. "The monster is not a category." @jeffreyjcohen. 28 December 2012. 2:11 p.m.

_____. "[T]axonomy is a kind of poetry." @jeffreyjcohen. 28 December 2012. 7:58 p.m.

_____. "Undead (A Zombie Oriented Ontology)." *Journal of the Fantastic in the Arts* 23.3 (2012): 397–412.

Collis, Clark and Chris Nashawaty. "Zombies A–Z: An Alphabetical Guide to the Living Dead." *EW*. Entertainment Weekly, 15 October 2009. http://www.ew.com/ew/gallery/0,,20310838_20311324_20687044,00.html#20687039.

Cronin, Justin. *The Passage*. 2010. St. Louis: Turtleback, 2012.

Cummins, June. "Hermione in the Bathroom: The Gothic, Menarche, and Female Development in the Harry Potter Series." In Jackson, Coats, and McGillis, *Gothic in Children's Literature*, 177–193.

Daly, Emma. "Could *In the Flesh* Be Saved by Amazon?" *RadioTimes*. Immediate Media Company, 19 January 2015. http://www.radiotimes.com/news/2015–01–19/could-in-the-flesh-be-saved-by-amazon.

Dargis, Manohla. Review of *Zombieland*. *The New York Times* 2 October 2009: C10.

Darwin, Charles. *On the Origin of Species: By Means of Natural Selection*. 1859. New York: Dover, 2006.

Davis, Wade. *The Serpent and the Rainbow*. New York: Simon and Shuster, 1985.

De Vise, Daniel. "Exploring the Undead: University of Baltimore to Offer English Class on Zombies." *The Washington Post*, 10 September 2010. http://www.washingtonpost.com/wp-dyn/content/article/2010/09/08/AR2010090802944.html.

Defoe, Daniel. *Robinson Crusoe*. 1719. New York: Penguin Books, 1985.

Delporte, Peyo, and Yvan Delporte. *The Purple Smurfs*. 1959. New York: Papercutz, 2010.

Dendle, Peter. "The Zombie as a Barometer of Cultural Anxiety." In Niall, *Monsters and the Monstrous*, 45–57.

_____. *The Zombie Movie Encyclopedia*. Jefferson, NC: McFarland, 2001.

_____. *The Zombie Movie Encyclopedia: 2000–2010*. Jefferson, NC: McFarland, 2012.

Department of Justice. "Highlights of the US Patriot Act." *Preserving Life & Liberty.* Department of Justice Website, n.d. http://www.justice.gov/archive/ll/high lights.htm.

Derksen, Craig and Darren Hudson Hick. "Your Zombie and You: Identity, Emotion, and the Undead." In Moreman and Rushton, *Zombies Are Us,* 11–23.

DeRosa, Aaron. "September 11 and Cold War Nostalgia." In *Portraying 9/11: Essays on Representations in Comics, Literature, Film and Theatre,* edited by Véronique Bragard, Christophe Dony, and Warren Rosenberg, 58–72. Jefferson, NC: McFarland, 2011.

Diehl, Digby, ed. *Tales from the Crypt.* New York: St. Martin's Press, 1996.

Dirks, Tim. "The 'Best Picture' Academy Awards: Genre Biases." *Filmsite.* American Movie Classics Company, 2010. http://www.filmsite.org/bestpics2.html.

Drezner, Daniel W. *Theories of International Politics and Zombies.* Princeton: Princeton University Press, 2011.

DuPrau, Jeanne. *The City of Ember.* New York: Random House, 2004.

Edwards, Justin D., and Agnieszka Soltysik Monnet. "Introduction: From Goth/ic to Pop Goth." In *The Gothic in Contemporary Literature and Popular Culture: Pop Goth,* edited by Justin D. Edwards and Agnieszka Soltysik Monnet, 1–18. New York: Routledge, 2012.

Egginton, William. "The Best of Worst of Our Nature: Reality TV and the Desire for Limitless Change." *Configurations* 15.2 (2007): 177–191.

Ellis-Davidson, Hilda Roderick. *The Road to Hel: A Study of the Conception of the Dead in Old Norse Literature.* Kindle ed. Ed. Carl Campbell. Idunnas Press, 2011.

"Europe's Zombie Banks: Blight of the Living Dead." *The Economist.* The Economist Newspaper Limited, 13 July 2013. http://www.economist.com/news/leaders/21581723-europes-financial-system-terrible-state-and-nothing-much-being-done-about-it-blight.

Evans, G. Blakemore and J. J. M. Tobin, eds. *The Riverside Shakespeare.* 2nd ed. Boston: Houghton Mifflin, 1997.

Farnell, Gary. "'Talking Bodies' in a Zombie Apocalypse: From the Discursive to the Shitty Sublime." In Keetley, *"We're All Infected,"* 173–185.

The Feature Creature. "Creating Evil Incarnate: The Making of *Resident Evil.*" *GamePro* 91 (1996): 32–33.

Feldstein, Al. "The Thing from the Grave." *Tales from the Crypt #22.* February 1951. In Diehl, *Tales from the Crypt,* 121–128.

Fetherston, Neil. "Addicts Depicted as 'Zombies' in Drug Treatment Clinic Row." *Dublin People,* 17 November 2014. http://www.dublinpeople.com/article.php?id=4270&l=100.

Foucault, Michel. *Discipline and Punish: The Birth of the Prison.* 1975. Translated by Alan Sheridan. New York: Vintage Books, 1995.

Fournier, Rasa. "Zombie Reality Show." *MidWeek.* Oahu Publications, 31 October 2012. http://www.midweek.com/hawaii-entertainment/zombie-reality-show.

Freud, Sigmund. "The Uncanny." 1919. In *The Uncanny,* 123–162. New York: Penguin Books, 2003.

Frye, Northrop. *Anatomy of Criticism: Four Essays.* Princeton: Princeton University Press, 2000.

Gaiman, Neil. *The Graveyard Book.* New York: HarperCollins, 2008.

Giroux, Henry A. *Zombie Politics and Culture in the Age of Casino Capitalism.* Popular Culture and Everyday Life. Vol. 23. New York: Peter Lang, 2010.

Goddard, Richard. *The Whistling Ancestors.* 1936. Vancleave, MS: Ramble House, 2009.

Golding, William. *Lord of the Flies.* New York: Perigree, 1954.

Grahame-Smith, Seth. *Pride and Prejudice and Zombies.* Philadelphia: Quirk Books, 2009.

Grossman, Leigh Ronald, ed. *Sense of Wonder: A Century of Science Fiction.* Rockville, MD: Wildside Press, 2011.

Haining, Peter, ed. *Zombie!: Stories of the Walking Dead.* London: Target, 1985.

Hand, Richard J. and Michael Wilson. *Grand-Guignol: The French Theatre of Horror.* Exeter: University of Exeter Press, 2002.

Harman, Chris. *Zombie Capitalism: Global Crisis and the Relevance of Marx.* Chicago: Haymarket Books, 2010.

Harrison, Christopher and Phil Pattison. *Night of the Living Dead Live.* 2013.

Harvey, Alex. *Attack of the Zombies!* New York: Simon Spotlight, 2011.

Harvey, David. "The City as a Body Politic." In *Wounded Cities: Destruction and Reconstruction in a Globalized World*, edited by Jane Schneider and Ida Susser, 25–46. Oxford: Berg Publishers, 2003.

Hill, Angela. "Undead Ahead: All Aboard West Sacramento's Zombie Train." *Oakland Tribune*. Woodland Daily Democrat, 6 August 2014. http://www.dailydemocrat.com/features/ci_26289196/undead-ahead-all-aboard-west-sacramentos-zombie-train.

Hill, Annette. *Reality TV: Audiences and Popular Factual Television*. London: Routledge, 2005.

Hoberek, Andrew. "Living with PASD." *Contemporary Literature* 53.2 (2012): 406–413.

Hogle, Jerrold E., ed. *The Cambridge Companion to Gothic Fiction*. Cambridge: Cambridge University Press, 2002.

_____. "The Ghost of the Counterfeit in the Genesis of the Gothic." In *Gothick Origins and Innovations*, edited by Allan Lloyd Smith and Victor Sage, 23–33. Amsterdam: Rodopi, 1994.

_____. "Introduction: The Gothic in Western Culture." In Hogle, *Cambridge Companion to Gothic Fiction*, 1–20.

Hubner, Laura, Marcus Leaning, and Paul Manning. "Introduction." In Hubner, Leaning, and Manning, *The Zombie Renaissance in Popular Culture*, 3–14.

_____, eds. *The Zombie Renaissance in Popular Culture*. Hampshire, UK: Palgrave Macmillan, 2015.

Hurston, Zora Neale. *Tell My Horse: Voodoo and Life in Haiti and Jamaica*. 1938. New York: Perennial Library, 1990.

Hutter, G. W. "Salt Is Not for Slaves." 1931. In Haining, *Zombie!: Stories of the Walking Dead*, 39–53.

"*In the Flesh* BBC Three, 10 p.m." *The Times*, 3 May 2014. http://search.proquest.com/docview/1520556133?accountid=28757.

Inguanzo, Ozzy. *Zombies on Film: The Definitive Story of Undead Cinema*. New York: Rizzoli, 2014.

"Islamist Cleric Anwar al-Awlaki Killed in Yemen." *News: Middle East*. BBC, 30 September 2011. http://www.bbc.co.uk/news/world-middle-east-15121879.

Jackson, Anna, Karen Coats, and Roderick McGillis, eds. *The Gothic in Children's Literature: Haunting the Borders*. New York: Routledge, 2009.

_____. "Introduction." In Jackson, Coats, and McGillis, *Gothic in Children's Literature*, 1–14.

Jacob, Jijo. "Anwar Al-Awlaki: Critics Say Killing Breaches Norms, Sets Wrong Precedent." *US*. International Business Times, 3 October 2011. http://www.ibtimes.com/articles/223724/20111003/anwar-al-awlaki-critics-say-killing-breaches-norms-sets-wrong-precedent-al-qaida-yemen-drone.htm

Jay, Stacey. *You Are So Undead to Me*. New York: Razorbill, 2009.

Jeffery, Morgan. "Everything We Know So Far about *The Walking Dead* Spinoff." *Digital Spy*. Hearst Magazines, 27 January 2015. http://www.digitalspy.com/tv/s135/the-walking-dead/feature/a624499/everything-we-know-so-far-about-the-walking-dead-spinoff.html#~p2MnwFJ-EUDVZ0g.

"Jiang Shi." *Mythical Creatures Guide*. WikiFoundry, 1 March 2011. http://www.mythicalcreaturesguide.com/page/Jiang+Shi.

Johnson, Katie N. "Televising the Panopticon: The Myth of 'Reality-Based' TV." *American Drama* 8.2 (1999): 1–26.

Jonason, Peter K., Gregory D. Webster, David P. Schmitt, Norman P. Li, and Laura Crysel. "The Antihero in Popular Culture: Life History Theory and the Dark Triad Personality Traits." *Review of General Psychology* 16.2 (2012): 192–199.

Kanazawa, Satoshi. "Why Do Some Battered Women Stay?" *The Scientific Fundamentalist*. Psychology Today, 13 April 2008. http://www.psychologytoday.com/blog/the-scientific-fundamentalist/2008/04/why-do-some-battered-women-stay.

Keene, Brian. *The Rising*. New York: Mass Market, 2004.

Keetley, Dawn. *"We're All Infected": Essays on AMC's* The Walking Dead *and the Fate of the Human*. Jefferson, NC: McFarland, 2014.

Kenemore, Scott. "Rick Grimes: A Zombie Among Men." In Lowder, *Triumph of The Walking Dead*, 185–199.

Kielpinski, Gerald. *Surviving the Zombie*

Outbreak: The Official Zombie Survival Field Manual. Edmonton, AB, Canada: Aquarius Publishing, 2011.

King, Stephen. *Cell.* New York: Scribner, 2006.

_____. *The Long Walk.* 1979. New York: Signet, 1999.

_____. *The Running Man.* 1982. London: Hodder Paperback, 2012.

Kirkman, Robert, Charlie Adlard, Stefano Gaudiano, and Cliff Rathburn. *A New Beginning.* The Walking Dead 22. Berkeley: Image Comics, 2014.

Kirkman, Robert, Charlie Adlard, and Cliff Rathburn. *The Heart's Desire.* The Walking Dead 4. Berkeley: Image Comics, 2005.

_____, _____, and _____. *Fear the Hunters.* The Walking Dead 11. Berkeley: Image Comics, 2009.

_____, _____, and _____. *Life Among Them.* The Walking Dead 12. Berkeley: Image Comics, 2010.

_____, _____, and _____. *Miles Behind Us.* The Walking Dead 2. Orange, CA: Image Comics, 2004.

_____, _____, and _____. *No Way Out.* The Walking Dead 14. Berkeley: Image Comics, 2011.

_____, _____, and _____. *Safety Behind Bars.* The Walking Dead 3. Berkeley: Image Comics, 2005.

_____, _____, and _____. *This Sorrowful Life.* The Walking Dead 6. Berkeley: Image Comics, 2007.

_____, _____, and _____. *Too Far Gone.* The Walking Dead 13. Berkeley: Image Comics, 2010.

_____, _____, and _____. *We Find Ourselves.* The Walking Dead 15. Berkeley: Image Comics, 2011.

_____, _____, and _____. *What We Become.* The Walking Dead 10. Berkeley: Image Comics, 2009.

Kirkman, Robert, and Tony Moore. *Days Gone Bye.* The Walking Dead 1. Orange, CA: Image Comics, 2004.

Kloepfer, John. *The Zombie Chasers.* New York: HarperCollins, 2010.

Koerth-Baker, Maggie. "Attack of the Zombie Maples." *Boing Boing.* Happy Mutants LLC, 18 June 2012. http://boingboing.net/2012/06/18/attack-of-the-zombie-maples.html.

Krzywinska, Tanya. "Zombies in Gamespace: Form, Context, and Meaning in Zombie-Based Video Games." In McIntosh and Leverette, *Zombie Culture,* 153–168.

Lamb, Robert. "How Ghouls Work." *How Stuff Works.* HowStuffWorks, Inc., n.d. http://science.howstuffworks.com/science-vs-myth/strange-creatures/ghoul.htm.

Landau, Elizabeth. "Inside Zombie Brains: Sci-fi Teaches Science." *CNN Health.* CNN, 25 April 2011. http://www.cnn.com/2011/HEALTH/04/25/zombie.virus.zombies.book.

Lauro, Sarah Juliet, and Karen Embry. "A Zombie Manifesto: The Nonhuman Condition in the Era of Advanced Capitalism." *boundary 2* 35.1 (2008): 85–108.

Le Diberder, Alain. "L'interactivité, une nouvelle frontier du cinema." *Cahiers du Cinéma* 503 (1996): 122–126.

Lecouteux, Claude. *The Return of the Dead: Ghosts, Ancestors, and the Transparent Veil of the Pagan Mind.* Rochester, VT: Inner Traditions, 2009.

Leverette, Marc. "The Funk of Forty Thousand Years; or, How the (Un)Dead Get Their Groove On." In McIntosh and Leverette, *Zombie Culture,* 185–212.

Lindqvist, John Ajvide. *Handling the Undead.* 2005. New York: Thomas Dunne Books, 2010.

Lovecraft, H. P. *The Dream-Quest of Unknown Kadath.* 1926. The H. P. Lovecraft Archive. Donovan K. Loucks, 2015. http://www.hplovecraft.com/writings/texts/fiction/dq.aspx.

_____. "Pickman's Model." 1926. The H. P. Lovecraft Archive. Donovan K. Loucks, 2015. http://www.hplovecraft.com/writings/texts/fiction/pm.aspx.

Lowder, James, ed. *Triumph of The Walking Dead: Robert Kirkman's Zombie Epic on Page and Screen.* Dallas: Benbella Books, 2011.

Lubar, David. *My Rotten Life.* Nathan Abercrombie, Accidental Zombie 1. New York: Starscape, 2009.

Ma, Roger. *The Zombie Combat Manual: A Guide to Fighting the Living Dead.* New York: Berkley Trade, 2010.

Maberry, Jonathan. *Rot & Ruin.* New York: Simon & Schuster, 2010.

Macintosh, Zoe. "Sun Eruption May Have

Spawned Zombie Satellite." *Space on MSNBC*. MSNBC, 14 July 2010. http://www.msnbc.msn.com/id/38242512/ns/technology_and_ science-space/t/sun-eruption-may-have-spawned-zombie-satellite/#.T-jQI5Hhd0I.

Magistrale, Tony. *Abject Terrors: Surveying the Modern and Postmodern Horror Film*. New York: Peter Lang, 2005.

Manning, Paul. "Zombies, Zomedies, Digital Fan Cultures and the Politics of Taste." In Hubner, Leaning, and Manning, *Zombie Renaissance in Popular Culture*, 160–173.

Marion, Isaac. *Warm Bodies*. New York: Atria Publishing, 2010.

Matheson, Richard. *I Am Legend*. 1954. New York: Tor, 1995.

Mathiesen, Thomas. "The Viewer Society: Michel Foucault's 'Panopticon' Revisited." *Theoretical Criminology* 1.2 (1997): 215–234.

McCarthy, Cormac. *The Road*. New York: Alfred A. Knopf, 2006.

McGillis, Roderick. "The Night Side of Nature: Gothic Spaces, Fearful Times." In Jackson, Coats, and McGillis, *Gothic in Children's Literature*, 227–241.

McIntosh, Shawn and Marc Leverette, eds. *Zombie Culture: Autopsies of the Living Dead*. Lanham, MD: Scarecrow, 2008.

Meyer, Stephenie. *Twilight*. 2005. New York: Little, Brown, 2006.

"Michigan College Offers Course in Zombies, Apocalypse." *Associated Press*. CBS News, 10 February 2014. http://www.cbsnews.com/news/michigan-college-offers-course-in-zombies-apocalypse.

Miller, Cynthia J. and A. Bowdoin Van Riper. *Undead in the West: Vampires, Zombies, Mummies, and Ghosts on the Cinematic Frontier*. Lanham, MD: Scarecrow, 2012.

Miller, Walter M., Jr. *A Canticle for Leibowitz*. 1960. New York: Harper Collins, 2006.

Moody, David. *Autumn*. 2001. New York: Thomas Dunne Books, 2010.

Moreman, Christopher M. and Cory James Rushton, eds. *Race, Oppression and the Zombie: Essays on Cross-Cultural Appropriations of the Caribbean Tradition*. Jefferson, NC: McFarland, 2011.

_____, eds. *Zombies Are Us: Essays on the Humanity of the Walking Dead*. Jefferson, NC: McFarland, 2011.

Mulvey, Laura. "Visual Pleasure and Narrative Cinema." *Screen* 16.3 (1975). In *Narrative, Apparatus, Ideology: A Film Theory Reader*, edited by Philip Rosen, 198–209. New York: Columbia University Press, 1986.

National Cancer Institute. "Understanding Cancer Series." *National Institutes of Health*. U. S. Department of Health and Human Services, 30 September 2009. http://www.cancer.gov/cancertopics/understandingcancer/cancer/page9.

"New Course Explores Use of Zombies in Pop Culture." *News Releases*. University of Baltimore, 7 September 2010. http://www.ubalt.edu/news/news-releases.cfm?id=1295.

Niall, Scott, ed. *Monsters and the Monstrous: Myths and Metaphors of Enduring Evil*. Amsterdam: Rodophi, 2007.

Nietzsche, Friedrich. *Beyond Good and Evil*. 1886. Translated by Marianne Cowan. Chicago: Gateway, 1955.

Nilsen, Alleen Pace and Kenneth L. Donelson. *Literature for Today's Young Adults*. 8th ed. Boston: Pearson, 2009.

Nora, Pierre. "Between Memory and History: Les Lieux de Mémoire." *Representations* 26 (1989): 7–24.

Pagano, David. "The Space of Apocalypse in Zombie Cinema." In McIntosh and Leverette, *Zombie Culture*, 71–86.

Patten, Dominic. "'Walking Dead' Shatters Winter Finales Ratings Record, Thrashes 'Sunday Night Football' Again." *Deadline Hollywood*. Penske Business Media, 1 December 2014. http://deadline.com/2014/12/the-walking-dead-ratings-season-5-finale-sunday-night-football-1201304308.

Paulhus, Delroy L. and Kevin M. Williams. "The Dark Triad of Personality: Narcissism, Machiavellianism, and Psychopathy." *Journal of Research in Personality* 36 (2002): 556–563.

Phillips, Erica E. "Feed Your Brain with Brains: Six Real Zombie College Classes." *Speakeasy. The Wall Street Journal*. Dow Jones & Company, Inc., 4 March 2014. http://blogs.wsj.com/speakeasy/2014/03/04/feed-your-brain-with-brains-six-real-zombie-college-classes.

_____. "Zombie Studies Gain Ground on College Campuses: Students, Professors Study Culture of Living Dead." *The Wall*

Street Journal. Dow Jones & Company, Inc., 3 March 2014. http://www.wsj.com/news/article_email/SB10001424052 7023048511045793614519513 84512-lMyQjAxMTA0MDAwNDEwNDQyWj.

Pierron, Agnès. *Le Grand Guignol: Le théâtre des peurs de la belle époque*. Paris: Robert Laffont, 1995.

Pifer, Lynn. "Slacker Bites Back: *Shaun of the Dead* Finds New Life for Deadbeats." In Christie and Lauro, *Better Off Dead*, 163–174.

Poe, Edgar Allan. "The Bells." 1848. *Poets*. Academy of American Poets, n.d. http://www.poets.org/poetsorg/poem/bells.

_____. "To _____. Ulalume: A Ballad." 1847. *The Poetry Foundation*, 2014. http://www.poetryfoundation.org/poem/174155.

Pokornowski, Steven. "Burying the Living with the Dead: Security, Survival and the Sanction of Violence." In Keetley, *"We're All Infected,"* 41–55.

Poole, W. Scott. *Monsters in America: Our Historical Obsession with the Hideous and the Haunting*. Waco, TX: Baylor University Press, 2011.

Priest, Cherie. *Boneshaker*. New York: Tor, 2009.

Quiggin, John. *Zombie Economics: How Dead Ideas Still Walk among Us*. Princeton: Princeton University Press, 2010.

Randall, Tom. "Bankers See $1 Trillion of Zombie Investments Stranded in the Oil Fields." *The Grid*. Bloomberg, 17 December 2014. http://www.bloomberg.com/news/2014-12-18/bankers-see-1-trillion-of-investments-stranded-in-the-oil-fields.html.

Renshaw, David. "G2: Reviews: Television: Your Next Box Set: *In the Flesh*." *The Guardian*, 23 January 2015. http://search.proquest.com/docview/1647648108?accountid=28757.

Rhodes, Gary D. *White Zombie: Anatomy of a Horror Film*. Jefferson, NC: McFarland, 2001.

Rice, Anne. *Interview with the Vampire*. 1976. New York: Ballantine Books, 1991.

Richards, Kim, ed. *The Zombie Cookbook*. Santa Rosa, CA: Damnation Books, 2009.

Riley, Brendan. "Zombie People." In Lowder, *Triumph of The Walking Dead*, 81–97.

Roach, Dr. *Night of the Zombie Goldfish*.

Monster Stories 1. New York: Scholastic, 2013.

Robertson, Chris, and Michael Allred. *iZombie: Dead to the World*. New York: DC Comics, 2011.

Rosen, Elizabeth K. *Apocalyptic Transformation: Apocalypse and the Postmodern Imagination*. Lanham, MD: Lexington Books, 2008.

Russell, Jamie. *Book of the Dead: The Complete History of Zombie Cinema*. Godalming, Surrey: FAB Press, 2006.

_____. *Book of the Dead: The Complete History of Zombie Cinema (Updated & Fully Revised Edition)*. London: Titan Books, 2014.

Ryan, Carrie. *The Dark and Hollow Places*. New York: Ember, 2012.

_____. *The Dead-Tossed Waves*. New York: Delacorte Books for Young Readers, 2011.

_____. *The Forest of Hands and Teeth*. New York: Delacorte Press, 2010.

Ryan, Patrick. "'Walking Dead' Comes Alive in the Online Classroom." *USA Today*. Garnett Company, 16 October 2013. http://www.usatoday.com/story/life/tv/2013/10/15/society-science-survival-walking-dead-online-course/2976427.

Savoy, Eric. "The Face of the Tenant: A Theory of American Gothic." In *American Gothic: New Interventions in a National Narrative*, edited by Robert K. Martin and Eric Savoy, 3–19. Iowa City: University of Iowa Press, 1998.

_____. "The Rise of American Gothic." In Hogle, *The Cambridge Companion to Gothic Fiction*, 167–188.

Schott, Gareth. "Digital Dead: Translating the Visceral and Satirical Elements of George A. Romero's *Dawn of the Dead* to Videogames." In Moreman and Rushton, *Zombies Are Us*, 141–150.

Schulman, Martha. "My Horrible '70s Apocalypse." *Publishers Weekly*, 15 July 2011. http://www.publishersweekly.com/pw/by-topic/authors/interviews/article/48015-my-horrible-70s-apocalypse-pw-talks-with-colson-whitehead.html.

Seabrook, W. B. *The Magic Island*. New York: The Literary Guild of America, 1929.

Selzer, Adam. *I Kissed a Zombie, and I Liked It*. New York: Delacorte Books for Young Readers, 2010.

Shakespeare, William. *King Lear*. 1606. In Evans and Tobin, *The Riverside Shakespeare*.

_____. *The Tragedy of Romeo and Juliet*. 1597. In Evans and Tobin, *The Riverside Shakespeare*, 1104–1145.

Shan, Darren. *Zom-B*. New York: Little, Brown Books, 2012.

Shandrow, Kim Lachance. "As 'The Walking Dead' Thrives, So Do Zombie Survival Camps." *Entrepreneur*. Entrepreneur Media, 10 October 2014. http://www.entrepreneur.com/article/238259.

Sheckley, Robert. "The Prize of Peril." 1958. *Store of Infinity*. Open Road Media, 2014. Amazon Digital Services.

Shelley, Mary. *Frankenstein*. 1818. Norton Critical Edition. Ed. J. Paul Hunter. 2nd ed. New York: Norton, 2012.

_____. *The Last Man*. 1826. New York: Oxford University Press, 1998.

Silver, Alain, and James Ursini. *The Zombie Film: From* White Zombie *to* World War Z. New York: Applause Theatre & Cinema, 2014.

Silverman, Kaja. *The Subject of Semiotics*. New York: Oxford University Press, 1983.

Simek, Rudolf. *Dictionary of Northern Mythology*. Translated by Angela Hall. Suffolk: D. S. Brewer, 1996.

Simon, Matt. "Absurd Creature of the Week: The Zombie Ant and the Fungus That Controls Its Mind." *Wired*. Condé Nast, 13 September 2013. http://www.wired.com/2013/09/absurd-creature-of-the-week-zombie-ant-fungus.

Singel, Ryan. "Zombie Computers Decried As Imminent National Threat." *Wired*. Conde Nast, 9 April 2008. http://www.wired.com/threatlevel/2008/04/zombie-computer/.

Skipp, John, and Craig Spector, eds. *Book of the Dead*. New York: Bantam Books, 1989.

Smith, Anna. "The Scary Tale Looks for a Family: Gary Crew's *Gothic Hospital* and Sonya Hartnett's *The Devil Latch*." In Jackson, Coats, and McGillis, *Gothic in Children's Literature*, 131–143.

"Special Panel: The Monstrous." Moderated by F. Brett Cox. 33rd International Conference on the Fantastic in the Arts. Orlando, FL. 22 March 2012.

Stevenson, Robert Louis. *Dr. Jekyll and Mr. Hyde*. 1886. New York: Signet Classic, 2003.

Stewart, George R. *Earth Abides*. 1949. New York: Del Rey, 2006.

Stine, R. L. *Why I Quit Zombie School*. Goosebumps Hall of Horrors 4. New York: Scholastic, 2011.

_____. *Zombie School*. Give Yourself Goosebumps 40. New York: Scholastic, 1999.

_____. *Zombie Town*. New York: Parachute Press, 2012.

"Storm Hits Fox's New 'Temptation Island.'" *The Atlanta Journal*, 8 January 2001. ProQuest Newsstand.

Streeter, Lin. "I Am a Zombie." *Adventures into the Unknown* #50. December 1953. In Yoe and Banes, *Zombies*, 11–17.

Strickland, Jonathan. "How Zombie Computers Work." *How Stuff Works*, 1998–2013. http://computer.howstuffworks.com/zombie-computer.htm.

"Survive the Apocalypse." *Zombie Survival Camp*. Tactical Training Services, 2010. http://www.zombiesurvivalcourse.com.

"SW290: Surviving the Coming Zombie Apocalypse." *Michigan State University*, 2015. http://zombie.msu.edu.

Swann, William B., Christine Chang-Schneider, and Sarah Angulo. "Self-Verification in Relationships as an Adaptive Process." In *Self and Social Relationships*, edited by Joanne V. Woods, Abraham Tesser, and John G. Holms, 29–72. New York: Psychology Press, 2007.

Swann, William B., and Stephen J. Read. "Self Verification Processes: How We Sustain Our Self-Conceptions." *Journal of Experimental Psychology* 17. 27 (1980): 351–372.

Sywenky, Irene. "After the End: Post-Apocalyptic Science Fiction." In Grossman, *Sense of Wonder*, 438–440.

Tadrowski, Keith. *Night of the Living Dead: The Play*. 1994.

Tenga, Angela and Elizabeth Zimmerman. "Vampire Gentlemen and Zombie Beasts: A Rendering of True Monstrosity." *Gothic Studies* 15.1 (2013): 76–87.

Trottier, Daniel. "Watching Yourself, Watching Others: Popular Representations of Panoptic Surveillance in Reality TV Programs." In *How Real Is Reality TV? Essays on Representation and Truth*, edited by

David S. Escoffery, 259–276. Jefferson, NC: McFarland, 2006.

Uncle Vanya and Zombies. Playbill. University of Hawai'i at Mānoa. 9 November 2012.

Verstynen, Timothy, and Bradley Voytek. *Do Zombies Dream of Undead Sheep? A Neuroscientific View of the Zombie Brain.* Princeton: Princeton University Press, 2014.

Wagenseil, Paul. "New OSX Trojan Lays Groundwork for Mac Zombie Army." *Tech-News Daily.* Tech Media Network, 23 September 2011. http://www.technewsdaily.com/7186-osx-trojan-mac-botnet.html.

"The Walking Dead: *Draugr* and *Aptrgangr* in Old Norse Literature." *The Viking Answer Lady.* Amazon, 18 October 2012. http://www.vikinganswerlady.com/ghosts.shtml.

Walsh, Kenneth T. "George W. Bush's 'Bullhorn' Moment." *U.S. News & World Report,* 25 April 2013. http://www.usnews.com/news/blogs/ken-walshs-washington/2013/04/25/george-w-bushs-bullhorn-moment.

Waters, Daniel. *Generation Dead.* New York: Simon and Schuster, 2008.

Webb, Kenneth S. *Zombie.* 1932.

Weise, Matthew J. "How the Zombie Changed Videogames." In Moreman and Rushton, *Zombies Are Us,* 151–168.

Welsh, Jennifer. "Zombie Caterpillars Rain Death from Treetops." *Live Science.* Tech Media Network, 8 September 2011. http://www.livescience.com/15962-zombie-caterpillar-virus.html.

Wessendorf, Markus. Email interview. 9 February 2014.

_____. *Uncle Vanya and Zombies.* 2012.

"What Is Humans vs Zombies." *Humans vs. Zombies,* n.d. http://humansvszombies.org.

Whelan, Andrew, Ruth Walker, and Christopher Moore, eds. *Zombies in the Academy: Living Death in Higher Education.* Wilmington, NC: Intellect Ltd., 2013.

Whitehead, Colson. *Zone One.* New York: Doubleday, 2011.

Whitman, Glen, and James Dow. *Economics of the Undead: Zombies, Vampires, and the Dismal Science.* Lanham, MD: Rowman & Littlefield, 2014.

William of Newburgh. *Historia rerum Anglicarum.* Book 5. Ed. Paul Halsall. Translated by Joseph Stevenson. Fordham University, 24 October 2000. http://legacy.fordham.edu/halsall/basis/williamofnewburgh-five.asp.

Wilson, Lauren, and Kristian Bauthus. *The Art of Eating through the Zombie Apocalypse: A Cookbook and Culinary Survival Guide.* Dallas: Smart Pop, 2014.

Wolf, Mark J. P., and Bernard Perron. "Introduction." In *The Video Game Theory Reader,* edited by Mark J. P. Wolf and Bernard Perron, 1–24. New York: Routledge, 2003.

Wood, Wally. "The Thing from the Sea." *Eerie* #16. June–July 1954. In Yoe and Banes, *Zombies,* 115–121.

Wyss, Johann David. *The Swiss Family Robinson.* 1812. New York: Sterling, 2007.

Yoe, Craig and Steve Banes. *Zombies.* The Chilling Archives of Horror Comics 3. San Diego: IDW Publishing, 2013.

Zed Events. Zed Events, nd. http://www.zedevents.co.uk.

Zimmer, Carl. "Could an Inner Zombie Be Controlling Your Brain?" *Discover.* Kalmbach Publishing, 8 September 2008. http://discovermagazine.com/2008/oct/15-could-an-inner-zombie-be-controlling-your-brain#.UmUjDhaxNFI.

"Zombie." *Box Office Mojo.* Internet Movie Database, n.d. http://www.boxofficemojo.com/genres/chart/?id=zombie.htm.

"A Zombie Infested 5K Obstacle Course Race." *Run for Your Lives.* Reed Street Productions, 2011. http://runforyourlives.com.

Zombie Research Society. 2013. http://www.zombieresearch.org.

Zombie Science: Zombie Institute for Theoretical Studies. Time-Tastical Productions, 2013. http://www.zombiescience.co.uk.

"'Zombie' Stars Cast Light on Dark Energy." *Space on MSNBC.* MSNBC, 28 July 2011. http://www.msnbc.msn.com/id/43932987/ns/technology_and_science-space/t/zombie-stars-cast-light-dark-energy/#.TjRn5Hhd0I.

Zombie Survival Course. Tactical Training Services, 2010. http://www.zombiesurvivalcourse.com.

"Zombieland (2009)." *Rotten Tomatoes.* Flixster, Inc., 2010. http://www.rottentomatoes.com/m/zombieland.

INDEX

217